KAYAK TOURING

Also by William Sanders
The Bicycle Racing Book
Guide To Inflatable Canoes And Kayaks
Backcountry Bikepacking

KAYAK
TOURING

William Sanders

Stackpole Books

Published by
STACKPOLE BOOKS
Cameron and Kelker Streets
P. O. Box 1831
Harrisburg, PA 17105

Cover photograph courtesy of J. Frank Dougherty

Printed in the U.S.A.

Library of Congress Cataloging in Publication Data
Sanders, William, 1942–
    Kayak touring.

    Bibliography: p.
    Includes index.
    1. Kayak touring.   2. Sea kayaking.   3. Camping.
I. Title.
GV789.S26   1984   797.1′22   83-18145

To My Mother

whose many contributions include driving me and my kayaks all over the map and off it, ruining her car's paint job with rooftop kayak racks and her tires on dirt access roads, and frequently exhorting me to be careful out there in that tippy little thing

Contents

1

Bow Waves

A quiet revolution is going on all over the United States on rivers, creeks, lakes, and even the open sea. Wherever there is clean water and wild, beautiful surroundings, sooner or later you will see them, moving singly or in pairs or even in pods, like killer whales: long, lean, streamlined shapes, low down in the water, sliding along with almost no sound or wake, while double-bladed paddles flash in the sun or slice through the mist like the wings of strange birds. People on the shore or in other boats fall silent, watching; then someone says softly, "Kayaks!"

The kayaks are here. They've been around a long time, of course—long before the white man arrived with his "superior" way of life (and immediately had to borrow Native American agriculture and small boat technology in order to stay alive). Only recently, however, have kayaks begun to come into their own in the United States.

Americans have always enjoyed traveling through wild and scenic country, and in recent years there has evolved a mass national passion for outdoor sports and wilderness travel—particularly travel by water, which is less work than backpacking, makes far less impact on the environment (canoes and kayaks don't leave footprints and rutted trails), and can take one through exceptionally beautiful surroundings.

The traditional vehicle has been the open canoe, a craft of impeccable lineage and enormous romantic associations. Unfortunately, the canoe is less than ideal in many respects. Except for a few expensive models, it tends to be rather heavy and clumsy. The paddle techniques are not easy to learn well, and most canoes are designed to be paddled by two people, requiring excellent teamwork. Worst of all, the open canoe suffers from being open; it swamps easily in even moderate waves, either on open water or in rapids. This inherent limitation has spoiled many trips, ruined a great deal of gear and supplies, and on occasion killed people. At the very least, it forces canoeists to carry their heavy boats and gear around rapids that could easily be run in decked craft.

None of this is meant as a putdown of the good old open canoe or the people who paddle it. It's just that some of us think there's something better.

A kayak can go anywhere an open canoe can go and a great many places the open boat had better avoid. In even moderately competent hands, it will live and prosper in waters that would swamp a canoe. It is light, fast, and easy on the back and shoulders; the paddle strokes are few and simple to learn for all but advanced whitewater running. Kayaks aren't tippy, as many believe, except for specialized designs. Actually, because the center of gravity is low, a touring kayak is very stable, and a few easily learned techniques make it even more so. You sit at water level, <u>wearing</u> your craft instead of merely perching atop it, <u>in</u> the water rather than on it, <u>experiencing</u> the water more totally than anyone but a swimmer. You become less a human in a boat than a kind of amphibious mammal, like a seal or an otter.

There are also many side benefits. If you're into physical fitness, the double paddle develops the upper body symmetrically, while practicing roll and brace techniques gives you a workout all over.

Courtesy Old Town

If you're interested in wildlife, the silent, low-lying kayak lets you approach wild animals closely; after all, it was originally designed for hunting.

Above all else, kayaks are fun. They look spectacularly classy with their long, fast lines, and you can make them dance across the water like hyper water bugs, yet you can sit in a kayak and drift quietly down a slow green river for hours on end, like Huckleberry Finn. If you like simply messing around in boats, then you'll love your kayak.

With all this going for it, why hasn't the kayak replaced the canoe and become the standard paddle-tripping craft in the U.S., as it is in Europe?

Some of us are working on it . . . but right now, a short history lesson.

As everyone surely knows, the kayak was invented by the Eskimo (more correctly called the Inuit) and Aleut peoples of the Arctic regions. Lacking materials for conventional boats, they constructed light frames of driftwood and covered them with skins, a system used in many other parts of the world. (Ireland, for example, has a long skin boat tradition.)

But the Arctic hunters had specialized needs. The kayak was never meant as a general-purpose boat; its original mission was as a hunting instrument, like a fighter plane or a submarine—which it came to resemble in overall lines. It had to be fast, it had to present a small silhouette, and it had to be capable of negotiating narrow leads in the ice. It also had to be built with a minimum of materials since wood was scarce. All this added up to a small, narrow, low-lying boat. But such a craft would be extremely dangerous in the Arctic seas if built in the usual open fashion.

Somehow these aboriginal geniuses conceived the idea of completely enclosing the boat, with only a small opening to accommodate the paddler, who was then fastened in by means of a waterproof garment. A boat made in this way could operate in heavy seas without swamping, and in time it was discovered that a paddler could even survive a capsize by righting himself with a flick of the paddle. (Who knows how many brave men died perfecting the Eskimo roll.) The Aleuts and the North Pacific

Inuit even hunted whales and routinely cruised back and forth between North America and Asia through the most dangerous waters on earth. In fact, the only thing they didn't do with their kayaks—it would have struck them as crazy—was play around in freshwater rapids. Few of them even lived on rivers.

When white men at last came in contact with these people, they were immediately and powerfully impressed by their boats. The very first white men to see Inuit must have been the Viking settlers of Greenland, and no Viking was ever slow to appreciate a slick small boat design. It was soon agreed that the kayak represented the finest boat developed by so-called primitive people, except possibly the canoes of Polynesia.

While white explorers quickly adopted the birchbark and dugout canoes of the Indians, the only whites to do much with the kayak were the Russians who opened up Alaska. During their conquest of the Aleutians, the Russians forced the Aleuts to build three-seat kayaks in which a Russian could ride around while a pair of Aleut slaves did all the work. (Nice guys.)

Modern European sport canoeing began in the 1860s with a British traveler named MacGregor. Inspired by seeing canoes in Canada and kayaks in Arctic Siberia, MacGregor designed a canoe which he called *Rob Roy* and toured extensively in Europe and the Middle East. His books were widely read and canoeing became popular in Britain and on the Continent. Most Americans today would call *Rob Roy* a kayak: full deck, two-foot beam, double-bladed paddle, and so on. Since MacGregor's day, canoe in most of Europe has referred to what we would call a kayak, and canoeing has been mostly done with decked boats. Only in France, with long traditions dating back to the Canadian fur trade, has the open canoe held its ground.

The great popularity of kayaking in modern times, however, is mostly the result of the work of a German tailor named Johann Klepper. In 1907 Klepper introduced the first successful folding kayak, the famous *Faltboot*. It was an instant success and Klepper got very, very rich. Few people in Europe had cars or places to store boats; a foldboat could be kept in a closet and carried on a train as luggage. Germans had a tradition of wandering in wild places anyway, so the *Faltboot* was a natural for the German university student.

Klepper's design was considerably fatter than the Eskimo boat, making it stabler. It could be used on rivers, lakes, or the ocean, or even fitted with sails. For some time there was even a foldboat event in the Olympics.

The foldboat movement never really caught on in the U.S., except for a brief vogue in a few areas. America was having its love affair with the internal combustion engine and motorboats were the big thing. The only people using canoes were hunters, trappers, and fishermen, who remained wedded to the open canoe tradition, or young men on moonlight paddles with girls and ukuleles, for whom the kayak would indeed have been impractical.

During World War II, in a bizarre and little-known phase, commando teams used folding kayaks to penetrate enemy harbors and blow up shipping. The fine film *The Cockleshell Heroes* dealt with such a raid.

In the fifties, whitewater river running became popular in the U.S., mostly done at first with war surplus inflatable rafts. A few brave types tried making big-water runs with folders. In Europe, however, there had been a dedicated whitewater kayaking movement since the twenties, and now this sport began to cross the Atlantic. About the same time, the first fiberglass kayaks appeared, greatly improving the possibilities of the sport. Americans have always been attracted by high-risk, high-tech sports; soon there was a genuine American whitewater kayaking subculture, small but fanatical.

This is when things started to get out of hand.

By the seventies, U.S. kayaking had become the exclusive province of an elite class of whitewater jocks interested only in the technical challenge of running and playing in difficult rapids, or in formal competition. The kayak became less a type of boat and more an item of athletic equipment, like a surfboard; in fact, the average seventies kayaker had more in common with a surfer than with a backpacker or canoeist. Whitewater touring was popular but usually done with inflatable rafts or, if the rivers were fairly easy, open canoes. Occasionally a group of kayakers would go on an extended paddle trip, but the usual procedure was to have a big raft following along with the camping gear and supplies so that the kayakers could play in the rapids with empty boats.

(Rather like the bicycle tourists of the period with their sag wagons—or Bwana trekking through the bush with his faithful native bearers.)

All of this was great, as far as it went; it was just a pretty limited approach. Oh, plenty of people still used kayaks for touring wild country, and the old foldboats were still seen on lakes and the like. But the general feeling was that whitewater was what kayaks were really all about, preferably the fastest whitewater available, and that people who had other ideas were lacking in moral fiber.

In time, like all popular trends, the whitewater movement peaked out and began to subside to more reasonable levels. Some of us began to wonder if there might not be more to life than an endless series of rocks, holes, and huge waves. In the last few years, American outdoors people have come to see the kayak in a more balanced light, as a versatile, efficient small boat with many interesting applications, especially moving through wild country. Kayak builders are getting more orders for the roomier, stabler touring models; there is even a growing wave of enthusiasm for sea kayaking in some areas. At the same time, advances in lightweight camping gear technology have now made it possible to carry an adequate camping kit for extended touring without having to paddle a big clumsy barge. You can have a light, agile boat and run whitewater to your heart's content and still be reasonably and smugly self-contained on your journey. And whitewater techniques and equipment have continued to evolve; paddlers with only a few months' experience and training now routinely run rapids and perform tricks once thought strictly for godlike superexperts.

What we seem to have here, in fact, is an authentic Movement. Welcome to the Mad Kayakers' Liberation Front . . . .

This is primarily a book on kayak touring—using the kayak to actually _go_ somewhere rather than just fooling around in rapids to impress the onlookers. I have tried to keep the orientation broad; however, we will not be covering any form of racing or other formal competition. Generally I have assumed the reader will want to be able to at least occasionally go on extended trips, carrying gear and camping supplies, but if you aren't interested in that we'll still have plenty for you too. This isn't strictly a whitewater kayaking manual by any means. There has been too much of that sort of thing already; you may well have no interest at all in the fast stuff, which is perfectly okay, but we will examine the techniques and principles of running various kinds of rapids, as well as open-water paddling. On the whole I imagine most people want to be able to do at least a little of everything. If not, feel free to skip and skim. This book is a kind of tool kit; you open it and select what <u>you</u> need.

We will consider what kind of kayak and other gear you need and how to use it. We'll try to distinguish between the things you have to have, the things you ought to have if you can manage it, the things you might like to have but can do without, and the things you ought to leave on the shelf. Our motto will be from Thoreau: "Simplify, simplify!"

One more point. This book is also written with the basic assumption that the reader is pretty much new to all this. I will be explaining some very basic things from time to time. No doubt many readers are more experienced and already know some of the things in this book. To them I say: you know what you know. Bear with me while I make sure we aren't leaving anybody behind.

To go kayaking, of course, you need a kayak. Let's look at the boats.

2

The Boats

To begin with, just what is a kayak, anyway?

I'm not being cute, rhetorical, or pedantic; a lot of people are genuinely uncertain about the precise meaning of the term. If you get into this sport, be prepared to be asked the question, "Is that a kayak?" with great frequency.

Some of this confusion arises from advertising hokey-pokey. Since kayaks have a certain glamorous, macho image, various flimflam men have stuck the label on diverse small craft (often, to be sure, excellent boats in their own right) which are as much kayaks as I am Zoltan, King of the Gypsies. To add to the mystery, one major kayak manufacturer denies that its boats are kayaks— afraid, I suppose, that the kayak's kamikaze image will hurt their sizeable family recreation business.

At the same time, modern developments have produced true canoes that look almost exactly like kayaks to the uninitiated eye, and which indeed share many of the true kayak's qualities and functions.

If we move beyond the American scene, the confusion multiplies. In British usage, what we call a kayak is known as a canoe, and the regular open canoe is called a Canadian canoe, with the term kayak usually reserved for native Arctic craft. Who was it who said that the Americans and the British are divided by a common language?

So—what exactly is a kayak?

The all-odds best explanation I have ever heard was given by a person who was neither kayaker nor lexicographer. I was sitting in front of a country store near an Ozark stream and a local fisherman was talking about me to the big, slightly retarded kid who pumped gas. "He come down the river in a kayak," I overheard. "You never seen a kayak? It's kind of a canoe, I guess, only real skinny and little, and it's got this deck over the top so the water can't get in, with just a little hole where you set. You set down flat on your hiney with your legs stuck out in front of you and paddle with this long old paddle that's got blades on both ends so you don't have to keep switching sides."

Now I defy anybody to beat that for clarity, precision, and conciseness. In two sentences that perceptive angler managed to nail down just about every single major characteristic of a kayak. With a little work on grammar it would do for a dictionary definition: a small, narrow boat of the canoe type, fully decked over, designed to be paddled from a seated position with a double-bladed paddle.

To most people the deck is probably the most obvious recognition feature. Not long ago, trying to explain these matters to a devoutly unamphibious friend, I began, "Now a kayak has a full deck—"

"Which," my friend interjected, "is more than you can say for people who paddle them."

Be that as it may, I must insist on the deck. There are boats, advertised as kayaks, which have only partial or even vestigial decks. I refuse to recognize them, and I am certain most authorities will back me up here. A kayak, by definition, is a <u>decked</u> boat. Now the size of the cockpit opening may vary considerably, and some entirely valid kayaks have pretty big holes in this area—particularly some of the two-seaters—but by any meaningful standards, I feel that more than half the total topside area ought to be decked over before the boat qualifies as a true kayak.

Decks do not a kayak make, however; lots of other decked small craft exist. The old duck hunter's "sneak box" looks rather like a kayak except for its broad beaminess, as do some of the small sailboats. Some canoes designed for competition or whitewater are fully decked and in general outline appear almost indistinguishable from kayaks.

Here is where the rest of our definition comes in. Sneak boxes, ordinary canoes fitted with spray decks, and other craft may be paddled in various ways, rowed, sailed, or fitted with motors, without losing their identities. But kayaks are special. The double-bladed paddle really has to be considered virtually an integral part of the kayak; in modern terminology, we might say that the kayak and paddle form a "system." A kayaker may, on occasion, use a single-bladed, canoe-type paddle for special applications, or fit a big foldboat with a sailing rig, but the true kayak is still basically designed to be used with the double paddle with the paddler sitting flat with legs extended, just as the man said. Decked whitewater canoes, so kayaklike in appearance, are used exclusively with single-bladed paddles and paddled from a peculiar kneeling position. Look inside the cockpit of one of these boats and you'll see the difference right away.

All right, so now we know what a kayak is—and isn't. But it does not follow that any boat fitting this description will put you in business. Kayaks are like dogs—lots of variations on the same basic pattern. You can easily spend a lot of money on a truly fine kayak that will prove as useful for your purposes as a bicycle would be for surfing.

Many of the boats on the market—particularly those sold to racers or people who hope to be mistaken for racers—are designed to do exactly one thing well, with all other considerations secondary. A slalom-racing 'yak is built for extreme maneuverability in turbulent water; an Olympic flatwater boat is meant to go fast as the devil in a straight line on sheltered waters; and so on.

Old Town touring kayak, a typical good all-around design. *Courtesy Old Town*

Life is more complicated for the designer or buyer of a recreational kayak which has to do quite a few different and often conflicting jobs. Ideally, a good touring kayak should:

(1) Have sufficient *capacity* to carry a basic camping kit and supplies for extended cruising. Loadspace should be easily accessible.
(2) *Track* well; that is, it should be easy for a competent paddler to keep the boat going in a straight line on calm water.
(3) Be *maneuverable* enough for safe handling in the conditions under which the boat is to be used.
(4) Have good inherent *speed*—not in the racing class, but enough to let a fit paddler cover reasonable distances without unnecessary fatigue.
(5) Be *strong* and durable, without excessive weight or clumsiness.
(6) Be reasonably *comfortable* to sit in and paddle on an all-day basis.

To this we may add a general quality that could be called "seaworthiness"—the boat should be so designed and constructed as to be safe and manageable in rough water, without any built-in tendencies to swamp, dive, capsize, or the like. This is, of course, important in *any* kind of boat, but it becomes especially critical if you are going to be moving through wild country with little chance of rescue. In the final analysis, however, it should always be remembered that safety—barring things like actual structural defects or genuinely dangerous designs—is primarily up to the paddler, not the boat.

Now it will be immediately obvious that these criteria set up several conflicts. If you build a boat so that it turns easily, it will be harder to keep it moving straight ahead, and vice versa. Improving capacity and comfort usually means making the boat bigger, but if you make it wider you lose speed and if you make it longer you reduce maneuverability, besides adding weight either way, to say nothing of expense, and the list goes on.

To some extent we set our own priorities; a whitewater river runner will cheerfully sacrifice tracking for maneuverability, while a sea kayaker will make the opposite trade any day. This is one reason I can't simply say, "Buy yourself an Elmo Quisenberry River Eater Mark XIII," or, "The Schimmelfarb Walrus is the finest touring kayak in the world," or whatever; you'll have to decide what your own personal wants and needs are before you can make a satisfying choice.

Most of us, however, do want a certain level of versatility; only very well-heeled or very single-minded kayakers need to get involved with specialized designs. The average reader probably wants to be able to cruise on open water such as lakes and bays, drift down slow rivers, *and* run fast wild streams with a fair amount of easy-to-intermediate whitewater—Class II or III on the International Scale—with the same boat. Of course, the designer also has to keep in mind a fairly wide range of customer interests in order to make any profits. So the true touring kayak represents a set of trade-offs and compromises. It's amazing, when you think of it, that the results are often so beautiful.

Let's look at what little kayaks are made of—and how.

DESIGN PRINCIPLES

Okay, relax; we aren't going to get into a lot of complex geometry or marine engineering here. The basic ideas are really very simple. After all, water is a pretty common substance, and we all have some idea how floating objects behave, right?

The characteristics of any boat are determined mainly by hull shape. A kayak is a "displacement" hull; that is, it rides in, not on top of, the water. Seemingly small differences in configuration can radically alter performance.

Looking back at our requirements for a moment, if we want an extremely maneuverable boat, we can design it so the bottom line sweeps sharply upward toward the ends. This is called rocker, and it is one of the chief reasons for the astonishing agility of a slalom kayak. A highly rockered boat, however, will also track about as well as a Frisbee, and paddling it for any distance over open water will be very tiring because you will have to keep fighting to keep it from swerving to one side.

On the other hand, if we make the bottom line of our kayak absolutely straight with no rocker at all, it will track as if on rails and be very easy to paddle in a straight line. (Straight-line racing boats—Olympic flatwater kayaks and downriver racers—are made this way.) But when you try to turn it you will be reminded of the old song, "Give Me Forty Acres and I'll Turn This Rig Around."

So if we want a reasonably versatile boat, we will need a bit of rocker toward the ends—enough to let us maneuver in all but very constricted rapids—but not enough to completely ruin its tracking qualities. This is a delicate business, and no totally satisfactory compromise has ever been invented—there being no loopholes in the laws of hydrodynamics—but the best modern boats are plenty good enough for the average person. The main thing is to avoid the specialized kayaks designed for racing or surfing.

Another important factor is hull length. Competition slalom boats are a bit over thirteen feet long because that is what the rules specify. Unfortunately, many makers have mindlessly followed these specs on boats which will never see a race. Thirteen feet, two inches is a handy length and makes a very maneuverable

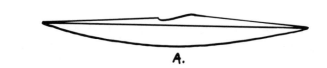

A.

B.

C.

Comparison of Kayak Hull Shapes

A. Slalom kayak for competition and advanced whitewater: short hull with pronouncedly "rockered" (upswept) bottom lines for maximum maneuverability. Relatively slow, extremely hard to paddle in straight line, but turns on preinflation dime.

B. Flatwater cruising kayak. Long hull is perfectly straight along bottom centerline, with "ship"-like bow and stern. Very fast, easy to hold on course, but reluctant to turn in close quarters.

C. General touring kayak: long and straight enough for reasonably good tracking on open water, but enough rocker at ends for maneuvering in intermediate-level whitewater.

boat for racing or very constricted whitewater, but it's a bit short for an all-round touring kayak. Not only is a short boat limited in cargo space, it's slow. All else being equal, a long kayak is faster than a short one and is less work to paddle over a long day. It will also track better and, while it will be less maneuverable, a bit of rocker at the ends will help keep it from being too clumsy.

Specific recommendations are hard to make because only you know what you want to do with the boat. But if you want to be able to tour on various kinds of water and don't expect to be running rapids above Class III, then I'd go for something about fourteen feet long. Slalom-length boats are still best for serious whitewater, and only a sea kayaker will need anything over fifteen.

Looking at the hull from another angle, the cross-sectional shape raises new questions. Beginners often think boats with flat bottoms will be safer and more stable, and you'd think this would be so, but in fact the opposite is true. A kayak with a round or inverted-arch bottom will feel a bit more unstable at first, but, if properly designed, it will have reserve stability; that is, as it tips to one side, more hull area enters the water, so it actually stabilizes itself. A flat bottom feels stable sitting on calm water, but the first time a wave or strong current hits it from one side the boat will tend to follow the contour of the surface. It will lurch and wallow and quite possibly capsize.

But we can go too far the other way. Very sharp, V-shaped hulls are wonderfully fast but lack inherent stability. It takes a really skilled paddler to handle one on a steady basis without getting dunked. You want to avoid the extremes of flat and sharp and look for something in between. What am I trying to tell you? Compromise equals versatility, provided the guy who made the compromise knew what he was talking about.

Volume is a term you may have heard tossed around. In kayaking it refers simply to the overall volume of the boat, both above and below the water; depth, deck contours, and general "fatness" of line come into the picture. This is mostly something that comes up in whitewater circles. A low-volume boat is very light and agile and thus popular for slalom racing because a crafty paddler can slip its low-slung ends under the dangling poles that mark the course, saving vital seconds. A high-volume kayak is the usual choice of non-racing paddlers, especially on big Western rivers, because it will rise out of keeper hydraulics and climb over big waves where a low-volume boat tends to act like a submarine. The high-volume 'yak, of course, also holds a lot more stuff, so if you're figuring on doing mostly whitewater touring and want a slalom-type boat, make sure you get the high-volume kind. Manufacturers' specifications will tell you these things (or should).

Viewed from above, any standard recreational kayak will be symmetrical and widest where the paddler sits. Some specialized racing designs have their greatest width back near the stern, but they are unsuitable for general touring for many reasons.

As for width, 24 inches is the standard or 25 inches in a few big boats. A very few models go considerably wider—mostly folders—but while a beam of 30 inches or so makes a very stable and roomy boat, it also makes a slow, clumsy one compared to narrower designs. On the other hand, some sea kayaks are a mere 22 inches wide, which makes them very fast but too tippy for the average casual paddler. Most people will do best to stay in the two-foot-beam class.

CONSTRUCTION

The original kayak construction of driftwood and sea mammal skin has given way to various modern materials, some more successful than others.

Wood frame kayaks are closest to the Arctic concept in that a skeletal wooden framework is covered with a flexible "skin," in this case a stout fabric, usually coated with plastic or rubber. (Some home builders successfully use ordinary canvas, waterproofed with a few coats of oil-base or polyurethane paint.) These can be extraordinarily beautiful boats; the complex, neatly fitted wooden frame, highly varnished, is something to see. The "organic" construction seems to impart a remarkable balance between stiffness and flexibility, and a well-made frame boat is very pleasant to paddle.

Frame kayaks used to be common, even standard, before fiberglass came in. Nowadays they are fairly rare, except for foldboats. Modern kayakers tend to dismiss them, not altogether justly. The main reason they have gone out of vogue is that they are far from ideal whitewater boats. It is difficult to get the wooden frame

Foxfire, a frame-and-fabric flatwater touring kayak designed and built by the author. Note long hull and raised wave-splitting bow. *Cordell Sanders*

to assume a shape that maneuvers really well, and the construction tends to be rather fragile compared with fiberglass. This can be corrected by using heavier materials, but then the boat becomes clumsy. I have used frame kayaks in rapids up through Class III, but it's true that they really aren't at their best amid the rocks and waves.

On the other hand, frame kayaks are splendid open-water touring craft. My own pet lake cruiser, *Foxfire,* is a frame boat; I built her myself to my own design. She is light—40 pounds, not bad for a 15-foot boat—comfortable, fast, and I love her passionately. I wouldn't take her down a rapid, though.

This is a good type of construction for the home builder, much easier and safer than fiberglass, and kits are available at low cost. In fact, this is by far the cheapest way to build a kayak at home— *Foxfire*'s materials cost me a whopping $150—so the would-be kayak tourist on a tight budget might want to look into the possibilities.

Wood veneer construction is very rarely seen except in Olympic racing models. Usually the hull is made by molding strips of veneer over a form to produce a very light, stiff shell, but a few outfits produce kayaks made of light plywood. These are easily the most beautiful kayaks of all; they positively glow.

The trouble, for most of us, is that they are entirely too pretty— and expensive—to drag around the boondocks. They don't take kindly to things like rocks, either; plywood lacks the flex of fiberglass or even fabric and it cracks. Keeping an all-wood 'yak in decent condition involves a lot of work and attention, far more than any other type. Moreover, the finished boats cost like the devil. However, a few companies sell kits for these kayaks at reasonable prices (see the appendix), and if you are good with woodworking tools and want to go the classy route, you might want to try building one.

Wood-veneer kayak built from Country Ways kit. *Courtesy Country Ways*

Fiberglass, to use the common though technically incorrect term, is the material used in the overwhelming majority of the kayaks in current use. If you set aside the folding models, you can almost say fiberglass has become universal. There are good reasons for this. Fiberglass (properly termed fiber-reinforced plastic, or FRP) is an extremely versatile material. It can be molded into virtually any shape and laid up to give different combinations of weight, stiffness, flexibility, and so on. It lends itself very well to mass production. And, properly made, it is tough, long lasting, and light. It is also somewhat unpleasant to work with, but that need not concern the buyer.

Fiberglass, or FRP, is not a single substance but a composite, consisting of fibers of glass (how *about* that) or other materials impregnated with some sort of plastic resin. The idea is rather like steel-reinforced concrete or the threads in your car's tires. The resin-based plastic is hard but brittle by itself, while the fiber is strong but lacks rigidity; put them together and you get the virtues of both.

There are various materials with which a fiberglass hull can be made. The resin used in most modern boats is a polyester, with some new vinyl-type esters gaining in popularity in recent years. Older boats, and a few new ones, may be made with epoxy; this makes a tremendously strong boat, but there are truly appalling health hazards involved in working with it, so epoxy is definitely on its way out, and none of us miss the poisonous stuff.

Most American kayak and canoe manufacturers use a glass fiber made by Owens-Corning. This may be put together in different ways. Strongest for weight is a clothlike woven fabric, rather pretty in its original state. Roving is a heavier, coarser cloth. Mat is just a sheet of mashed-together random fibers without any weave at all; it is cheaper than cloth but not nearly as strong.

A really first-class kayak will be built entirely of cloth in several layers—four will make a good strong boat—usually the 6- or 10-ounce type. The maker may substitute a layer of roving for one or two of the cloth layers; this is entirely satisfactory if done properly and should hold the price down. A few may use a layer of mat or even a cloth-mat-roving sandwich, but this is less than ideal construction and tends to make a heavy, clumsy, brittle boat.

Some cheap kayaks (and a few not so cheap) have been made by spraying chopped-up fiber mat into a mold. Such construction works fairly well in the cheapest open canoes, perhaps, but in a kayak it is just no good at all. Chopped-mat construction should be considered unacceptable. You can check for this by looking into the boat in strong light; you ought to be able to make out a clear, definite weave pattern. If you can't, and especially if this is a brand you have never heard of, you may be about to get ripped off.

It used to be standard practice to have a gel coat on the outside of kayak hulls, and most commercial builders still apply them. This is merely a layer of resin, rather thin, with no fiber content, and the pigment is mixed in so the boat does not have to be painted. Large fiberglass craft such as yachts, which have to be in the water all the time, need this coat to keep water from slowly soaking into the fibers, but in a kayak, canoe, or other small craft, a gel coat serves an almost wholly cosmetic purpose. In plain English, it makes the boat look pretty. If the manufacturer got a little sloppy or fudged on the materials, it may help hide that too. It adds weight and expense and must be ground off to apply any sizeable patching. A lot of people are starting to question whether it's worth it, and some very fine kayaks are now being made without any gel coat. Consider this a plus; it holds down the weight and the price and it forces the maker to do a clean job on the laminations.

The kayak will be molded in two main components, the hull and the deck. The deck will be somewhat more lightly constructed than the bottom, but should have sufficient strength to keep the boat from collapsing and trapping the paddler in an accident. These halves are joined by an internal seam (putting this in place is one of the most loathsome jobs known) and a separate molded cockpit-coaming-and-seat piece is fitted. It's all very neat and simple and, admittedly, about as romantic as a bathtub, but then we don't have to harpoon any walruses to get the materials, either.

It is worth giving some careful scrutiny to fiberglass boats when shopping for your kayak; frankly, there is a good deal of sloppy

There's one in every crowd . . . this baroque effect is not a paint job but was done by laminating a paisley fabric into the fiberglass under a clear gel coat. Lines of this boat are extremely good for touring. *Courtesy Old Town*

work floating around. And some of it is no longer floating, or even in one piece. One bad sign: whitish patches, which often mean the cloth did not get sufficiently impregnated with resin. More resin isn't necessarily better, though; resin by itself is brittle. If you see unusually thick, shiny areas on the inside of the boat, where the liquid resin appears to have puddled up before setting, you've got a poorly made boat. Slight imperfections might be acceptable in a home-built job, but when you're going to lay out several hundred bucks you have a right to expect proper workmanship. Anyway, if there's an obvious flaw where you can see it, what other sloppiness may be hidden up in the recesses of the hull, or under a slick gel coat? Pressure on the hull and deck should produce a slight springy flex; the boat should be neither rubbery soft nor absolutely unyielding. There certainly should be no ominous crackling noises when you push against the fiberglass.

There are many more aspects to fiberglass construction, but these general remarks should let you make an intelligent evaluation. If you're interested in further study, check the reading list in back.

Various **soft plastics,** mostly some form of polyethylene, have been used in kayak construction; old-school river people tend to use snide terms like "Tupperware," "Frisbee material," and others too colorful to print. The boats are tremendously durable, if not indestructible, with roughly five times the impact strength of fiberglass. They are therefore attractive to novice whitewater paddlers, who bounce off a lot of rocks. The hull can be molded in one piece, eliminating the seam that is such a headache in glass boats, and making kits for these boats much less work to assemble. The interior is smooth, which is easier on waterproof stowage bags.

Reaction to these boats has been very mixed; they are not quite as wonderful as they look. Their soft, flexy bottoms make them considerably slower and harder work to paddle than more rigid boats; this pretty much takes them out of the running as open-water touring 'yaks. At the same time, a lot of people are very nervous about using them in dangerous rapids because there is a very real fear that the soft deck and hull will collapse and fold if the boat gets pinned against a rock, trapping and drowning the occupant. This has happened—and not just with soft-plastic boats, either. The problem can be solved, more or less, by adding rigid bulkheads of Ethafoam—this has, in fact, become standard practice with this type of kayak—but these interfere with internal storage and add weight; and the polyethylene boats are heavier than FRP to begin with. Finally, existing models are designed strictly for whitewater use and have less than optimum hull geometry for general cruising.

A few exotic materials are used in kayak construction, if you want to pay the hefty tab to obtain their undeniable virtues. Kevlar

49, which most of us call simply Kevlar, is an astonishingly light, strong, stiff fiber made by DuPont (an aramid, whatever that may mean) and used by top kayak and canoe builders to replace one or more layers of fiberglass (or even to build the whole boat, which really gets you into the Rolls-Royce class.). It makes a truly wonderful boat—very light, stiff, and responsive; you also have to figure that any manufacturer who goes to the expense of using Kevlar will apply extra attention to things like lamination and seams.

Kevlar, however, is fabulously expensive stuff, and a Kevlar boat may easily be several hundred dollars more than the equivalent all-FRP model (though the difference has come down somewhat in recent years). Few ordinary kayakers really *need* the added advantages—it's really a racer's material—so don't cry if you can't have it. But if you've got the money and the taste for Kevlar, you'll glow a little every time you even think about your new boat.

Carbon fiber was considered a promising material some years back, and you still see it now and then, mostly in racing boats. Even more expensive than Kevlar, and very difficult to work with, it has mostly been used in small amounts as hull reinforcement rather than as a major structural material.

OTHER MATTERS

The **cockpit** area deserves some special attention; after all, that is where you are going to spend your time. You can't move around in a 'yak as in other types of boats. Here is where we get back to comfort, which, to be sure, is a subjective question, but a vital one all the same. I once wrote, in a book on bicycle racing, "*Anything* will make your butt hurt if you sit on it long enough," and this is true of kayaks as well; all the same, you don't want to wind up with some kind of Spanish Inquisition torture machine. This is another point where we lose the racing boats; competition events are short, and racers are thinking about other things anyway, so these craft are definitely built for speed and not comfort.

Large people need to be particularly attentive to cockpit designs; some models are extremely tight. (Though some cockpit layouts are tight to get into they're quite comfortable once you're in.) Every time I ease my 6'-3", 200-pound frame into my old Lettmann Mark I slalom boat, I feel like a fat woman pulling on a too-small pair of pantyhose. If you stand over six feet tall or just run to legs, you might well consider one of the bigger boats with oversized cockpits.

But don't get a bigger cockpit than you actually need; it adds hassle. A larger-than-standard cockpit requires an outside spray cover. These are not always easy to get in the better models, and the nylon varieties tend to form regular little swimming pools which drip through the seams onto your knees all day—lots of fun when it's cold. Also, if you have any hopes at all of ever learning the Eskimo roll, don't get more cockpit than you have to have; it will increase the tendency to fall out of the boat in a capsize.

Perhaps I should pause here and add that you *won't* get stuck in the boat if you dump it, even if getting in was a bit of a squeeze. If you got in, you'll come out, and probably so fast you won't even remember how you did it. I've seen a fair amount of skin left on coamings during panic exits, but this doesn't seem to have much to do with cockpit size. You just want to be able to get in and out with reasonable ease, without wishing for a can opener every time.

A few really first-class kayaks have adjustable seats—wonderful, and well worth paying for.

Except for the big folders, nearly all modern kayaks incorporate some kind of system of **braces**—fittings against which the paddler can press the feet, knees, hips, and sometimes thighs. The purpose of the bracing system is to let you lock yourself securely to the boat, so that you become one unit; the kayak becomes an extension of your lower body and you can control it with your hips, knees, and feet, not just the paddle. Since you are applying force down near the waterline rather than from your shoulders, this is a very efficient and safe system; it is also absolutely necessary in order to do the modern strokes such as the high brace and the famous Eskimo roll. It does not jam you in so you can't get out; a mere relaxation of muscle pressure is enough to free you.

Foot braces used to take the form of a straight bar across the inside of the bow, but paddlers began to wonder if it might not be possible to get a foot caught under this, trapping the kayaker. After a few such cases were actually reported, the bar brace fell from favor. Today most kayakers use pedal-type braces—little footrests fastened to the sides of the hull. (This system also permits a bit of gear to be stored up in the bow, so it is better for touring.) These may be homemade arrangements, or commercial foot braces are obtainable. Adjustable models are particularly worth having, since they let several people use the same kayak—a valuable feature in a family, club, or group tour.

The knee braces are simply pockets in the underside of the deck, though a few kayaks are fitted with foam pads and the like for greater comfort. The hip braces are formed by the same fiberglass struts that suspend the seat from the cockpit coaming; a few boats have separate seats, and these must be fitted with hip braces, usually in the form of glued-in blocks of foam. Thigh braces are specialized equipment used by a few heavy-water river runners, unnecessary in a touring boat.

Rudders are fitted to some big flatwater kayaks and virtually all sea boats. You don't really need a rudder to turn a kayak—the paddle does that—and a rudder adds moving parts and complexities of lines and pedals, greatly detracting from the simplicity that is part of the kayak's original charm. While a rudder may help keep an otherwise recalcitrant boat on course, this is basically something that should not be necessary if you've got a decent boat.

In some situations, though, rudders are worth having. If you're having to cover a large expanse of open water, and there is a strong pattern of waves or tide coming in from the bow quarter trying to shove you off course, it is very fatiguing to have to keep making corrective strokes. A rudder lets you hold your course through quartering waves and still use all your energy for going where you want to go. This may sound very off-the-wall, but believe me, strong quartering wave patterns are an extremely—and maddeningly—common fact of life in open-water cruising. Unless you expect to do a great deal of this sort of thing, though, I wouldn't bother with a rudder. Remember, a rudder has no business at all in any kind of rapids. It will catch on rocks and be ripped off or cause you to dump. So if you do get one, make sure it's readily removable, or else give up even modest whitewater.

Skegs are, on the whole, nasty little bits of work. If you don't know, a skeg is a kind of fixed rudder—a vertical fin that sticks down under the kayak's stern. The idea is to give the boat better tracking qualities, but the idea rarely works. If the hull is properly designed for linear stability—good length-to-width ratio, not a lot of rocker—and the paddler is competent, it will go straight without needing any added-on gadgets. If it's a hull designed for maneuverability and never mind tracking—or if it's simply a badly designed hull, no good for anything—then a skeg won't do all that much good either.

Some makers have tried marketing add-on skegs to fit their general-purpose kayaks. Supposedly this lets you use the same boat for a wider range of jobs, and you can whip the skeg off to run rivers, and so on. I remain unimpressed. A kind of temporary skeg, however, is sometimes used by beginners. Made of scrap metal, wood, or even flattened cans, and taped to the underside of the stern, this cheap-and-dirty rig helps keep the kayak on course while the novice is getting the hand of the forward paddle stroke. Nothing wrong with this; in fact, I wish I'd thought of it when I was learning.

BUYING A KAYAK

Let's add it all up. A good all-round touring kayak for a paddler of average size and ability will be about 14 feet long and 24 inches wide at the cockpit, relatively straight along the bottom centerline, but rockered upward somewhat at the ends. In cross-section the bottom will be rounded or shaped like an inverted, squashed-out Gothic arch. The hull will be deep enough to provide room for gear and the cockpit opening big enough for reasonable ease in entry and exit. Such a boat will weigh 30 to 40 pounds, depending on materials used.

A boat on these lines will be fine for cruising on lakes, slow rivers, and most whitewater streams of Class I and II difficulty. (The easier grades in other words—the classification system is explained in chapter 6.) It may or may not work out in more difficult whitewater; on large rivers on the western pattern, where the passage is broad and the obstacles are mostly hydraulic in nature, it ought to be okay in strong hands, but it will be too big and clumsy for narrow rocky streams where maneuvering is tight.

If the boat is bought primarily as a whitewater craft, it should be a bit shorter—slightly over 13 feet is standard—and have a more rounded, rockered hull design. If, on the other hand, it is bought strictly for open-water cruising, then it can be as long as 15 or 16 feet and should have no rocker at all.

All this assumes you are going to buy a new boat for touring. If you already own a kayak, chances are you can use it even if it doesn't exactly fit specs. Just know its limitations; don't take an old 16-foot flatwater boat down a squirmy Class IV stream, for instance, or try to go to sea in a slalom 'yak. Even older racing designs often make quite good touring boats if you are careful about your choice of gear. My old Mark I was considered quite a hot item in its day; now I take it on camping trips. Competition designs have changed so much in the last decade that kayaks designed for racing have often evolved into touring boats. It is only the extreme low-volume boats that are really hopeless for touring. If you own one of these you already know what it is and isn't for, and you probably paid a lot of money for it and wouldn't dream of dragging it around the wilderness anyway.

The point of this book is to get you to go out and do it, not to persuade you to spend money, and certainly not to make you give up the idea because the budget won't stretch to cover a new boat. If you already own *any* halfway decent 'yak or have a chance to pick up one at a good price, go to it.

This homily out of the way, we'll get back to our original assumption—that you're about to go buy yourself a touring boat.

Beyond the remarks I've already made about design and construction, my main advice is: get what you want. Get a boat in which you feel comfortable, one which will be suited to the kind of kayaking you want to do—and not what somebody else thinks you ought to have. There is an awful lot of label-sniffing snobbery in the outdoor field nowadays, and you can very easily meet many people who will disparage anything but the hottest, costliest, most "in" boat on the markets. There is also a pervasive elitism, particularly among specialized groups like whitewater jocks and sea kayakers, that looks down on practitioners of less extreme branches of the sport. For that matter, most of the available books on kayaking practically tell you that kayakers are divided into two groups: whitewater cowboys and wimps. Ignore all of this. No one has a right to downgrade the value of another's trip, because no one knows what the other person was looking for or whether or not he or she found it.

On a more mundane level, unless you want to do a lot of driving every time you want to get your kayak wet, you ought to consider what kind of kayak touring water is likely to be available where you live. I live in Arkansas, so I get to run rather narrow, rocky little mountain streams, or cruise around on big man-made lakes, or occasionally poke my way along a bottomland stream or swamp. A sea kayak, or one designed for the Homeric hydraulics of western rivers, would be pretty pointless for me. If you live in, say, southern Florida, you probably won't get much use out of a slalom boat. And so on; you see what I'm saying.

How do you go about picking your own 'yak, your floating home and soul mate, that you will spend some of the best times of your life in and probably get scared half to death in and talk to and sleep beside and the rest of it? Take your time. There are plenty of people willing to take your money. Get the catalogs from the leading makers, check the list of addresses in the back of the book, look for ads in magazines, and pore over the specs. Ask the guy who owns one, being careful to allow for the usual tendency of kayakers to lie about nearly everything relating to their boats and the water they've run. Go to outdoor shops and look at boats, but don't let yourself be pressured—unless, of course, you find one which is absolutely and undeniably magnificent at a price you can't pass up.

If at all possible, try some kayaks out. Shops probably won't let you do this, but there are other ways. Along many popular float streams, some of the better rental concerns are now renting kayaks as alternatives to their usual clunky canoes; sometimes outdoor shops have kayaks for rent too. Rent what you can find for simple day trips—this will also give you a chance to practice basic paddling—and note the makes and how they perform.

Another way to try out kayaks is at a class. In most cities, if you ask around at outdoor shops and the like, you can find kayak classes, usually run by the local canoe clubs. Not only can you learn a lot about kayak technique, including the tricky Eskimo roll, but such classes nearly always have some boats and paddles on hand for people who don't have their own 'yaks yet. Ask to try different ones and note to yourself how they feel.

This business of "feel" is very difficult to put into words but very important all the same. Sometimes a boat is technically perfect and seems to fit you as if it were made just for you, yet there is some indefinable quality about it that makes you feel awkward and alien when you sit in it. Another boat may be all wrong for you by any objective standards, yet the moment you get in something inside you says: this is *my* boat. The Javanese, who carry daggers as ritual custom, believe that for each man there is a dagger which is meant for him, even though it may have been made before his birth, and that a dagger in the hands of any but its intended owner will be useless and may even turn against the bearer. I'm not at all sure they aren't onto something—at least if you apply the idea to kayaks.

Less mystically, do try to get a boat that fits you. We've already noted that big or long-legged people need more cockpit space, and the foredeck must be high enough to let a long pair of legs extend properly, especially if the big guy also has big feet, as most of us do. On the flip side, if you're rather small, don't get more boat than you can handle, or something that makes you feel like a bug in a bathtub.

Don't be ashamed to give some weight to things like color and general looks. You want something you can be proud of and enjoy looking at. Why not? After all, it's your money.

If you're still confused, just get something from a reputable manufacturer such as Phoenix, Seda, Easy Rider, or Old Town, to name but a few. I always felt Dick Held's Clearwater was the best all-round touring 'yak, but I am told it is out of production, although you might find one in a shop. Excellent boats in this class are the Phoenix Appalachian, Seda Vagabond, and Old Town Prijon 420. For open water, Easy Rider's big Dolphin is a fine cruising boat with serious seagoing capability as well; indeed, some of the true sea kayaks, such as the Sea Otter or Seda's Viking, make superb lake cruisers. If your interest is strictly in whitewater, there are several high-volume slalom boats around;

Easy Rider Dolphin, shown at Glacier Bay, Alaska, but a fine cruising boat for any open water, fresh or salt. Definitely not for whitewater, however. *Courtesy Easy Rider*

Old Town's slalom model is a good one, and Easy Rider's Augsburg II is, for my money, the best and most comfortable big-volume whitewater touring kayak on the market, especially for big, long-legged men.

All of these are expensive. Well, remember, a boat will get you through a time of no money better than money will get you through a time of no boat.

USED KAYAKS

If you're hard up for money, there are good deals in the used kayak market. Many people start with touring boats, get into racing, and sell their little-used touring 'yaks at low prices to raise money for racing boats. Not long ago I saw a Hollowform River Chaser going for a mere $120; I'm not crazy about the River Chaser or any other soft plastic boat, but for the price I think I could live with its faults. About the same time, I met another guy selling a Phoenix Appalachian, a really good touring boat, for $200—less than half the list price even then.

All of this assumes the boat is in clean condition. If it has been patched, you'd better be extremely cautious. An awful lot of people don't know how to patch fiberglass so it stays patched. I had originally found my old Mark I lying neglected in a backyard with several poorly done patches in a state of advanced delamination; I had to grind the old patches off then clean up the breaks— and there were several big ones—with a grinder before doing the job properly. I was willing to do this because the boat was something of a classic. It was made back in the early seventies by Hyperform, a company long out of business, and it was one of the finest designs of Klaus Lettmann. But I wouldn't advise anyone to take on this sort of project under normal circumstances. I could have rented a mold and built myself a new boat with less work.

If there are a few small patches but the hull appears basically sound, examine the work closely. Are the patches holding solidly all around? If you can slip a knife blade, or even force it, between the patch and the hull, forget it. As with the boat itself, there should be no white patches or resin pooling. If the break was in the area of the seam between deck and hull, check the inside and see if the seam is still solid, or, if there was damage, whether this was repaired. How extensive is the damage? One or two little patches, even if badly done, could be removed and replaced if the boat is otherwise a bargain, but if the 'yak has been really crunched then I'd pass it up unless you have good reason to know the work was done by a real expert. Press firmly against the patched area; it should have about the same slight flex as the rest of the hull. The hull doesn't flex either? Forget it—it's a lousy boat. If you get a snap, crackle, and pop, tell the guy thanks but no thanks.

Wood boats are not usually good buys when used. There is no way to tell whether they have been properly cared for, and dry rot is a possibility. Soft plastic kayaks are almost impossible to damage, but once holed they are very difficult to patch properly. I'd be particularly wary of any repaired boat of this material.

Despite these cautions, used kayaks are definitely worth considering. Even if you can afford a new boat, remember that you're going to need some other things—a paddle, camping gear, and so on—and you might prefer to get a used 'yak and put the money you save into other areas. Good luck, and remember to bring to your quest the kind of faith and trust you would bestow on a person trying to sell you real estate in Florida or a Spanish treasure map.

HOME BUILDING

Building your own kayak sound attractive. You can save money, maybe, and there's certainly a thrill in paddling a boat you made yourself, but it's not always as easy as it looks.

Building a fiberglass boat is a complex and fairly demanding business. It is possible to put in a great deal of work and come up with a brittle, heavy, lumpy klutz of a boat that delaminates in two years. It is also very possible to do your health a lot of harm, as some of the chemicals involved are pretty nasty. For one thing, the fibers themselves will play havoc with your lungs, so you have to wear a respirator for some operations. You have to rent a mold, which usually means going through a club or a private builder. In the end you will have saved some money, but not as much as you might think—not as much as you would probably have saved by getting a used boat, anyway.

There is certainly no space here to go into the details of building a fiberglass boat; check the reading list. And read these books before you make a definite decision, let alone buy any materials, so you'll know what you're getting into; you may decide to forget it.

Frame boats, if you can live with their limitations, are much easier to build at home and can be bought in kit form. Folbot puts out several such kits; their wildly misnamed "Racer" is quite a good touring boat. You can also get some plans and build your kayak from scratch.

One last point: all this material has been aimed at the one-boat paddler. I have assumed, somewhat arbitrarily, that the reader will want a single kayak that can be used in a wide variety of applications, even though this means a certain amount of compromise in the final design.

However, if for some reason—unusual affluence, luck in acquiring bargains, or whatever—you should find yourself able to own more than one kayak, you can ignore quite a bit of the material in this chapter. A big open-water cruising kayak and a high-volume whitewater boat will make an almost perfect combination, and either of them will perform better in its intended environment than any general-purpose boat ever can.

This is my own current situation, as it happens; at the time of writing I no longer own any all-round boats. I use my 15-foot cruiser, *Foxfire,* for lake and open-river travel, and my old Mark I slalom boat, *Lady Mary,* for whitewater. (The whitewater streams in my area are all short, so I don't have to carry supplies for really extended trips in the little 'yak.) Since I built *Foxfire* myself to my own design, and rebuilt *Lady Mary* after getting her for next to nothing, the total investment probably works out to less than the cost of a new touring kayak of the better sort. Perhaps you might be lucky enough to work out a similar arrangement.

There are a few other possibilities for kayaks that we ought to discuss. They lie so far outside the mainstream that I have given them a chapter of their own.

3

The Oddballs

Kayaks have, on the whole, become pretty standardized—long, banana-shaped hollow shells of synthetic materials or, more rarely, wooden boats based more or less on Inuit designs. Still, there are a few designs and categories that differ radically from anything else on the market. It would be simple enough to pass these mutants by as "not true kayaks" or of little interest to the serious kayaker, and indeed this is what has happened in a lot of kayak literature. But in fact most have definite advantages in their own specialized way, and all deserve at least a brief look.

FOLDBOATS

Yes indeed, Herr Klepper's brainchild is still very much afloat and doing extremely well—in fact, enjoying a definite revival of interest, both in the boats that bear his name and other craft

sharing the folding concept. At first glance the appeal of the folders would seem to be that of convenience and portability. Nowadays an increasing number of people live in small apartments
and have no good place to store rigid boats. There is also a trend
toward smaller cars which are not always well adapted to carrying
rooftop racks. A foldboat can also be carried on a large motorcycle, a bus, or an airplane.

The folder has a lot going for it, however, beyond the simple
fact that it folds. Current designs are very big by kayak standards—broad in the beam and exceptionally roomy in the cockpit.
This makes them very comfortable to sit in, a point of particular
interest to long-range cruisers. You can store enormous loads
below those canvas decks—enormous for a kayak, anyway—so
the foldboat traveler can live in far more luxurious style than any
other kayak camper and can go on very long trips without re-
plenishing supplies.

The wide hull also makes the typical folder extremely stable;

Klepper Aerius II—the Rolls-Royce of folders. *Courtesy Klepper America*

given the low center of gravity, the foldboat is probably even more stable than the open canoe. This is very appealing to people who for various reasons find normal kayaks a little too tiddly, or those who simply can't take chances, such as elderly or handicapped people or those with small children along. The increased stability, coupled with the generous cockpit, makes the foldboat handier for fishing than smaller designs. You can even fit sails to some models. Many sea kayakers swear by Kleppers. A successful Atlantic crossing was done in a Klepper double by a guy named Lindemann back in 1956. It is possible that more miles have been paddled in Kleppers than in any other type of kayak.

But foldboats, like humans, have their failings. The big drawback, in handling terms, is the very stability that makes most folders so safe. A big foldboat is easy to paddle in a straight line on open water—especially if fitted with a rudder, as many are—and will go surprisingly fast. But in close spots with things happening in a hurry, they are clumsy. Whitewater expert Earl Perry once wrote that they have "all the maneuverability of a fired bullet . . . once they start down a rapid, only God and solid objects alter their course." A bit overstated, but not much. Folders can run surprisingly big rapids if the passage is wide and unobstructed—fitted with spray skirts and handled with skill, they handle big waves very well—but they are not suitable for any situation demanding rapid maneuvering because they just can't hack it. Basically the typical folder is an open-water boat and an excellent one.

There is another problem: price. Folders are, on the whole, excruciatingly expensive compared to other kayaks. At the time of writing, a Klepper Aerius costs around fifteen hundred dollars. A lot of people simply can't afford it. I don't mean to imply any criticism here. The expense is largely inherent in the concept; the frame requires much hand labor, which is expensive, as is good wood. All the current makes come from countries like Germany or the U.S. where labor is not cheap. It is also fair to point out that a good folder will last a lifetime with proper care, as the skin can be replaced, whereas fiberglass eventually becomes brittle.

You do get a lot of boat for the money. A Klepper Aerius is a magnificent human artifact, in a class with the Rolls-Royce. Both materials and workmanship are absolutely impeccable. For some people the associations are worth something, too; Kleppers are the only kayaks with a really long tradition behind them, one that includes Arctic and Antarctic exploration, ocean crossings, and jungle expeditions by famous explorers. It could be argued that the Klepper Aerius is the only commercially made kayak to have qualified as an authentic classic small craft. It says something, I suppose, that Kleppers almost never turn up on the secondhand market; their owners seem to become fanatically devoted to them. The price is a big barrier, as I say, but my observation has been that those who are authentic "Klepper people" eventually manage to talk themselves into making the purchase, no matter how hard it is to come up with the money.

Folbot, an American company, makes folders which usually run a bit less than half the price of Kleppers. They aren't copies but original designs. Despite the maker's claims—Folbots in my opinion are not in a class with Kleppers as to details of finish and fitting. I have examined a great many (they are very popular in the South) and found quite a few small discrepancies: saw marks, screw heads not quite flush, and the like. On the other hand, the difference in price might seem worth the difference in finish standards; certainly Folbots are on the whole serviceable and sturdy boats and many people have paddled many miles in them.

A few Folbots—not all or even most, just a few—seem to have problems with imprecisely fitted skins. A loose skin will slow the boat down, while a tight one can warp the frame, so this isn't just a cosmetic problem. I've seen this a couple of times myself. However, Folbot may have eliminated this by now, and for that matter, some cases may have been caused by improper assembly by owners.

Incidentally, not all Folbots are foldboats; they make rigid versions of all their boats, at lower prices. If you are attracted by the roominess and stability but have no particular need for a folder, you might look into these non-folding Folbots. They also come in kits at very reasonable prices.

The English-made Tyne folders used to be popular and were outstanding in quality and design, but I don't see them around any more, and I have been unable to find a U.S. source. Let's hope they come back.

All folders work on the same basic principle: the skin is in one piece, like a sock, and the framework is assembled with various joints and pushed into the skin. A toggle arrangement, like a huge shoe tree, snaps it all taut and rigid. Most people can get the time down to fifteen minutes with practice.

Kleppers have long inflated tubes built into the skin under the gunwales. These provide added stability, snap the skin nicely taut, absorb impacts when coming alongside a dock or another boat, and eliminate the need for float bags. Folbots lack this feature and their literature even ridicules it (though it would go far to eliminate the baggy skin problem) and they need float bags added for safety.

Folders are often used without spray skirts; their stability and high cockpit coamings permit this in normal conditions. In rough water a spray skirt is still essential and is always nice to have to keep paddle drip off your lap.

Do you want a foldboat, then? Not if you're into whitewater beyond the simplest levels. But if your interest is in open-water cruising, especially long-range cruising, or if you have transportation or storage problems, you may want to get one of the good old battleships.

And then you might just decide the class alone is worth it.

K-2s

Strictly speaking, a K-2 is a type of Olympic racing kayak, but most people use the term for any two-seat kayak; we'll do so in the interests of space. After all, any true kayaker has to be conscious of saving space.

It has often been said and written that K-2s are outside the mainstream of kayak tradition, that Eskimos didn't use them, and so on. That's not entirely true. The all-time kayak champions of the aboriginal world were the Aleuts, who raised sea kayaking to a level never attained by anyone else, then or now. They cruised the North Pacific between Siberia and Alaska as casually as you'd walk down your driveway and also developed a whole amphibious culture based on the kayak. They used the regular single-sea. kayak like their Inuit cousins, but they also built and used very advanced two-seat kayaks with which they hunted sea mammals, even including the mighty whale. They usually hunted with a paddler in the rear cockpit and a spearman or archer in the bow, but for covering distances both men would paddle together. Later the Russians forced them to install a third cockpit for the use of a Russian overlord; in these three-seaters—*baidarkas,* the Russians called them, but this is not an Aleut word—the white invaders and their slaves hunted furs as far south as San Francisco Bay.

In our own time, the two-seaters have managed to hold a small but steady following among paddlers. There is a special appeal to a K-2, rather like a tandem bicycle. If nothing else, people are guaranteed to turn and look when you go by, and some of the looks will be frankly envious.

Let's get one thing very straight—K-2s are strictly open-water boats. Dick Held once built a whitewater K-2 (I saw him demonstrate it) but it required two absolutely expert paddlers and a great deal of special training and practice; even then the idea did not catch on. The two-seaters are just too long and heavy to maneuver well. While two people can maneuver a canoe handily, this is because they sit at extreme ends of the boat and exert great leverage. In a K-2 the paddlers are close together, reducing their mechanical advantage. Held tried putting the cockpits far apart, but this resulted in too little legroom for the bowman.

On flat water with no need to maneuver quickly, two strong paddlers with good rhythm can really make a K-2 move out. You've got two paddles going with about the same hull geometry as a single-seater, so the power-to-water resistance ratio is very favorable. And a lot of people are bothered by the solitary aspect of normal kayaking and feel happier when sharing a boat with somebody else. Such people will probably prefer the K-2. Finally, the cargo capacity of the average K-2 is nothing short of mammoth, at least by kayak standards.

There are serious drawbacks to the doubles, though. A K-2 is very heavy, clumsy to carry and load atop a car, and over a long day's paddling with no current, this weight can be very tiring to paddle. They take their time about turning; a rudder is pretty much standard. And most models are so big that you really lose a lot of the kayak experience—the unity with the water and the boat, the porpoise-like grace. You <u>wear</u> a standard kayak, but you ride around <u>in</u> a K-2. This isn't always bad—for rough water, especially sea paddling, it can be a plus—but it may run counter to your taste.

Two-seaters are expensive and you could get two good single-seaters for about the same cost. With normal kayaks you can go off by yourself, but with the K-2 you need to find a partner; if one of you doesn't feel like going or can't go, you're stuck. (It is often said that a single person can paddle a K-2, using the other seat for cargo. This is true, provided the person is going down a river with a strong steady current but no rapids and can just drift, or will be using a sailing rig, or has arms and shoulders like Mr. Universe. Paddling a K-2 single-handed is as much fun as wrestling a walrus.) And developing a good steady two-paddle stroke is pretty demanding and requires considerable practice if you don't want to knock each other's heads off. In fact, mastering a K-2 is easily equivalent to working up an exhibition dance routine with a chance of winning a contest.

This last point is worth pondering. I have seen the same situation come up with tandem bicycles, to bring them up again. Two

Easy Rider Sea Eagle two-seater in Desolation Sound, Canada. Except for really remote runs like this, carrying cargo on deck shouldn't be necessary. *Courtesy Easy Rider*

people—especially a married couple—decide the togetherness of the thing would be lots of fun, until they get into the hassles and struggles of actually operating it in unison and harmony, and the hollering and arm-waving begins—

"Whatta you, asleep back there?"

"Hey, watch that paddle hitting mine, will you—"

"I said right, don't you know your right from—"

"—idiot—"

"—fascist—"

Etc., etc., etc. I mean, you can put a lot of strain on a relationship. You had better like each other a lot before you start. And wear helmets while learning to paddle though you don't need them otherwise; not one K-2 team in a thousand can roll one of these boats.

In addition to all the above, it should be pointed out that most of the K-2s on the market are folders, so all the remarks about foldboats should be considered as well. The price is even more staggering, though not actually all that far above the single-seater folders. If you're interested in sailing, Klepper recommends the two-seater Aerius II as better for this purpose than their single; really, only a K-2 has enough cockpit space to allow decent sail handling.

There are a few rigid K-2s around. Klepper also makes a fiberglass K-2, the Kamerad, very nice looking and not a bad price (half that of the Aerius II), while Folbot's non-folding version of their big Super is a real bargain, especially in kit form. Their other big models—the Glider series—are not real kayaks, though, just small open boats. Country Ways has a kit for a two-seat, all-wood kayak that is so beautiful it takes your breath away, for a very low price. Several other companies make two-seaters. The best one I've ever seen was the touring K-2 put out by the defunct (and much mourned) Hyperform Works. If you find an old one in good shape in somebody's garage, grab it.

KIWIS

Kiwis are delightful little one-holers which have recently appeared on the American scene, mostly in California. The design is originally from New Zealand, of all places. Several different

The unique Minnow kayak, a.k.a. Kiwi. Carrying a child as shown is strictly for calm, shallow, close-to-shore waters—and this one definitely should have a life jacket. *Courtesy California Rivers*

models have been offered, but basically they are all very short, fat, funny-looking kayaks with big cockpit openings and full decks. Length is usually about eight feet. Despite their toylike appearance, these are very well-made boats of hand-laid fiberglass and can be used for serious kayaking within their limitations. The Minnow, the most popular model, has such useful features as adjustable seat and foot braces (which you may not get in much bigger boats) and is said to be very comfortable.

You'd think a boat this short would track badly, but the Minnow has a V bottom and straight keel line, so it tracks pretty well—better than some slalom kayaks—yet the extreme shortness of the hull still makes the boat turn easily. Extremely stable, these are excellent kayaks for children—probably the ideal first boat for a child, in fact—but a lot of cautious adults like them too. They can be rolled and used in serious whitewater if the paddler is competent. Prices are lower than conventional kayaks.

I would have thought these little boats very limited in cargo space and suitable only for daytripping, but apparently this is not so. At least one man has taken a Kiwi Minnow down the lower Colorado for 318 miles and 2½ weeks without outside support. This is interesting since this stretch of the big river has little current, so the Kiwi must have reasonably good flatwater qualities.

These funny-looking boats are being used now by some western guided tour outfits as they are easy for beginners to operate. This might offer a way to try out a Kiwi in the field, if you think you might be interested in getting one.

INFLATABLES

Small inflatable boats are very popular nowadays, and one interesting type features a canoe-shaped hull to improve performance. Some hustlers have called them inflatable kayaks. As noted earlier in this book, this is a gross misnomer, and most makers are now calling them inflatable canoes instead.

I don't mean to put inflatable canoes down. On the contrary, I love them. I've owned as many as four; come to think of it, I own three right now. For some whitewater situations they are delightful. All I'm saying is that they fall outside the scope of this book, though some of the techniques described herein can be adapted to them.

But authentic inflatable kayaks do exist. The most spectacular example is the Metzeler Spezi. This is nothing more or less than a slalom kayak which happens to be made of inflatable Hypalon material rather than FRP. Once you blow it up, you have, for all practical purposes, a rigid kayak—a bit *more* rigid than some of the soft plastic 'yaks. There is a fiberglass seat and knee braces. The boat can be rolled as readily as any standard kayak, though it takes a little bit more muscle.

The Spezi is a fine boat for someone who wants to run whitewater and needs a portable, stowable boat. It can be carried on a motorcycle or by air, and in capable hands it will handle any level of whitewater. But it isn't in any sense a touring boat. It's strictly a serious whitewater design, being very short and broad, heavily rockered, and rounded in section. Its directional stability is terrible. The air chambers take up a lot of internal space, which

Metzeler Spezi, a true inflatable kayak. *Courtesy Ski Hut*

is lousy enough in *any* slalom-style boat, so there really isn't enough room to carry even the most marginal, Spartan camping outfit. This is a boat for day trips or for cruising with raft support. It is also *very* expensive, almost as high as a Klepper Aerius.

The only inflatable touring kayak on the current market is the Semperit Dolphin, a truly impressive product. The boat can be set up as a single or double; the rear seat can be deflated and converted into a deck extension for the solo configuration—very ingenious indeed.

The Dolphin has a narrow, streamlined hull for an inflatable and tracks far better than an inflatable canoe or a Spezi. The Hypalon material allows you to pump it to high pressures, making the boat very rigid. Price is only a little higher than the average good-quality FRP boat and much cheaper than the better folders.

It might be thought that the air chambers of an inflatable would be vulnerable to damage from rocks and snags. Don't worry about it; this is a non-issue. I have never owned a Dolphin, but I have, as I said, a lot of experience with other inflatables—I even wrote a book on them once—and their ruggedness often amazes me. I have had a Sea Eagle Explorer, an old one with many miles on it, wrapped around a tree in a flood-swollen river and got it off to find it completely undamaged. A fiberglass kayak or aluminum canoe would have been destroyed. Inflatables bounce off rocks and the like rather than cracking or denting; they are actually more durable than rigid boats in many ways. And the Dolphin is made of materials of equal, if not somewhat superior, durability to those used in the older Sea Eagles.

The big plus with an inflatable, of course, is the portability. If you need something you can stash in your closet and check as luggage on a plane, or toss in the back of a VW, or lash atop a motorcycle, and yet you can't quite afford a folder, give the Dolphin a very close look. If you're interested in fast water, the Dolphin is a much better whitewater boat than anything in the folder class. Even for open water, the Dolphin isn't bad, though not as good for extended paddling as the foldboats.

The main problem is cargo capacity; inflatables just don't have it. Those big airlocks take up a lot of interior space. A Dolphin is only about 12 feet long to begin with, and 26 inches wide. After you subtract airlock thickness you don't get as much useful space as you'd get with a touring boat of rigid construction, let alone the bargelike folders. And however clever the seating arrangements, forget any idea of using a Dolphin as a double on extended trips; there just isn't room for two people and camping gear. The rear-seat area is excellent for storing your kit, though.

Despite this drawback, I think highly of the Dolphin; it offers the same advantages of portability and compactness as the folders at a much lower price (under $500). It has no provision for fitting a spray skirt and therefore can't be rolled properly, but it's still a good boat for up to intermediate whitewater—one group even managed to get a Dolphin through Lava Falls in the Grand Canyon, one of the meanest rapids on the planet—and yet it will track much better on open water than any other inflatable. A kind of "missing link" between the inflatable raft and the kayak, I suppose, but unlike most hybrids this one is a definite winner.

DECKED CANOES

As we saw earlier in this book, there are small canoes, decked over for use in whitewater, that closely resemble kayaks in many ways. While they are not kayaks, there is enough similarity that we might give them a brief glance here.

The single-seat decked canoe or C-1 is the most kayaklike of canoes, especially in the modern low-volume configurations meant for competition. The international racing rules used to specify that the ends had to be raised a certain amount to qualify the boat as a canoe, but this has been changed, resulting in an even more kayakish generation of C-1 designs.

The C-1 is somewhat wider than most kayaks. Beyond this, the difference is primarily in the mode of operation. A C-1 paddler kneels astride a weird-looking sort of saddle, with knees and feet braced by various fittings, and wields a single-bladed canoe paddle. In this high position the paddler has excellent vision; whitewater groups often let a C-boat run lead in rapids because the operator can see farther ahead than any kayaker. Also, since the paddler can lean far out to one side and exert tremendous leverage on the paddle, the C-1 can be turned very rapidly. In expert hands these boats are even more maneuverable than kayaks.

However, in any but expert hands they are a joke. The paddle technique is very, very demanding and hard to learn. The short-coupled, heavily rockered boat tries to turn with every paddle stroke and you have to rudder like mad. The kneeling position is not very comfortable for most people, and you can't shift around to regain circulation.

This is too bad, because the basic idea has much potential for touring. Being wider than a kayak, a C-1 has improved cargo capacity and is a bit stabler. The improved vision is both safer and more pleasant—you can see your surroundings better—and the single-bladed paddle is light and somewhat less tiring to use, though slow.

A couple of companies are now bringing out craft that seem to lie somewhere between the canoe and kayak categories. Fully decked, and narrower than most canoes, they can be paddled from either position with either type of paddle. The Sawyer Loon and, apparently, the new Mad River Monarch are examples of this interesting new class. So far they are dreadfully expensive but the price may come down in time. At any rate, this is a promising development.

As to the larger two-seat decked canoes—C-2s—the technique is even more difficult since it requires absolutely perfect teamwork at all times and a precise balance of power. To give you an idea, the fore-and-aft trim of a competition C-2 is so critical that they come with the cockpit moldings separate. You have to find out exactly where the two paddlers are going to sit, depending on their relative body weights, and then install the cockpit fittings! Once set up for a particular twosome, a C-2 is nearly useless for anybody else. There is potentially a lot of cargo space in there but no good way to get at it. Anyway, these things are canoes—period.

HOT RODS

Slalom kayaks are designed and built to run a competitive event in which a series of poles are suspended in pairs over a whitewater stream. The racer has to negotiate these "gates" in sequence, and touching a pole means losing points.

Some years ago it was discovered that a very small, low-volume kayak had a peculiar advantage in this event. With certain tricky techniques, it could be made to slip *under* the ends of the dangling poles. This was decried by many people. Dick Held once said to me, "The original idea was to simulate a rocky stream, and it's pretty hard to slip under a rock!"—but it became the standard technique: So modern slalom kayaks are designed to permit this rather weird practice.

Many people refer to any small whitewater kayak with a 13-foot rockered hull as a slalom boat, but the true modern slalom 'yak is something else. Decks are very low and ends are very pointy and sharp. (Some whitewater paddlers will not let you join a group with one of these because of those sharp ends.) The boat is comprehensively useless for actually going anywhere unless you have another, bigger boat or raft carrying all your gear; low-volume slalom boats have the cargo space of pogo sticks. It has too little volume to cope with big hydraulics and keeper holes, and it cannot be paddled in a straight line on flat water without great concentrated effort.

Older slalom kayaks, such as the old Lettmann Mark I and

Low-volume slalom kayak—strictly for racing, useless for touring. *William Sanders*

Mark IV or the earlier Prijon designs, are larger in volume and can be used for touring on fast streams (not open water unless you like to curse and go in circles) if the equipment and supplies are kept to an absolute minimum. These models occasionally turn up fairly cheap—paddlers wanting to get hotter boats for racing usually sell theirs—and are worth considering if you can live with their limitations.

Downriver kayaks, also called wildwater boats, are even more specialized. Wildwater racing is run straight down a fast river, with no gates or turns, like a bicycle time trial or a marathon run. A downriver racer has no intention of turning aside for anything less substantial than a large rock; he will go right through waves and ignore them. The racer wants a boat that will cut through the water rather than riding over it, and he doesn't want to waste any energy keeping the boat in line, so he wants a kayak that tracks by itself.

The result is a long, narrow, V-bottomed kayak that looks like something out of *Star Wars*. Usually it will be widest behind the cockpit and taper straight to a needlelike bow. It will be so tippy the average untrained person cannot keep it upright for long. In fact, some of the more extreme designs are almost like bicycles in that they are only stable when in forward motion. These boats are very hard to turn; however, there is a trick technique involving leaning sharply to one side, creating the effect of rocker, but anyone but an expert will promptly capsize trying this. They lack any useful cargo space.

A very few people, experienced in downriver racing, use these boats for touring and claim certain advantages. Undoubtedly they are enjoyable to paddle if you can do it—they go where you point them and are shockingly fast—but on the whole they aren't touring boats. The average person shouldn't even think about getting one. If you're at home in a downriver kayak, you already own one anyway.

Flatwater racing boats are seen in the Olympics and other international events. Made of very thin wood veneer, they are expensive and fragile. (You might as well take a set of antique bone china into the boondocks.) But they are also extremely fast. They come in singles, doubles, and the awesome K-4s, which look like centipedes or Roman galleys and can tow a water skier. All are madly unstable, even more so than the downriver boats, and hopelessly impractical for any kind of touring. Don't worry about it—nobody is going to try to sell you one.

Another very specialized type of kayak, not intended for racing but perhaps in the hot rod category, is the **surf kayak** seen along beaches. These boats are no doubt great fun but totally useless for anything but surfing. Some guys in Idaho tried taking one on a whitewater trip; they reported it was great—if you liked going down the river backwards.

Sea kayaks are yet another class, but they're covered in chapter 8.

4

Gear

Well, you've digested all the information in the last two chapters, and shopped around and asked questions, and you've finally got yourself the kayak of your dreams. That's about it, right?

Sorry. It comes hard for me to have to talk about things that are going to cost you more of your money—believe me, I know how this stuff can add up—but there are some things you've absolutely got to have and some others you ought to at least think about. I'll try to make this as painless as I can. . . .

PADDLES

You've got to have a paddle, of course; there is nowhere to clamp an outboard to one of these things, so you'd better get yourself a good one. A kayak is only as good as the paddle you use to propel and control it. Every now and then I see somebody who spent a pile on a fine kayak and didn't have enough left to buy a decent paddle, and it's so depressing to see him struggling with an off-balance piece of warped plastic or a monstrous club the size of a telephone pole, with that lovely 'yak completely wasted.

You're going to be lifting, dipping, pushing, and pulling that paddle several thousand times a day. It's going to be your motor, brakes, steering, and transmission. It will be the means by which energy leaves your body and is converted into linear motion. It is the paddle, not the boat, that represents your real interface with the water. So figure on a good paddle—not necessarily the most expensive custom job around, but a well-made, well-designed paddle that fits you and your boat—as a basic part of your outfit. If that means settling for a less expensive kayak to get a decent paddle, do it.

No doubt it goes without saying that a kayak is propelled by a double-bladed paddle. For the benefit of the occasional person who asks—no, it isn't feasible to use a standard canoe paddle. You sit so low that you can't reach out and get leverage on the paddle. Ask any kayaker who has had to use a broken paddle.

If you look at a selection of paddles, probably the first thing you will notice will be that some of the blades are flat like canoe paddles and others are shaped like gigantic salad spoons, with varying degrees of "scoop." You may wonder which is best. Well, you can get up a good argument on that around kayak circles— I've seen a few I thought might turn into fist fights—but much depends on your interests. Whitewater paddlers, especially beginners, often like the flat blade for various reasons, most of which boil down to having one less thing to have to think about when it gets hairy. A flat-bladed paddle is easier to orient underwater for an emergency roll-up, especially if the upset has loosened your grip, and you can brace with it without having to contort your wrists and elbows. In backpaddling, a flat blade actually delivers superior power, and this is important in back-ferrying techniques. (Explained in chapter 5.) Finally, if cost is an object, anybody can make a flat blade, but cheap scooped blades can be awfully bad. But spoon blades are virtually universal among flatwater paddlers, being considerably more efficient in grabbing the water; in fact, flat blades on open water just don't make much sense unless that's all you can get.

Most kayakers wind up using spoon blades. Part of the reason is the heavy influence of the racing community, who use spoon blades for obvious reasons. Partly it's because spoon blades are more efficient and powerful. It takes a split second longer to get set up for a roll or brace, perhaps, but once you do, the spoon blade delivers a lot more purchase. For general touring I recommend a paddle with mildly scooped blades, but I must admit that I myself use spoon blades for open water and flat blades for whitewater, and you may find yourself doing likewise. To some extent it comes down to paddling styles.

The very best touring and flatwater paddles are asymmetric—the blade is slightly offset and the end is cut at an angle rather than square—for clean entry and exit. A good feature if you've got the money, but not essential.

You may also notice that the blades are set at right angles to each other on the shaft axis. The idea is to keep you from having to fight air resistance with one blade while the other is down in the water doing the work. A paddle made in this way is said to be feathered, and all good modern paddles have this feature.

This brings up an important point. A feathered paddle is rotated with each stroke to bring the blades into alignment, using a technique that we will detail in chapter 5—don't panic, it's very simple. Part of this technique involves holding the paddle shaft firmly with one hand and letting it rotate within the grasp of the other. The hand which maintains the solid grip is said to be the control hand. Now it will be obvious that a spoon-bladed paddle has to go into the water facing a certain way because it has a front and back face. So, for reasons that will become clear when we learn to use the paddle, a spoon-bladed paddle has to be made for either left- or right-hand control. And thus if you hear somebody talk about a left-handed paddle, he's right; there really is such a thing.

But this has absolutely nothing to do with whether the paddler is right or left-handed. Many left-handed people use right-handed paddles. On the other hand, I am right-handed, yet because I started kayaking on my own and learned to paddle with a left-handed paddle—merely because that was what I got hold of and nobody told me differently until it was too late—I use a left-handed control. It's purely a matter of which way you start out. It requires no particular extra dexterity on either hand.

Therefore, unless you have already learned to paddle with a left-hand control, I strongly advise you to get a right-hand paddle and learn to use it. Whatever way you start out, it will quickly become almost impossible to change over (I've tried enough), and left-handed paddles are much harder to find. Some very good paddles are not even available in left-hand setups. Besides, if you are on a group trip, everyone else will probably have right-handed paddles, and interchangeability is an important safety factor.

If you still don't know how to use a feathered paddle, you won't be able to tell which is which just by looking. But most of the paddles in the average shop will be right-handers; in fact, the lefties are usually special-order jobs, another reason to learn to use a rightie. Ask the sales help or take an experienced friend along. If a salesman unloads a left-handed paddle on you by swearing it's a right-hander, you have my permission to go back and wrap it around his neck with not inconsiderable force.

Flat-bladed paddles, of course, are the same for right or left control. If you learn on a flat paddle, use it right-handed so you can switch if you later decide to go to spoon blades. Take-apart foldboat paddles can be set up either way, so be sure to set them up for right-hand control.

It is important to be able to orient the paddle correctly without having to look at the blades. Otherwise, you might find yourself trying to paddle with the edge of the blade, and of course you can't roll in turbulent water unless you can instantly orient the blades by feel. Many good paddles have shafts made slightly oval in section to assist in this; the feature is well worth paying for. Many whitewater paddlers tape a strip of foam along the shaft where the control hand goes, for the same purpose.

Paddles are made of various combinations of materials. The cheapest ones use aluminum shafts and plastic blades. These are all right for spares or for beginners in very rocky streams; they are rugged and the blades are nearly unbreakable. But they flex in use, being soft, and this robs power from your stroke and makes control imprecise.

Fiberglass paddles are much better if correctly shaped, being very stiff and strong. The best ones are excellent and cost accordingly. Cheaper models tend to be rather heavy and have a harsh feel in hard paddling. Fiberglass paddles are favored for rocky whitewater streams for their durability. Indeed, nearly all current fiberglass paddles are designed for whitewater use, with large square-ended blades, adequate but less than ideal for flat-water touring. If you expect to be running a lot of rocky, fast little streams (not necessarily advanced whitewater; there are quite a few creeks and rivers, especially in the East, which are easy enough to run but so shallow and rocky they eat paddles) you probably ought to get a fiberglass job. If you're going to be paddling primarily on deep rivers and open water, most FRP paddles are unnecessarily heavy.

Some fiberglass paddles have shafts of aluminum tubing; these are cheaper, but their lack of resiliency makes them rather tiring to use. Far better is the "pole vault" type shaft, which is made of tubular wrapped fiberglass; this gives the whole paddle a slight springiness and give, besides being inherently stronger. But the fiberglass shaft paddles also cost quite a bit more.

On the whole I think most kayakers will be better off with wooden paddles. In all these thousands of years, nobody has ever come up with a better paddle material, though the invention of reliable waterproof glue has been responsible for the best shapes. (Inuit and Aleut paddlers, lacking trees for large, broad planks, used rather skinny paddles; this makes their accomplishments even more impressive.) A really good wooden paddle has a feel like nothing else on the scene; it has just enough stiffness without being dead and clunky. I suppose some modern people would say it feels "organic," and certainly a good wooden paddle feels alive compared to plastic, FRP, or aluminum. Besides, wood is beautiful when well finished, and a wooden shaft doesn't blister your hands as easily or freeze them on a cold day. An aluminum shaft, in particular, forms a dreadful heat sink, one reason most of us avoid them.

Wood does demand a little more care—an occasional bit of sanding and varnishing, even a bit of epoxy in an embryo crack—but not all that much. Wooden paddles sometimes fail to survive use by inexperienced whitewater kayakers, who tend to use their paddles as push poles, but the answer to this—except perhaps in the very rockiest conditions, or low water—is better training and technique, not indestructible paddles.

For general touring and recreational paddling on open water and rapids up through Class III except, as noted, the narrow, rocky, or shallow kind, one of the best answers is a paddle designed for downriver (wildwater) racing. The requirements are about the same and the paddles are beautifully light and well balanced, while the blade forms represent decades of research, testing, and high-level technology. The top-line models are very expensive, but there are less expensive versions intended for beginning wildwater racers and still superb for touring. Nor is there anything flimsy about these light paddles; wildwater racers have to negotiate quite powerful whitewater streams and certainly can't win with broken paddles.

Foldboats usually come with two-piece takedown paddles. Klepper's are excellent. Takedown paddles are irritating to use because the joint always works loose sooner or later, but sometimes you have no choice. Still, if you have a Klepper or other folder but the fold-up feature isn't really a big concern—maybe you just liked its qualities—you might prefer to get solid paddles. Takedowns do make good spares. Iliad makes the best ones I've seen. But some of the very cheap plastic-blade takedown paddles are no good even as spares. They're like Vice-Presidents; lose the main one and you're almost worse off than if you had nothing else. Dolphin owners may find it hard to reach over those fat sides with Iliad paddles; Klepper paddles might work well.

What is the proper length? Just long enough to reach the water, the old gag goes. Mountain ranges of literature have been published on this. Actually, most people can use a fair range of sizes. Whitewater paddlers use paddles about 81 to 84 inches long for easier handling and to keep from hitting rocks and the like. (Short paddles are also valuable when passing through willow jungles or exploring swamps; overhead limbs can really snag a long paddle.) For general open-water cruising, something longer is better unless you have short arms. A longer paddle lets you cover more ground. Something like 84 to 86 inches is a good all-round size but may be too long for tight rapids. Tall men may go to 88 inches.

Folders, K-2s, inflatables, and the beamier sea kayaks will need longer paddles to clear their sides. Eight feet is common in this class. But it's very hard to get good paddles in lengths over 88 inches; fortunately, the sea-kayaking movement has been responsible for new developments in longer paddles, so this may soon change.

A person going on a mixed-water cruise—for example, in some

parts of the North and Canada there are large lakes separated by fast, rocky rapids—might like to have a good light touring paddle, fairly long, and carry a takedown fiberglass whitewater paddle as a spare. Then he could switch to the takedown for running rapids and save the good paddle for the open stretches.

Whatever you get, handle it a lot before deciding. Paddles tend to be very subjective things with many intangible factors involved. Pay special attention to lightness and balance. Balance is, if anything, more important than lightness; it should feel neither blade-heavy nor shaft-heavy, or it will tire you out regardless of weight. FRP blades and aluminum shafts make a very nasty combination in this respect, being nearly always blade-heavy. You'll have to lift that paddle many thousands of times. . . .

Be wary about used paddles. A tiny crack might be hard to spot. A solid-looking shaft might break in use. Because of the long thin shaft, the great leverage exerted by the paddler, and techniques such as rolls and braces, kayak paddles are subjected to tremendous stresses compared to canoe paddles, and in rough water a broken paddle could be very dangerous. At the very least it's distinctly unnerving—I had it happen to me once. Take your time, spend whatever it takes, and get a good paddle you can depend on; you can keep it and treasure it while you go through three or four kayaks.

BOAT GEAR

Spray skirts are those little doodads that go around your waist and keep water out of the cockpit. You definitely need one unless you are operating a very large, stable, high-sided boat such as a Klepper or a K-2. Normal kayaks sit low in the water and have very rounded, slick sides and decks. Even a small wave or splash will wash right up over the deck and slop into the boat, forcing you to bail. In choppy, open water the situation can be dangerous, and in a rapid even more so. For most kayaks a spray skirt is essentially part of the boat rather than an accessory; they are designed with the assumption that they will be used with spray skirts.

Some beginners are nervous about getting trapped in the boat in case of a capsize, but the spray skirt will not delay your exit unless you have foolishly tightened it down too much or tried to use a spray skirt too small for your cockpit. It will come right off in an emergency—more of this in chapter 5.

Spray skirts of coated nylon are light, cheap, and pleasant on hot days, but they tend to leak after extended use and to wear out where they contact the hard fiberglass coaming. They also tend to collect little puddles of water, followed by a steady drip through pinhole leaks—unpleasant if the water is cold. Nylon spray skirts are okay for most open-water touring, though, or for use with larger boats where they mostly serve to keep paddle drip off your lap.

Most kayakers—and virtually all whitewater types—use spray skirts made of neoprene foam, the same stuff they use in wet suits. Neoprene spray skirts are durable, don't leak unless ripped or burned, and provide a little extra warmth if the water is cold. They also shed water so it doesn't pool up in the cockpit area. A few people with small hands have trouble getting them on and off the cockpit coaming in cold weather, and this might be dangerous in an upset; such people might do better with nylon.

Make sure your spray skirt fits your cockpit. Most commercial spray skirts are built to fit the standard whitewater kayak cockpit, with a coaming circumference of not more than 72 inches. Some touring 'yaks have cockpits larger than this. Measure yours by running a tape measure all the way around the lip of the coaming. If it's over 72 inches you will have to get one of the special spray skirts made for outsize cockpits. In the larger sizes, neoprene is advised if you're going to be running anything rough; big nylon spray skirts tend to accumulate sizeable pools of water, making the boat top-heavy.

It should also fit you around the waist. Nylon models adjust easily, neoprene less so. In case of an extreme mismatch to waist or cockpit you may have to do some work with neoprene cement and wet-suit-patch material. Most good spray skirts come in a range of waist sizes.

The skirt will snap around the cockpit coaming by means of an elastic band. This should be adjustable. Adjust it until you have a firm but not unyielding fit. It should be tight enough to keep out water but you should not be able to pick up the empty kayak by the spray skirt. If you can, loosen it, or one day it will kill you. This is very important. Get it tight around the waist because if you capsize and have to swim, a loose spray skirt can work down around your ankles with fatal results.

Flotation bags must be considered standard in fiberglass kayaks. A swamped kayak in moving water is a terrifying thing, like a runaway torpedo. An ordinary slalom kayak full of water weighs half a ton! It can crush a swimmer, hole another boat, or destroy itself against a rock. On flatwater this may not be a problem, but fiberglass has no inherent buoyancy, so you still need the air bags to keep from sinking after an accident.

Anyway, you need some kind of waterproof bags to keep your camping kit dry. You can get flotation bags that double as storage bags—details in chapter 9—so for once you get two necessary accessories for the price of one.

Ropes are handy with any boat, but for the most part it's risky to have a lot of line around a boat in moving water; they can tangle a foot or leg in a capsize. On flatwater bow and stern painters are all right but should be firmly secured. Many people like to rig a line from bow to stern, passing alongside the cockpit coaming, to give them something to grab in an upset. If you do this, get it down tight so it can't snare a foot. Larger braided polypropylene rope is less prone to wrap around ankles than thin line.

The bow and stern of any kayak should be fitted with loops of nylon line, large enough to admit a hand but too small to hold a foot. Tubular nylon, used by mountain climbers, is perfect for this if you can find a source.

Racks for carrying kayaks atop a car should employ either contoured cradles or an inverted T design. The best of the racks is made by Yakima Products and is expensive. But you can construct an entirely valid rack for little money. Buy a set of Quik-N-Easy brackets, which mount on a car's rain gutters. Outdoor shops usually have them, or you can order them through the mail from one of the houses listed in the back of this book. The simplest approach is to construct a simple inverted T rack—a crossbar with a vertical member in the middle. Ordinary 2 × 4s can be used for this. Bolt, don't nail or screw, and cover the wood with pieces of carpet material or foam to prevent scratching. The advantage of the inverted T is that it lets you carry the kayaks on edge, which for various engineering reasons is easier on them than laying them flat on a rigid bar.

If a car lacks rain gutters you've got a serious problem. (A lot of folders and inflatables get sold this way.) However, the cartop racks that use straps and metal hooks, while less than ideal, will work fairly well if the driver will hold speeds to reasonable limits and if little rough road driving is involved. I've carried *Foxfire* atop a Plymouth Volare in this way for considerable distances, and she's a big 'yak.

You do need a rack. Don't try to lash a kayak directly to the top of a car, as people sometimes do with canoes. It just won't work and you'll damage the boat and quite possibly cause a serious auto accident.

PERSONAL EQUIPMENT

YOU HAVE TO HAVE A LIFE JACKET. Not only is this mandated by law in many areas; it is required by common sense anywhere, unless the water is so shallow and completely calm you can wade. I don't care how well you swim. If you capsize out on a lake or bay, it may be miles to shore, and the wind and waves will make things much worse. As for whitewater, the stuff that makes it white in the first place—dissolved air—drastically reduces its capacity to support floating bodies. In real whitewater you simply cannot swim in the normal sense of the term without additional flotation.

Anyway, regulations require life jackets in most places nowadays. On any seacoast, large lake, or river controlled by the government, the Coast Guard will slap you with a hefty fine if you are caught in a boat—including a kayak—without a life jacket which they call a Personal Flotation Device or PFD. This choice bit of bureaucratese is followed by many otherwise good writers. It will not be followed in this book; I want you to remember that a *life* jacket is meant to save your *life*.

The usual horsecollar-shaped life jackets sold in hardware stores provide adequate flotation and don't cost much; the older models used a kapok filling which could be ruined by rough handling, but

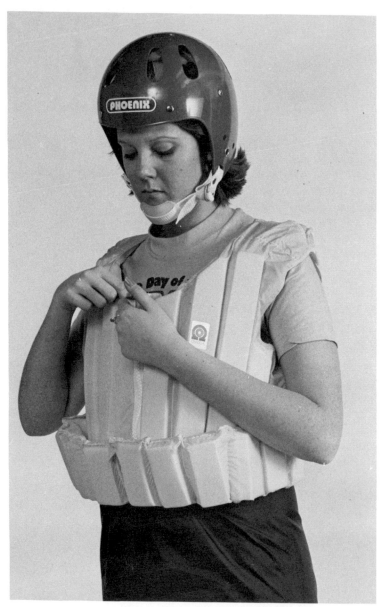

Two necessities—a life jacket and a helmet. *Courtesy Phoenix Products*

newer ones, using foam blocks, are much better. However, most people find this style of life jacket rather clumsy and uncomfortable for kayaking; it does get in the way in some strokes, and that pad around the neck is pretty hot and sweaty in the summer.

Most kayakers use rather skimpy vests made up of lots of small foam blocks in a shiny nylon casing, looking like Japanese samurai armor. These are very comfortable and sharp-looking and work well for fairly small people, or fat people with plenty of natural flotation, in relatively calm water. They do not usually provide very much flotation, and big, bony men often find that they are not adequate to support them in heavy whitewater. I nearly got killed once because I trusted one of these things. If you like this style of life jacket, test it under controlled conditions such as a swimming pool before taking it into the rough stuff.

There are, however, vests of this general type which provide extra flotation. Charlie Walbridge of Wildwater Designs has brought out what I consider the best whitewater kayaking vest around; it provides more flotation than any other kayak vest and fastens firmly so it won't come off in an upset.

The flat foam block vests made by Stearns and Gladding, sold in sporting goods stores, are comfortable and provide good flotation for medium-size people; get only the kind with securing straps or belts, or add these, because without such straps a vest can come off in precisely the conditions where it is needed.

Large, kapok-filled "Mae West" life jackets provide tremendous flotation and are worn by many rafters and kayakers on big western rivers such as the Colorado, where huge waves and holes can make a joke of little skimpy racing vests. Some sea kayakers also favor them. Most kayakers find them too clumsy for ordinary use. I have never found these vests at all unpleasant to wear; indeed, this is what I usually prefer. Maybe body size comes into it. The late, legendary Walt Blackadar also favored the big vests of this type. One thing about these vests, they are relatively easily damaged, whereas foam vests are almost indestructible.

In even moderately bumpy water, a life jacket must have ten pounds of flotation for each pound of body weight. Flotation should be listed on the label or supplied by the maker or dealer. Many popular vests do not meet this standard, especially for big people. I weigh 200 pounds, so I need a life jacket with at least

20 pounds of flotation; yet few commercial makes go above 16 or 17.

I have successfully added flotation to a Stearns vest by splitting open the lining and inserting rectangles of Ensolite foam. In theory this makes the vest illegal, but I've never seen the Coast Guard checking that closely. In coastal waters you just might run into trouble, though.

Helmets are required in shallow streams and any whitewater. When a kayak turns over, the paddler's head is suddenly down there among all the rocks and sunken logs, and if any sort of impact should knock the paddler unconscious, it doesn't take much imagination to figure out the results. Get yourself a helmet if you have any plans to run even the simplest whitewater, and get a good one.

Kayakers used to be seen wearing flimsy hockey helmets and the like, and no doubt these crude improvisations saved some lives, but basically you need something better. Kayakers are lucky in that several of our most dedicated whitewater exponents have also been brain surgeons, and they have done a lot of work in figuring out our head protection needs. Nowadays there are many excellent helmets designed especially for kayaking, such as the Pro-Tec and the Nona. A kayak helmet needs a layer of crushable foam (not resilient) and a solidly constructed one-piece outer shell, with a dependable strap system so it doesn't come off when you need it. Most kayakers also like to have drainage holes so they don't try to roll up with several pounds of water on their heads.

The old police-type motorcycle helmet is okay for kayaking, though a bit heavy—some moped dealers sell them—but a full motorcycle helmet that covers the ears is dangerous. If water is trapped between the helmet and your ear and the helmet then receives a blow, the hydraulic pressure can burst your eardrum! Some of the bicycle helmets work pretty well—I've used an MSR bicycle helmet successfully—but basically I recommend a helmet designed especially for kayaking.

Open-water paddlers don't need helmets, though it might be good to have one when coming in for a landing on a rocky shore with surf or heavy waves up. Wear whatever you like on your head when you're on the briny or non-briny deep.

Below the neck, you can wear whatever sort of clothing seems appropriate. If it's chilly, remember that wool is much warmer when wet than any other fabric. Kayaks sit low in the water and catch a lot of splash and spray, so you'll need to dress warmly. At the same time, when it's hot weather, you can wear shorts all day long without worrying about sunburn, but you'll need an upper garment with long sleeves if you burn easily.

Except in very warm weather, you'll be more comfortable with a water-resistant shell jacket of some sort. An ordinary wind-breaker will help, but in cool weather you might prefer a water-proof paddle jacket made for kayaking. A good paddle jacket has elasticized cuffs and collar to keep water from seeping in. This is especially nice to put a stop to that trickle of water down the sleeve every time you raise your arm for another stroke. Or you might prefer a hooded coated nylon rain jacket, which will also be useful around camp; you could carry a pair of rain pants to go with it and be set for any weather.

Wet suits are a comfort if the water is cool and a necessity when water temperatures get below about 50°F. Yes, *fifty*. Water conducts heat away from the body faster than air, so you can get hypothermia—and possibly die of it—at water temperatures that would not be considered particularly cold on dry land. If the water is down to forty or below, a full-length wet suit represents your only reasonable chance of survival if you are in the water more than a few minutes. Hypothermia is very, very dangerous, nothing to kid around with. Get yourself a wet suit if you're planning to paddle in any but warm weather.

Don't be too sure you won't want to do this. If you can get out in the cooler months you'll have a lot more privacy and peace and quiet—the water skiers and canoe renters and beer can tossers have gone home—and the water birds are migrating and the leaves are incredibly beautiful. Try it and you'll be glad you bought the wet suit. Wet suits are also advisable, even in summer, on certain streams which are fed from springs or snow melt, or from the bottoms of dams; they can be cold all year, and sudden immersion in cold water on a hot day is very dangerous.

You don't need or want the thick wet suits made for skin divers; get the kind made for whitewater paddlers, 3/16 of an inch thick, with nylon backing. Except in really cold conditions, you probably won't need a full-length wet suit; for most purposes a short-legged "bod pod" with short or no sleeves is adequate, and you can add a wet suit jacket if you like. The better wet suits are now made in women's models with extra room in the chest.

As for foot covering, tennis shoes are okay. Wear something, at least, because the inside of a fiberglass kayak is often a bit rough for bare feet. (Wood-frame boats are something else; I always take off my shoes in *Foxfire*. Aaaah.) Boots are dangerous, as they may hang up in a wet exit or drag you down if you have to swim. If it's cold, try neoprene wet suit booties. There are also the new wet shoes which combine a neoprene boot with a tennis shoelike sole, heel, and toe unit. These look wonderful, and I think I'm about to send off for a pair myself.

I always wear soft leather gloves when paddling, but a lot of kayakers say this interferes with their feel of what the paddle is doing. It's up to you. In windy conditions you might want to try pogies—a kind of open-palmed mitten which closes with Velcro over your whole hand, while your palms remain in contact with the paddle. There are also neoprene wet suit mittens.

One other thing which might be considered clothing: If you wear glasses, don't forget to wear some kind of retaining strap or band, or you'll lose them in the first capsize—a very bad time to go blind.

5

Driving Lessons

Now—finally—you actually get to do something with all this stuff. We're going to learn how to paddle that kayak. If you've never operated any sort of boat before, relax—you're in the best situation of all because you don't have anything to unlearn.

If you've paddled a conventional canoe, you'll be pleasantly surprised how much simpler the kayak strokes are. A kayak is really very simple to operate and the basic strokes are easy to learn. For advanced whitewater, there are indeed techniques that take some work, but you can paddle happily all your life and never need them.

For your first lessons, try hard to get the use of a swimming pool. Failing that—and most of us do fail it, I imagine—go to a very calm, shallow lake or pond. If you absolutely have to make do with a stream, then at least find yourself a long, quiet area with no perceptible current. Don't try to start on moving water.

And find, if you can, a bit of clean, clear, unpolluted water, so you can get wet without getting dirty.

Wear your life jacket unless you're in a pool, and have somebody with you. An experienced kayaker would be ideal, of course, but if you can't find one, then just take a friend. The main thing is to have somebody there who can give you a hand if you get in trouble. If you are going to be learning on a body of water of any size, somebody ought to be on hand with another boat of some sort, to chase down drifting paddles, kayaks, or whatever.

GETTING IN—AND OUT

The first big mystery for most people is often expressed as, "How do you get into this thing?" This is not infrequently shouted from a position somewhere near the bank of a river, lake, or pool, by a person with water streaming from hair, nose, and clothing, while a still-unoccupied kayak bobs irritatingly nearby.

Actually, boarding a kayak is quite easy, once you know the trick. You just can't go clambering aboard any old way; there's a technique, devised by the Inuit long ago. Pull your kayak up parallel to the water's edge. Get it right up to the shoreline, but not so far that the bottom will ground out with your weight; in most lakes and ponds you'll have to wade in the shallows a bit.

Lay your paddle across the boat just behind the cockpit, next to the lip of the coaming. One blade should be resting on the bank or pool lip or on the bottom in an inch or two of water.

Crouch down beside the cockpit, facing forward, with the paddle behind you. Reach across the boat with the hand nearest to the boat and grasp the paddle shaft and cockpit coaming, holding them together in your grip. Most people hold the paddle with the thumb and the cockpit coaming with the fingers, a few do it the other way. It makes no real difference; just do whatever feels natural for you.

Now you will see that the paddle, clamped to the boat by your hand, forms an extension of the boat, bracing it, like a bicycle kickstand. Keeping your grip firm, still in a crouching position, raise the foot nearest to the boat and put it into the cockpit. Put it on the floor, dead center, as far forward as you can get with your shinbone still vertical, but don't try to slide it up under the deck yet. Keep your weight on the grounded foot until you have your foot centered in the boat. Now swing your body over, smoothly and steadily, and lower your backside into the seat. As your weight leaves the grounded foot and comes onto the foot in the boat, let the extended paddle brace you; you may want to put your free hand on the bank or grasp the paddle shaft for added support. Let your weight come vertically on the foot in the boat; don't let yourself push sideways with either foot or the kayak will try to slide out from under you. But don't try to hold the kayak absolutely balanced; tip it slightly toward the land side so a little weight comes on the paddle.

Once you have your behind planted firmly in the seat, it is a simple matter to hoist the other leg aboard and shove your feet forward into position.

One important caution: your weight during this entire maneuver is supported *by your legs*. You should only put enough weight on the paddle to steady you. Do not use the paddle as a handrail to hoist yourself up and down by arm power; this puts an excessive strain on the paddle for no good reason.

This very first time out, leave off the spray skirt; you won't need it yet. Get your paddle around in front of you and make sure your life jacket is securely fastened.

Next, get yourself into waist-deep water and turn over. Quit screaming and waving your arms. I'm not crazy—there's a reason for this. If you're like most beginners, somewhere in your subconscious a little voice is telling you that you will never get out of this thing if it capsizes. This buried fear is going to make you stiff and nervous every time you get in the boat and will seriously hinder your attempts to learn to paddle. So the first thing to learn is the wet exit.

What you must do is this: as the boat turns over, hold onto your paddle with one hand—holding it out a bit from your side, parallel to the boat, so it doesn't get in your way—and with the other, reach behind you and push against the cockpit coaming so that you simply slide out of the boat backwards. Bend your knees as soon as they clear the cockpit edge. There you are, free and clear. As you bob up beside the kayak, grab it with your free hand so it doesn't float away. No big deal, was it?

It's best to bend your body forward when you capsize; that

way, you are less likely to hit your head on submerged objects. Not that this should come up in these early lessons—surely you made certain there were no such objects in the practice area— but it's better to start right off forming these habits. Anyway, the wet exit is easier in this position.

Probably, the first time or two, you'll blow it—let go of the paddle, thrash wildly around, and so on. If your boat has a fairly large cockpit or you're on the small side, you may well fall out of the kayak before it's completely over. That's okay too. We're not trying for style here, but only convincing you that you can get out of your 'yak in an emergency.

After you've done it without the spray skirt, put the skirt on and try it. The only difference is that you have to reach forward with your free hand, grab the loop at the front of the spray skirt, and pop the skirt loose from the coaming. This job is a lot easier if you'll get one of those perforated whiffle balls and tie it to the grabloop. They are easier to find by feel.

You may want to wear a nose clip and/or ear plugs for this operation. You'll probably need them later anyway if you decide to learn to roll.

This business leaves you with a partly flooded kayak each time. You did remember to install and inflate those float bags, didn't you? Empty it out by raising one end repeatedly in a seesaw motion until most of the water is out. Then turn it rightside up and get the rest out with a big sponge.

The first couple of times you try the wet exit, have a friend standing by in the waist-deep water just in case.

THE FORWARD STROKE

The key to successful and efficient kayak paddling is to forget the concept of sticking the paddle into the water and dragging it through the fluid medium. It's better to think of the water as if it were virtually solid—which it is, compared to you and your kayak— and to picture yourself using the paddle as a lever with which you push and pull yourself around. The idea is to move yourself, not rearrange the river. It may be instructive, in fact, to replace the paddle for a moment with a long pole such as a broomstick, sit in very shallow water, and try pushing yourself about, so you get the feel of how the kayak responds to various forces.

Sit in your kayak now and experiment with the paddle. See how easily it moves? With your light, streamlined, shallow-draft boat and the leverage of that long paddle, you simply do not need a lot of muscle power to move around on calm water. It will be much easier to learn the strokes and develop a smooth technique, and you'll be less likely to develop bad habits, if you will paddle gently, using only enough force to get the job done. Most novices paddle too vigorously and then can't understand why they have so little control. With a kayak, the more force is applied to a stroke, the more perfect the technique has to be. In the forward stroke, for example, any tendency to go off course will be multiplied by extra effort.

The beginner, seeing that the last stroke has put him off course, responds by stroking even more violently to compensate and then gets frustrated and angry when this doesn't work, making him thrash even harder. Soon he is going in circles, and finally he explodes in a welter of foam, sweat, and obscenities and hurls his paddle at the first person to venture a suggestion. Don't let this be you. Take it easy. There's time to develop power later.

The basic forward stroke is pretty much obvious. The paddle blade enters the water near the bow of the boat and moves backward in a line parallel to the centerline of the kayak, making the boat move in the opposite direction.

Don't try to accomplish this by pulling and heaving back on the paddle. The hand nearest the blade in the water, rather than hauling backward, is primarily a fulcrum. The real power is provided by the upper hand, which *pushes forward* against the paddle shaft. This introduces the principle of leverage and also lets us use bigger, more efficient muscle groups.

Let's run through the basic sequence, ignoring for the moment the feathered blades, which we'll get to in a minute.

The paddle blade—let's say, arbitrarily, the left blade—enters the water up near the bow of the boat. Your left arm is fully extended and your upper body is bent slightly forward. The blade is far enough from the boat that it can move straight back without having to follow the curvature of the hull, but no farther. Your right arm is bent and raised. Your right hand, gripping the paddle shaft, is up in the neighborhood of your right ear; you can just see it out of the corner of your right eye. Your hands are about shoulder-width on the paddle shaft, with equal hand-to-blade distance on either side.

Now you begin to push forward with the right hand, as if throwing a punch. The boat begins to move forward, and you continue to push the right hand forward, while the left hand starts to move toward the rear. You are now pushing with your right hand and pulling with your left. Yes, there is some element of pulling involved; the error is in letting it become dominant. The movement of the paddle blade is in a straight line to the rear, parallel to the boat's centerline, not in a sweeping arc like an oar. Your right hand moves over as it travels forward and is now in front of your face; your left elbow starts to bend.

When the paddle blade is even with your body the power stroke is over. Beyond this point, for complex hydrodynamic reasons, you won't get enough power to be worth the energy expended. You can follow through if you like, letting the movement of the boat and the water take the paddle on back somewhat, but once the blade passes your hips, quit applying any force to it. It's just a waste of effort. After this point the blade begins to leave the water.

This process has automatically brought the other paddle blade forward through the air, and now the right blade dips toward the water and the sequence is repeated. Stroking on alternate sides, you cancel out the kayak's tendency to turn away from a stroke, and if you have kept your strokes even and smooth and applied the same force on both sides, the kayak will move in a straight line for as long as you keep it up.

You will observe that the motion of the hands is not exactly linear. Rather than a reciprocating push-and-pull action, the hands actually follow circular or elliptical paths, as if turning the cranks of a gigantic bicycle. Think about this as you paddle; as my aikido teacher used to tell us, "Think circles." It's easier on your arms and shoulders, and more powerful too.

Novices usually have trouble keeping the kayak on a straight course, especially with shorter boats with any appreciable rocker at all. I feel sorry for those people who start out to learn with slalom 'yaks. Common reasons are: letting the paddle swing out farther from the boat on one side, putting more force into the stroke on one side, holding the paddle off center, sitting off center in the boat or leaning to one side, or failing to maintain an even rhythm. Cures for these faults are: making sure to move the paddle straight back parallel to the boat's centerline on both sides, taking care to apply equal energy on both sides (much easier if you don't paddle too hard!), checking hand positions on the shaft, sitting square and centered, and paddling in a steady cadence. This last is hard for some people, but if you have a lot of irregular pauses between strokes the boat will never go straight. If you think it will help, count cadence to yourself, or even sing. I've got an Inuit tune I hum on long flatwater trips—drives everyone bananas.

If the boat wanders off course, minor corrections can be made by applying a little extra force on the side to which it is trying to turn, or bringing the paddle blade out a bit farther on that side. Major course changes require other techniques, discussed later.

A useful trick, recommended by my daughter Eileen—who swings a pretty fair paddle—is to pick out a landmark on the far shore, such as a tree, and try to keep the bow of your kayak aligned with that. This is easier than trying to keep a straight course while looking at the water, which can be disorienting. Don't paddle along looking down at your hands or the paddle; this is as bad as trying to learn to ride a bicycle while looking at your feet! You will notice, if you've got a kayak with any rocker at all, that the boat swings a little from side to side as you paddle. Don't panic; only very long, straight hulls will track absolutely straight. With practice you will reduce this swing but it will never go entirely away. Just make sure it isn't swinging more one way than the other, or through a really wide arc.

Now to the business I promised to explain—how do you deal with a feathered paddle?

I'm going to assume you have a right-hand or at least flat-bladed paddle. If you are already stuck with a lefty and do not want to try to replace it, you'll have to figure out for yourself how to reverse all the following instructions.

The procedure is basically this: the *left hand* holds the paddle firmly but just loosely enough to allow the shaft to turn in its grasp. The *left wrist* is held straight at all times so that the back of the hand is in line with the forearm. The *right hand* holds the paddle shaft tight and *does not* let it turn; the *right wrist,* the key to the whole process, is bent or straightened to rotate the paddle through 90 degrees to orient the blades.

Taking it through in sequence: as the *right* paddle blade enters the water, *both* wrists are straight. The right blade moves back through the water, its scooped power face to the rear. Meanwhile tbe left blade is moving forward in an edgewise manner, slicing through the air.

At the end of this stroke, the right blade leaves the water and the left blade is lowered. At this point, *while both blades are out of the water,* the *right* wrist is suddenly and smoothly cocked *back,* exactly like the movement of rolling a motorcycle throttle on. This motion rotates the paddle shaft 90 degrees on its long axis; the *left* blade is now oriented for a power stroke, while the right blade is now presenting its edge to the air. *All this time the left wrist has remained straight. The right hand has at no time relaxed its grip.* The left hand has relaxed just enough to let the shaft turn for a second, but the grip has not been actually loose.

At the conclusion of the left-side stroke, the *right* wrist *straightens* again—still holding that grip—and we're ready for another cycle.

The movement always follows this sequence: right wrist straight for a right-side stroke, right wrist cocked back for a left-side stroke. The paddle rotates back and forth through a 90-degree arc; it is not rotated around and around, as some people try to do. The left wrist remains straight for power strokes and is not used to rotate the paddle; it is only bent for certain brace and roll situations, covered later. The right wrist is cocked back or straightened, never bent downward in a chicken neck position for a power stroke. The only occasion for bending either wrist downward is in the Eskimo roll, covered later.

The most common error of confused neophytes is to try to juggle the shaft around and around. Fix it in your head that you never relax your grip with the control hand. If all else fails, tape your control hand to the shaft for a few practice sessions, until it becomes automatic.

I strongly recommend that you practice this technique at home

Study this racer's hands and wrists. Note how right wrist is cocked back to orient feathered paddle. To use other blade he simply straightens right wrist. Do **not** imitate his lack of life jacket, or that perfectly useless leather bicycle helmet! *Courtesy Klepper America*

in a chair for some time before venturing on the water. If you can just learn the basic trick of operating a feathered paddle before you do anything else, you'll have an easier time. You won't have to think about which way the blades go every time you take a stroke, and that will let you concentrate on technique. This is another reason beginners go in circles—they get hung up on orienting the paddle and can't maintain cadence, and while they're doing their juggling acts the boat is spinning all over the lake.

If you have a folder or inflatable with a takedown paddle, you may be tempted to set it up unfeathered "just to learn with." I don't suggest this; in fact, I think it is harmful. It only gives you something to unlearn. Learn to use a feathered paddle from the start; in the long run, it's less work.

THE BACKSTROKE

If you can do the forward stroke, the backstroke is easy; it is the same stroke in reverse. Just stick the paddle into the water back near the stern and move it forward, using the same feathering techniques you already learned.

With a spooned paddle, don't try to turn the blades over; just paddle with the back of the blade. It isn't as efficient as the power face, but it will do the job adequately.

This stroke is your brake—the only brake you've got—and it is also important in certain ferry techniques we'll study later, so work on it a bit. It's a bit less natural than the forward stroke and people tend to do it weakly. Learn to lean on a backstroke as strongly as you would a power stroke because one day you may need it badly. Practice paddling backward for short stretches. Don't worry if you swerve a bit; you seldom need to paddle backward in a straight line anyway.

THE SWEEP

This is your basic turning stroke. Just reach out and plant your paddle near the bow as if for a power stroke, but instead of bringing it straight back, swing it out in a wide arc away from the boat, ending up at the stern. You should have drawn a big letter *C* on the water with your paddle. This will whip the boat around;

do it hard enough and you can turn a slalom kayak in its own length. (Impresses the bystanders mightily.)

Experiment a bit and you will discover that you can get very precise, subtle control by varying the power of this stroke, the radius of the sweep (you can even reach across your body with your upper hand to get a wider sweep), the angle of the blade, and other factors. This is also a good way to correct your course if you wander; simply put a sweep stroke into your power sequence, without breaking rhythm. The sweep is your basic open-water control stroke, so practice it.

You can also do a *reverse sweep*—the same stroke, but it starts at the stern and ends at the bow. This is very effective if you're trying to miss an obstacle in moving water, as it both turns and slows the boat, but you don't want to use it on flatwater because of the braking effect.

THE DRAW

This one is dead easy. Stick the blade into the water out to the side of your boat, but with the blade facing you rather than in power stroke position. Pull the paddle toward you as if sweeping with a broom. The kayak will move sidewise. It is a very useful stroke for dodging rocks in rapids or pulling the boat over to a bank when you want to get out.

You can whip the kayak's nose over smartly by executing a draw stroke up next to the bow. Now try this: do a bow draw stroke and at the end, without a break or lifting the paddle from the water, rotate the paddle into power mode and go into your forward stroke. This will make the boat change directions and accelerate snappily without loss of forward momentum; this is very handy in tight spots. Indeed, all these strokes can be combined in many different ways, and you should experiment along these lines, because combination techniques are the sign of a really slick kayaker.

If you are moving slower than the current—often a wise tactic— and need to do a quick hard draw stroke, give the blade some angle, so that the trailing edge is an inch or so farther from you than the leading edge. This angle will catch the current coming from behind you, and the pressure of the water will greatly augment the power of your draw. It is a valuable trick in rapids.

BRACE STROKES

The strokes outlined so far are enough to get you around on open water and even through easy rapids. If you have a big folder or other large 'yak, they may be the only strokes possible. But for advanced whitewater, sea kayaking in narrow boats, or turbulent open water, brace strokes are very valuable and may save you many cold swims and soggy lunches.

Fortunately, braces are really rather simple in themselves. In fact, even the high brace is easier than doing a really smooth undeviating forward stroke. The real problem for many beginners is the psychological one; it's just so hard to believe you really can put your weight on the paddle. It looks faintly miraculous, akin to walking on water—and, come to think of it, it does require some faith.

Maybe it will help to explain how it works. Have you seen those pictures of kayakers leaning way out to one side, with half the bottom of the boat showing, apparently hanging on that paddle? The secret is that the guy in the picture is also pressing against those braces inside the boat with his hips and knees, with a swivelling motion of his whole lower body. The water offers more resistance to the flat, broad paddle than to the sliding, rolling motion of the smooth, rounded kayak bottom, so the kayak comes upright rather than turning over. If there is a strong current, the kayaker can brace downstream, using the current's pressure against the paddle blade for added support, and hold the brace for a remarkable time.

Before you can do brace strokes, you have to have the braces inside your boat adjusted properly to fit you. They should have done it for you at the shop when you bought the boat; but if not, it's something you've got to do. Try to hand a proper brace without being solidly wedged into your boat and you'll probably just lever yourself out of the 'yak while it capsizes.

Sitting in the seat in your normal paddling position, put your feet firmly on the pedallike foot braces. When you do this, your knees should automatically be jammed solidly against the underside of the foredeck; if your boat is at all properly designed, there will be pocketlike places for your knees to fit. If the knees do not touch the deck, you may tape pieces of Ensolite foam to the inside of the boat—this is good for comfort anyway—but if this still doesn't get it, your foot braces are too far forward and must be moved back. On the other hand, if you can't get your feet onto the braces at all, obviously they need to move forward.

A really good kayak should come with adjustable foot braces, and it is simple enough (if awkward work) to get these where you want them. If you're getting a kayak which comes with either type of braces, spend the extra money and get the adjustable kind. If you buy one which has only fixed foot braces, insist that the shop where you buy it must install them for you without extra charge, and make sure they fit correctly before you accept the boat.

If you order a boat through the mail, build one from a kit, or buy a used one with fixed braces that don't fit you, then you'll have to have them installed. I strongly advise against doing this job yourself; it involves using potentially toxic substances inside a cramped, unventilated space and is difficult to do correctly if you have no related experience. Weakly installed foot braces are likely to rip out at a bad moment. It is better to take the boat to a shop and pay a professional to do it. If you're having the braces changed on a used boat, have them put in adjustable braces while you're at it. Yakima adjustable braces are particularly good; they may seem expensive, but not compared to the cost of a kayak or even a good paddle.

Hip braces in most kayaks are formed by the sides of the bucket seat. If your backside is so small you can slide around from side to side in the seat, you'll need to add some foam and duct tape until you get a snug fit. Make sure you're centered.

Now we're ready to do it. I suggest practicing these techniques in shallow water at first—not so shallow you crack your head if you turn over, of course—and have someone around. You shouldn't be in much danger of capsizing, but the added safety will give you peace of mind.

A *low brace,* in its simplest form, is rather like the reverse sweep; it starts near the stern and moves forward and outward in a broad arc. But instead of the normal power attitude, with the blade surface vertical, we tilt the blade so that it lies at a shallow angle—45 degrees or less—to the surface of the water like the wing of an airplane taking off. The resemblance, as we shall see, is far from coincidental. Now, when we sweep the paddle smartly forward, the climbing angle of the blade causes it to ride along the surface. And if we lean on the paddle a bit, we find that this climbing effect is powerful enough to support a fair amount of weight.

So try it. Set the angle of your paddle blade as described—remember, the front or leading edge is higher than the trailing edge—and sweep it out in a reverse sweep motion. As you feel it generate resistance, lean your weight out on that side; let your upper arm come across your chest and stretch your other arm out to give you plenty of radius. As you lean on the paddle shaft, apply sidewise pressure against the hip and knee braces. Swing your hips toward the paddle side with a rolling motion, not unlike the classic stripper's move. The kayak will rock back upright and there you are.

You probably won't be able to make yourself lean out very much at first; in fact you'll probably be rather timid. That's okay; you want to start out small and work your way up, gradually increasing the degree of lean. You'll find that the farther you lean, the harder you have to swing the paddle to get enough force to bring you back upright.

The trick, you'll find, is to quit thinking of getting your body back up over the center of the boat, and instead use your hips to move the boat under you.

If you keep pushing it, eventually you will discover the point beyond which the simple low brace is not enough to hold you. You certainly won't be able to do one of those armpit-soakers like the guy in the picture. But the low brace is still useful for a quick recovery when you feel yourself tipping. It is handy in whitewater, and sometimes elsewhere too—as when some clown in a motorboat hits you with an unexpected side wake.

The *high brace* is different, and not just because of the height of the paddle. In a high brace you do not sweep the paddle blade along the surface; you bring it downward in an arc, with the power side of the blade facing toward the bottom of the river. The paddle shaft is held high, at shoulder level or even above the head, depending on how far out you are leaning. Hip action is absolutely vital to this one and must be coordinated with the paddle movement so that the two forces act together to bring you upright. The paddle motion may remind you of the draw stroke, but it is much more powerful because you get your whole body into it.

The high brace is not just for recovery, though it's certainly useful for that too. In many fast water situations, it is valuable to be able to lay your boat on its side, so that the force of the current comes against the bottom of the kayak rather than the side. An expert kayaker can lean downstream and take the force of a fast jet of water on his boat's rounded bottom while he turns out of an eddy, for example. It is also often necessary to use the high brace to negotiate holes—more of this next chapter.

The high brace is a somewhat advanced technique, and you can go ahead and do a good deal of kayaking—even in the easier kinds of whitewater—without having mastered it. But you definitely need to work on it if you have any hopes of ever running serious rapids, or else get ready for a lot of swimming. It is also basic preparation for learning the Eskimo roll, which, as we will see, is in a sense an extended sort of brace. But even if you have no interest in running the kind of water where braces and rolls are needed, learning these things will give you a great feeling of control over the boat.

Both these braces are limited in duration. Practice will let you hold a brace longer, up to a point, but as you'll quickly learn, you have to get the boat back up into its arc of stability with that hip snap by the time the high- or low-braced paddle overcomes the resistance of the water. After that point, over you go.

But there is a way to extend the brace and hang out there quite some time, even in still water. You adopt the basic high brace, but instead of bringing the paddle blade downward, you move it rapidly from side to side while twisting the shaft repeatedly through

Frank Barton demonstrates the high brace. *William Sanders*

a few degrees so the blade is always "climbing." That is, the position is that of the high brace, but the actual motion of the blade against the water is more that of the low brace. The blade describes a kind of flattened horizontal figure eight. This is hard to describe or visualize if you've never seen it done, but get an experienced kayaker to demonstrate for you and you'll get it immediately. It really is a simple technique.

As long as you maintain that rapid back-and-forth sweep with the blade always "climbing"—raise the front edge as the blade moves forward, then raise the rear edge as you reverse the motion, the whole sweep just a foot or two—you can hang out there on that brace even with no current. This is known as the sculling brace and is well worth learning. An unsuccessful low or high brace quite often can be salvaged by going into this sculling movement long enough to complete the recovery. It is also great fun when playing in rapids and gives you a feeling of mastery and confidence. Try it.

In the low brace, it is sufficient to use the back of the paddle rather than trying to get the power face into play. But the high brace and sculling brace will require more power. So in the high brace position, not only are both wrists cocked back, but the elbows are bent as well to present the power face downward. Unless, of course, you have made a permanent commitment to flat-bladed paddles, in which case there's no point worrying about it. In any of these strokes that require a paddle-blade angle different from the basic power stroke, the adjustment is made by bending wrists and elbows and even, if necessary, raising the arms over the head. Don't alter the grip of the hands on the shaft, no matter what. If the water is turbulent enough to require a brace in the first place, it's no place to be juggling the paddle and changing your grip; when you bob up out of that brace you're probably going to need your power stroke, fast. Note, too, that the position of the arms and wrists will be different for braces on right or left, owing to the wrist-cocking motion required to orient the feathered paddle, so be sure to practice these techniques thoroughly on both sides.

But do only what is necessary to execute a smooth, efficient brace. Some hotdoggers get into grotesque, contorted postures— paddle shaft behind the head, and the like—which serve no purpose except to impress spectators (and then only if the spectators are wholly ignorant of kayaking). These weird gymnastics do no good and can cause shoulder injuries.

One last caution—in moving water, never brace upstream. The current will snatch the blade and have you over in a very wet flash.

THE ESKIMO ROLL

The Eskimo roll is a pastry popular in Alaska; beginning kayakers who try it sometimes feel they have bitten off more than they can chew.

Puns aside, the roll is the one kayak technique above all others which fascinates the public. It looks so neat to be able to turn over and pop back up with a stroke of the paddle. And it is a valuable skill in many ways. Not only is it necessary in advanced whitewater work and a possible lifesaver on open water, it also gives the kayaker a great feeling of confidence and unity with the boat. Really master the roll and you'll find yourself having less trouble in all situations. The feeling that you can handle an upset lets you relax and go with the flow.

But do you have to learn to roll? Many seem to think so; I've even heard it said that you aren't a real kayaker if you can't roll. Bull. You can do a great deal of kayaking without a roll; in fact, you could paddle all your life without ever getting into the sort of water where you really need one. For cruising on lakes, wide slow rivers, sheltered coastal waters, and even whitewater streams of Class I and II difficulty, a roll is nice to have but far from necessary. Even Class III whitewater (intermediate) seldom mandates a reliable roll; you might one day have to do a wet exit and swim a little, when a solid roll would have saved you the trouble, but if you've packed your gear right and followed basic safety rules, this shouldn't be too traumatic. And with beamy foldboats, the roll is seldom even possible.

The greatest sea kayakers of all time, the Aleuts, did not roll their kayaks like their Eskimo cousins; instead they practiced a deep-water remount. And if you think you're more kayaker than an Aleut—

A dependable roll is essential in any situation in which swimming is dangerous or otherwise unacceptable, such as advanced rapids (Class IV and up), sea kayaking with the narrower boats, or cold water.

But the roll has been overemphasized. Many contemporary teachers begin by teaching the roll even before they teach the basic paddle strokes. Some people spend their summers in swimming pools trying to learn to roll and neglect the other techniques such as a solid backferry, which might reduce the chance of needing a roll to begin with. They spend their rare trips feeling inadequate because some hotdogger has convinced them that a real kayaker can roll up at the bottom of Niagara Falls with two broken arms and anyone who can't roll should stay off the rivers. You almost get the idea that the kayak is primarily a device in which to do the Eskimo roll. And I suspect that all this emphasis on the roll gives people the idea that kayaks go around capsizing all the time. This simply isn't true of the ordinary touring kayaks, and causes much unwarranted anxiety all around.

I suggest, then, that you go ahead and learn normal paddling techniques and do some cruising in easier waters, getting the feel of your kayak and building up your paddling muscles and so on. Then plan to enroll in a class next chance you get—or, if you're lucky enough to have a skilled friend, get one-on-one instruction that way—and make a reliable roll one of your goals. It will be easier to learn to roll, anyway, if the cockpit of a kayak is a familiar and pleasant place to be, rather than something new and maybe unnerving.

But do figure on getting some kind of personal training; this is something that is nearly impossible to teach yourself, no matter how athletic you are. A very few people have learned to roll without teachers (obviously somebody originally did) but it's terribly hard and rather dangerous, too, in that you might teach yourself something that works all right in the pool but gets you in big trouble the first time you try it in a rapid. And if you have a lot of bad, frustrating experiences trying to learn on your own, you could build up a mental block that makes it impossible for anyone to help you later on. So the following remarks are intended strictly as general guidance, *not* as a teach-yourself-the-Eskimo-roll-in-ten-easy-lessons course.

The basic principle of the Eskimo roll is fairly simple, but it does not work quite the way it may look to an observer; the kayaker does not simply haul the boat over by main force. It's true that a few strong paddlers have mastered a version of the roll that uses a simple lateral stroke, like a huge high brace, but in the roll used by most kayakers, the paddle sweeps around in an arc, with the blade edge on to the water and at an angle. The principle is the same as in the low brace; the angle of the paddle blade against the water creates a camming effect, like changing the angle of a helicopter's rotor blades to make it rise.

This is how it is done. The paddler turns to one side, putting the paddle across and laying it alongside the kayak hull, the shaft parallel to the long axis of the boat, one blade up by the bow. For example, if the paddler is holding the paddle on the left side of the boat, then the right paddle blade will be up by the bow, the right arm will be stretched across the chest, and the roll will

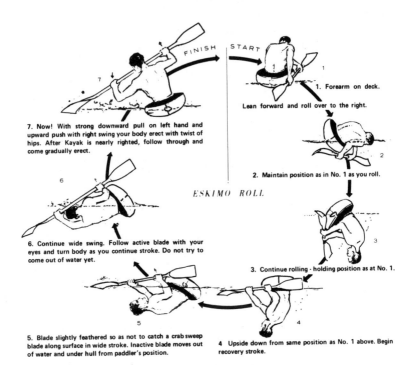

7. Now! With strong downward pull on left hand and upward push with right swing your body erect with twist of hips. After Kayak is nearly righted, follow through and come gradually erect.

1. Forearm on deck.

Lean forward and roll over to the right.

2. Maintain position as in No. 1 as you roll.

ESKIMO ROLL

6. Continue wide swing. Follow active blade with your eyes and turn body as you continue stroke. Do not try to come out of water yet.

3. Continue rolling - holding position as at No. 1.

5. Blade slightly feathered so as not to catch a crab sweep blade along surface in wide stroke. Inactive blade moves out of water and under hull from paddler's position.

4 Upside down from same position as No. 1 above. Begin recovery stroke.

Courtesy Old Town

end with the paddler coming up on the right side of the boat. If the roll begins with the paddle on the right side, everything is reversed. It doesn't matter which way you go because in time you have to learn to roll both ways anyway.

The paddler's body will be bent somewhat forward, the paddle extended for maximum leverage—this last depending on which variant of the roll is being used.

This whole position, when you're still learning, is assumed before capsizing, but of course in a real upset you have to set it up underwater.

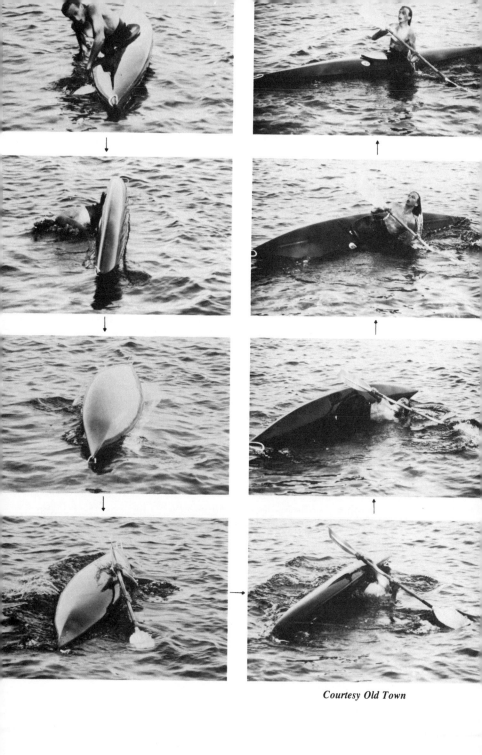

Courtesy Old Town

Now pay close attention to the position of that paddle blade up by the bow, the one that will be doing all the work. It is basically flat—roughly parallel to the water's surface—rather than in the normal power stroke mode. But the paddler's wrists are cocked outward just enough to cause it to assume an angle, so that the edge toward the boat—the leading edge in the actual roll—is tilted upwards (we're assuming you're still upright) and the outside edge tilts downwards. It looks backwards, but once you turn over, up will be down and vice versa—which is the main reason this whole business is so hard to describe in print! Still confused? Just hold the paddle so the blade is flat, parallel to the surface, and then bend your wrists a bit to rotate the paddle shaft out away from you, as if rolling a motorcycle throttle to the off position or using a screwdriver to tighten a screw. That will get the right angle; the precise degree of tilt is relatively unimportant. The main thing is to make sure you don't tilt it the wrong way.

Now, the paddle sweeps out away from the boat in a big arc, the blade staying close to the surface. It will dive a little from the paddler's weight at first, but no great harm if it isn't too much. The action of the angled blade, like the bow plane of a submarine, makes the paddle blade try to ride up in the water, pulling the boat and its occupant around to begin the roll. The whole maneuver forces the arms and shoulders into some awkward positions at a couple of points, so it is necessary to swing the whole body from the waist in order to get enough power into the stroke. It is nearly impossible to do this with arm power alone unless you are unusually powerful.

The other paddle blade comes out of the water, past the bottom of the boat and plays no active part in the roll.

The entire maneuver sounds grotesque and looks impossible—as if you need another elbow—but this is exactly where a teacher comes in—to take you through the sequence and show you how it works. Almost any teacher can make the whole thing clearer than all the books ever written on the subject.

All this time the paddler has also been exerting lateral pressure with hips and knees to help roll the boat. Naturally this requires solid and well-fitted braces, or you'll just jack yourself out of the boat. You must <u>consciously</u> lock yourself into the kayak with knee and foot pressure to roll.

As the paddler's body comes near tbe surface, there is an instinctive tendency to want to get the head out of the water as quickly as possible and to sit upright. This *must* be resisted; it is the single most common reason why beginners' roll efforts fail. At this point the kayak has not yet reached its arc of stability. It still wants to go back to the inverted position, and if you went limp at this point that is what it would do. Once you try to haul your upper body out of the water, then the water is no longer supporting your weight, and the paddle blade is now in a weak low-brace position that just won't hold you up. The minute you try to sit up or raise your head, the roll will collapse and over you'll go again.

What you must do is resist instinct and *leave your head underwater,* keep your upper body *low,* and use that lateral hip snap action to roll the kayak on over into its normal upright attitude. Once you rotate it past a certain point and once it reaches its basic arc of stability, it will pull you the rest of the way up if you've done the roll right. Even if you haven't quite got it down that well, a quick bracing action at the end of the sweep will generally take care of any remaining problems. Rather than trying to climb frantically on top of your kayak, use your hips to pull it over under you.

If you will just remember to do this—keep your head low and wait until the boat rolls up before trying to sit upright—you can often succeed with an otherwise sloppy and incorrect roll technique. On the other hand, as long as you don't keep that head and upper body down and snap those hips, you can do everything else textbook-perfect and probably still blow it.

To sum up, then, the keys to an effective sweep roll are not, as you might think, the arms and shoulders, but rather the wrists, which must set and hold the blade angle, and the pelvis, which must execute that finishing lateral snap.

There are several variants on this pattern. The Greenland Inuit practiced ten different rolls. Most classes teach beginners the extended paddle roll, sometimes called the Pawlata roll after the European kayaker who pioneered modern roll techniques. In this version the paddle is fully extended so that one hand actually grips the non-powered blade rather than the shaft. This gives great leverage, as well as making it easier to orient the power blade and hold the correct angle; it is thus considered easier for novices to master.

Unfortunately, the Pawlata roll, or its numerous variants, must be considered pretty useless for any situation except dead calm water with no need to hurry. Marginally feasible for ocean or flatwater use, in other words, but a bust on any level of moving water. Trying to change your grip on the paddle while upside down in a rapid, let alone sliding both hands clear down to the end of the shaft, is almost certain to result in a lost paddle. Besides, even if you did bring it off—and I've never seen anyone make it work in the field—you would not be ready to control your kayak, and chances are you'd get flipped again before you could get your hands back in power mode.

The real idea is to give the beginner the basic feel of what the roll is all about, the theory being that later on he or she can gradually master the more practical roll techniques. But many feel this gives the beginner just one more bad habit to unlearn. Frankly, I'm not sure how I feel on this question. Go with whatever system they use in your class unless it seems to be really messing you up; then, perhaps, you could look around for another teacher. In most cities you'll have few choices anyway.

Remember that mastery of the extended paddle roll does *not* qualify you for the big whitewater. As long as the extended paddle roll is the only roll you can execute, stay out of anything you wouldn't want to swim in, just as if you had no roll at all. It is not a really dependable technique in heavy rapids.

The effective form of the Eskimo roll is usually called the screw roll. Some experts say this term should only refer to one variant, but they all seem to disagree on exactly which variant this is! Whatever you call it, the basic idea is to do the roll with your hands on the paddle shaft in normal paddling position. This is faster (an important point with your head underwater!) and reduces the chance of losing your paddle, while leaving you set up for the next hazard once you get upright. This is the one you want to shoot for. Many of the best teachers now begin right away with this roll and say it is not really that much harder to learn.

One variation seems worth mentioning here. The usual sweeping roll technique, in its final movements, causes the paddler to finish the roll lying back on the rear deck facing the sky. I still remember my teacher telling me, "If you don't see blue sky in your eyes when you finish, you did it wrong!" Some point out, convincingly enough, that this is not a very good position to be in when negotiating a tough bit of whitewater. If, as very often happens, a wave or rock should cause a second upset before the paddler can get set, then there the poor guy is with his face aimed right at all those submerged rocks. Eegh! The answer, it is claimed, is some variation of the sweep-type roll which eliminates this face-up ending. This is done, in most such variants, by turning the last half of the sweep into something rather like the high brace—a straight down swing of the flat paddle blade. But this is definitely advanced country here, and only a really expert teacher can even discuss this sort of thing, let alone teach it.

There is also the no-paddle roll, which is mostly a stunt. Any water violent enough to take the paddle away from you is a bad place to be drifting around out of control, which is what you'll be doing if you roll up without a paddle. The broken paddle roll, on the other hand, is a very valuable skill indeed, though difficult to master.

As I say, you need a teacher, and not just for the roll; a good instructor can help you perfect all your paddling skills, though only the roll really demands personal guidance. In most cities there are classes at some time of the year, sponsored by the local canoe club, the Y, or the like; ask at an outdoor shop. Or you may be able to find a skilled kayaker who will give you private lessons for a reasonable fee.

There are also several whitewater schools around the country, located on major whitewater streams, and if you've got the money, and maybe a vacation coming up, you might consider signing up for one of these. This is by far the best approach of all; the instructors are usually first-rate. Check the outdoor magazines such as *Canoe* and *Outside* for addresses.

If you absolutely must try to teach yourself to roll, then at least have somebody along for safety. A strong, intelligent friend standing by in case of trouble will at the very least add to your peace

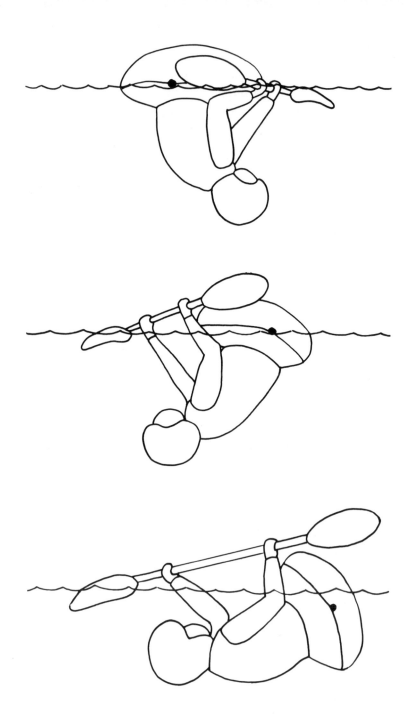

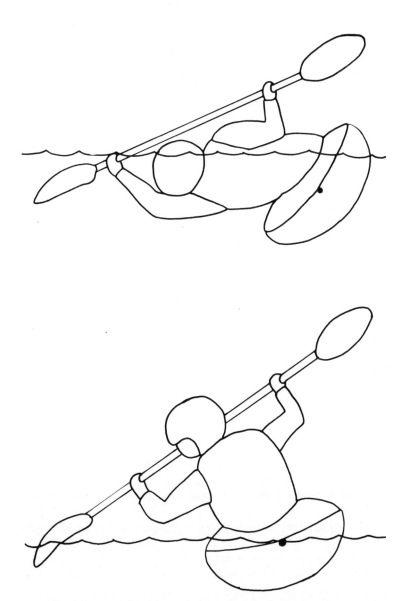

Complete screw roll sequence. Paddler sets up underwater, sweeps paddle out and around in arc while simultaneously exerting lateral pressure with lower body, and finishes with snap of hips in position similar to high brace. Note that upper body is kept low even when kayak has begun to come right side up, and that paddle blade is kept near surface throughout. Do not be misled by stylized sequential diagrams such as this; entire maneuver must be performed in single smooth movement.

of mind; he doesn't even have to be a good swimmer since you need to do your practicing in water no more than chest-deep, and preferably in a pool.

A few tips that may help, if you're forced to go the self-teaching route: get yourself a nose clip and goggles, or a skin diving mask, or the water in your nose and eyes will irritate and distract you. This is particularly important if you have any tendency to sinus trouble, as I do. The goggles or mask will let you see what you're doing. Pay particular attention to the angle of that paddle blade; this is perhaps the hardest thing of all to get right without a teacher.

There is a tendency, unless you've done a lot of diving and the like, to panic a bit in this strange submerged position. Most beginners, even in classes, get in too much of a hurry to begin the roll and don't get set up properly. So I suggest you begin by simply turning over and hanging there a little, without trying to roll, until you start really needing air. Do this a few times—you will be getting useful wet exit practice, anyway—until you get over the worst of that oh-my-God instinctive panic at being submerged and trapped in a capsized boat. Then, when you begin trying to roll, take your time and wait until the kayak has quit wallowing and the water has cleared a bit, study your blade angle and the position of your hands and make your move. Any healthy person can do this on a deep breath, without danger or real discomfort. I personally found yoga breathing exercises very helpful; with enough practice, many people can hold their breath up to three minutes. One minute is within easy grasp. So you've got plenty of time down there, and you can always bail out if it gets too bad.

It may also help to have your friend hold the paddle blade steady at surface level while you hang on it, laying the boat on its side, and practice that hip-snap action. Also, have an agreed-on signal—usually a slap on the bottom of the boat—that means, "I'm in trouble—get me out of here."

All this is speaking of trying to learn from scratch. Once you've learned even a wobbly, unreliable roll, though, there's certainly nothing wrong with practicing on your own, trying to perfect your technique. In fact, it's something everyone should do—with, of course, somebody standing by for safety. You need to practice that roll until it's instinctive and automatic; otherwise, don't waste your time learning it at all because once you flip in a real rapid, you won't be able to think things out.

Practice rolling on both sides; after all, you can't tell which way you're going to flip. Learn the screw roll—most people will be able to work out the conversion from the extended-paddle roll on their own, if they don't get the screw roll in class—and then start practicing it from positions of unreadiness, as if actually paddling, rather than always carefully setting up before turning over. One trick when you think you're getting good: have your friend stand at the stern and suddenly capsize you, without warning, in either direction at random, so you don't know which way you're going to go. It gets harder, but it's perfect preparation for the real thing.

You will probably learn to roll without life jacket or helmet—most people find it easier this way—but when you get the hang of things, practice with full safety gear on. You'll note that the life jacket actually helps you a bit, as it wants to come to the surface, but the helmet may slow you down. Try to simulate field conditions as much as possible.

Remember, finally, that while this is a lot of hard work and results may not be quick in coming, you can still go out and have a lot of fun on easier streams without a solid roll. If you do capsize on one of these runs, try to roll before bailing out. You might surprise yourself or get lucky. In fact, a moving current makes a roll easier, if you can remember to roll in a downstream direction; the current helps push your body around. If you fail, though, don't let it discourage you.

6

Water in a Hurry

The central fact about water is that it is heavy. Try picking up a few gallons of it and see. Like all heavy things, it tends to move downward with the force of gravity. And you know what happens when you get something big and heavy moving downhill and then interfere with its course.

When something—irregularities in the streambed, a sharp curve, fallen boulders, any natural obstacle or barrier—interferes with the flow of fast-moving water, we get a rapid. When the turbulence thus caused mixes a lot of air into the water, we get whitewater. The rest is just a matter of degrees.

Running whitewater is fun, and at the simpler levels it isn't really all that dangerous if you observe basic safety rules. All the same, never forget what's going on. Even a simple little riffle has mind-blowing tons of water behind it, trying to get off the continent and back into the ocean. Enjoy the river, but never fail to respect its power.

A fast stream is like a horse. If you can stay on top and go with its movement, you can have a wonderful ride. If you get in its way, you will probably get stomped. If you get between it and something solid, you're in big trouble. And if you get crazy and try to fight it head-on, you'll lose.

Essentially there are two approaches to whitewater kayaking. The hard-core whitewater freak basically sees a rapid as a playground where various stunts and advanced techniques may be practiced. He or she looks at a rapid much the way a surfer looks at surf. A kayaker of this persuasion will quite commonly choose the most difficult route through a rapid, or work back upstream to run it several times, or poke the kayak into turbulent holes and get tossed around just for the sensation. Such a person may go on wilderness tours and enjoy the scenery, but the real thrill, the final reward, will still be in that interface of kayak and paddle and water.

The touring kayaker, on the other hand, has to view a rapid primarily as an obstacle. He may well have a great deal of fun running a fast stretch, but the object of the game will be to get through in the safest, easiest, most direct way. In a way, it is the difference between the rock climber, looking for the most difficult route up a mountain, and the high country backpacker to whom the mountain is mostly something to get over without breaking any bones just because there's a great view from the top.

Many whitewater jocks, unable to understand how anyone could fail to share their goals and values, assume the touring kayaker is simply afraid or an incompetent paddler. But the cruiser is neither a wimp nor a turkey; he is just rising to a different set of challenges. When you've got all your food, bedding, and other life-support systems on board, you *have* to paddle conservatively, especially in remote country with perhaps a cold night coming on. Anyway, a loaded touring kayak isn't a suitable mount for doing stunts. The whitewater hotdogger and the tourist may take different lines through the same rapid, yet each may be operating at the maximum potential of their respective craft. We need more mutual respect on the rivers.

In this chapter we will consider how rapids work and how to negotiate them without having to learn to breathe under water. Nothing more. For one thing, this book is primarily oriented toward the touring kayaker—using the term in its broadest sense—and, for another, you have to learn the basic techniques of simply getting through a rapid before you can get into the fancy stuff. If you want to go on to learn how to do pop-ups, endos, and the like, you'll need to find experts to teach you; advanced whitewater play techniques are definitely not teach-yourself material. By the time you're ready for that sort of thing, you shouldn't need to read books like this any more.

WHITEWATER CLASSIFICATIONS

Whitewater is classified according to the International Scale from I to VI. This was inspired by the scale used by climbers, though they have now added a seventh class to cover all-but-impossible climbs and still leave something unclimbable. Some have argued for a seventh whitewater class.

The scale may be applied to an entire stream or to a particular rapid. Strictly speaking, the scale refers to degree of difficulty

Running a simple Class I chute. Even in such easy water, this young man should have a life jacket and a helmet. *Courtesy Old Town*

rather than degree of danger—difficulty deals with the likelihood of failure, danger with the severity of failure's consequences—but in practice these concepts tend to overlap and blur.

Here's how the classes break down:

Class I. Easy water. Moving, perhaps fairly fast, but without great force or volume. Few obstructions and these easy to miss; correct route obvious and easy to follow. Small waves, minor turbulence, short drops with safe runout pool below. Typical configuration: narrow or shallow neck between slow pools, short patch of waves up to a foot in height. Suitable for beginners; requires only basic control of boat. Can be run by virtually any kayak, even folders or K-2s in competent hands. Rapids usually called riffles.

Class II. Still easy, but getting tougher. Faster current, enough to require reasonably quick decisions and reactions. May include narrow channel, with some obstructions and/or sharp turns, but correct course will still be clear and easy for competent paddlers to follow. Waves may be a foot or two in height and water may be fairly turbulent, especially on outside of curves. Typical configuration: sharp or blind turn in short rapid, a few large boulders requiring maneuvering, string of standing waves at bottom. Requires good control of boat and elementary water-reading skills; may be run by beginners but preferably in company with more experienced paddlers. Usually requires too much maneuvering for the average K-2 team, but single folders can probably get through. The lowest level to which the term rapid really applies.

Class III. Intermediate, which is *not* to say easy. Fast, strong current, sizeable drops, obstructions numerous and/or large. At least one clear channel, but some definite skill required to follow it; complex maneuvers often involved. Waves may be unnervingly high (up to 4 feet) and irregular; considerable turbulence and eddies strong enough to cause upsets. Typical configuration: short, steep drop with boulders or rocks creating zigzag course, waves capable of swamping open canoes, possibly some small holes. Too much for beginners; requires excellent boat-handling and water-reading skills, though not expert level, and some experience in easier whitewater. Paddler should be competent to run lead boat in Class II rapids. Spray skirt mandatory; roll not essential but probably useful, and paddler should have good mastery of low braces, ferry strokes, and eddy turns, with some grasp of high brace. Definitely no place for folders, K-2s, or other large flatwater boats; some of the bigger touring kayaks (over 14 feet) may not be sufficiently maneuverable for this kind of water.

Class IV. Difficult. Powerful, very fast current, many obstructions and these hard to miss. Course difficult to recognize, requiring scouting from bank; superb kayak handling necessary to follow correct course. Very large waves, vicious turbulence. Various possible configurations—short drop of greater difficulty than Class III, or very long stretches of rapids equal to Class III in difficulty, therefore more tiring to the paddler, affecting strength and judgment. Requires very advanced skills, with solid roll, and first-class outfit. Too difficult for large touring kayaks with gear aboard, except perhaps in expert hands. Anyone who can run

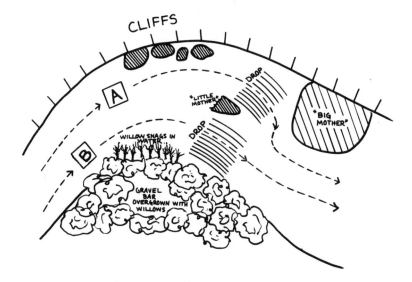

A Class III rapid. The "Devil's Elbow" on Big Piney Creek illustrates some typical aspects of intermediate whitewater. Basic problem is missing "Little Mother," a sharp spur of rock protruding from the ledge that forms the drop. Following Line A requires a powerful ferry to the right to miss "Big Mother," a Winnebago-sized boulder at the bottom of the drop. Line B is a straight shot but must be set up early as the current tends to push boats toward the outside of the curve; it is also necessary to pass close to some dangerous willow snags. Indecisive paddlers wait too long to go either way, and pile up on "Little Mother"—nervous beginners, intimidated by fast drop and size of "Big Mother," often fail to see "Little Mother" at all until they hit it. Quiet pool downstream allows safe recovery.

Class IV water regularly and reliably knows enough to teach a class or work as a professional guide.

Class V. Woo. Scary. Huge waves, long passages, giant hydraulic forces, everything. Don't lend any money to anyone who is about to go run Class V water. Strictly for experts (brave ones) with top equipment and coordinated teams; extremely dangerous even then. Distinct possibility of death in case of an accident, and not really much fun even for experts—more a rite of initiation than a sport. Definitely not tourist water.

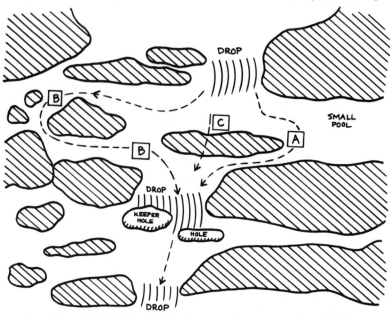

A Class IV rapid. "Washing Machine" is part of a nasty complex called Cossatot Falls, on the Cossatot River in western Arkansas. A series of ledges and boulders creates a Class IV rapid of the type called a "rock garden" calling for precise and fast maneuvering. Kayaker may run lines A or B. Line A is usually easier to get into but you come out at a poorer angle to run the drop. Line B requires a strong backferry when coming out of the preceding rapid. Line C is sometimes possible at high water but at this level the rapid is extremely dangerous. Final chute between keeper hole and rock is only about one paddle length wide. Another powerful Class III-IV rapid immediately below allows little time for recovery. Reliable roll is essential in case of capsize—this is a very bad place to swim. Flow is very powerful and often cold. Only experienced paddlers in good slalom kayaks should attempt such water.

Class VI. Unrunnable or nearly so; may be successfully run by a very few experts under ideal conditions, but even they will owe much to luck. Very strong chance of death. Stay away.

The big jump is between III and IV. Anywhere beyond III, beginner skills are not adequate. A relatively inexperienced paddler with a good boat can probably manage to blunder down the average Class III rapid after a fashion if he or she takes the time to scout it first; and even if this ends in an upset, chances are nothing worse than a rough swim and a swamped boat will result.

But anyone who enters a Class IV rapid without a solid grasp of kayak technique and excellent control of the boat is almost certainly going to dump it, and swimming through a Class IV rapid is a terrifying and brutal experience. In fact, this is why I say you need a reliable roll above Class III—Class IV represents the point at which swimming becomes unacceptably dangerous. It is also the point at which a free-floating boat is likely to suffer major structural damage.

Class IV, to be absolutely frank, is the level at which running whitewater becomes genuinely dangerous—not mortally so, if you're good enough, but dangerous all the same. Don't let anyone talk you into attempting a Class IV run if you lack the experience and skills; the penalty for failure starts to climb very sharply at this point, and you could make a permanent mistake.

It should be noted here that these classifications apply either to rivers or to individual rapids, or sometimes to particular stretches along a stream. In referring to a longer stretch of water, the classification will be based on the *upper* level of difficulty commonly encountered; that is, a rating of Class III for a river doesn't mean it's continuous III rapids all the way, merely that there are several III-grade rapids on the course. However, there may be one or two rapids of higher grades, in which case this should be specified. If the Class III river has a couple of Class IV rapids, it will usually be described as "III with a little IV." This is sometimes reduced to a simple "III-IV," but really this should be used to refer to variations in possible difficulty. A typical example is if the river is Class III at lower levels but IV at spring flood stages.

These classes may also be broken down further by adding plus or minus signs. "Class II+" means the rapid or river is a bit harder than what would usually be considered Class II, but still not hard enough to rate a III. Obviously, the line between II+ and III— is not always easy to draw.

There is an unfortunate tendency among some American kayakers and rafters to downgrade rapids, referring to an obvious and difficult Class IV rapid as "hard III" and the like. This no doubt makes them feel very tough and macho, but it can lead unwary novices into serious danger. Be a little skeptical about accepting ratings assigned by a hot young kayaker with an obviously high opinion of himself. And experts tend to get pretty vague about anything under Class IV because it all looks pretty easy to them. On the other hand, many new paddlers wildly exaggerate the dangers and difficulties of the rapids they've run. Naturally, a three-foot wave looks enormous if you've never run one before. The best information is usually found in maps and guidebooks put out by responsible canoe clubs.

READING WATER

A successful whitewater paddler must be able to study the water—either from the boat or from the bank—and recognize obstacles, understand what the current is doing, and figure out the best route. This skill is called reading water and it is a *sine qua non* of becoming a good fast-water kayaker. In fact it is more important than the fine points of paddling technique. Any paddler who knows the basic strokes and has practiced them a reasonable time can usually get through rapids of Class II and even III difficulty, *if* this is coupled with really good water reading ability. This is sometimes seen when a veteran rafter or open-canoe paddler tries a little kayaking. But even a highly skilled paddler would be in trouble in a relatively simple rapid if he did not know which way he ought to go.

This portion, then, is mostly about reading water. Let's look at some of the most common obstacles and hazards in rapids:

Standing waves are the simplest phenomenon of fast-water physics. When water suddenly accelerates, due to a steepened gradient in the river bed, and then runs into a relatively slow pool below, the water in the chute is compressed vertically, like the hood of a car in a collision. This takes the form of standing waves; unlike sea waves, they do not move but remain in place while you run into them. They can also be caused by a shallow bottom, a submerged rock or ledge too deep to cause more obvious effects, and various other causes. When they are really gigantic they are called haystacks. Beginners and excitable writers often refer to little 3-foot waves as haystacks, but the real thing is the size of your house.

It's fun to run standing waves if they aren't too huge; don't fear them even though they may look scary at first. Kayaks are great for this because the long sharp bow tends to poke through the wave instead of riding over it—an exciting sensation, and no harm done if your spray skirt is in place. Kayaks can run standing waves that would instantly swamp open boats.

In fact, in most rapids, the standing waves mark the deepest, safest passage. If you aim toward the biggest, most regular pattern of these waves, you'll be pretty sure of missing any submerged rocks. But watch out for any standing waves that don't seem to fit the overall pattern; something is under there waiting to bite you.

When hitting big waves, try to keep the boat lined up squarely rather than at an angle. If the bow hits a wave at an angle, you could flip. However, if you do get sideways, don't panic; just reach over the top of the wave and hang a light brace on the downstream side. Just a quick pat of the blade is usually enough. In fact, you can drift sideways down a chute full of waves in this manner if you have a good brace and the passage is clear; in some situations, it is a good way to take the run.

Whitewater players like to surf on standing waves. Unlike the ocean surfer, the whitewater surfer is sitting in one place, more or less, in relation to the solid world on the banks rather than being propelled by the waves. The trick is to balance the various forces acting on the kayak until they cancel each other out—gravity, water pressure, paddle action, and so on. The current is trying to carry the kayak downstream, but the water sliding down the upstream face of the wave is going in the other direction. A top kayaker can find the point at which these forces are in equilibrium and hang there with little effort—an impressive trick and lots of fun, though without real practical use.

Rocks, and other solid obstacles, can be spotted even though they lie just below the surface. Watch for a V-shaped pattern on the surface, pointing upstream; there will be a rock or other solid object at the point. A submerged or semi-submerged rock will also leave a patch of white foam on the surface in fast water, but this may mislead the unwary. The foam patch will be downstream from the object itself. How far will depend on the water's speed. If you steer to miss the foam patches, you could still hit the rocks. Aim to clear these patches by a generous margin upstream. Actually, it's wise to leave plenty of room in this direction in dodging any obstacle anyway, since you might misjudge the water's speed or your own reaction time.

A rock lying just at the surface can be hard to spot from upstream, as the water piles up on the upstream side to form a "pillow" which can hide the rock. If you spot such a rock while scouting from the bank, note a reference point or two along the bank so you don't begin the run and discover you can't see it after all. Kayaks, being low in the water, intensify this problem, so figure on scouting more than you would with a canoe or raft.

If you do hit a rock, lean <u>towards</u> it, <u>never</u> away. The force of the water deflecting off the rock will usually push you clear. But if you lean away from the rock, the current will get up over your deck, pin the kayak, and possibly either break the boat in two or trap you underwater. Fix this rule in your mind.

Strainers and *sweepers* are the most vicious hazards of all. A strainer is an obstacle through which the water passes without checking its force—a fallen tree, a wire fence, a patch of willows. If you get caught in a strainer, the water can pin you and drown you. Strainers can occur on any stream, regardless of its rating, and a fallen tree can turn a simple Class II run into a deathtrap— another reason never to rely entirely on printed guides. And, because many strainers are formed by temporary phenomena such as logjams, there's no way to predict them or warn others, nor will they be marked on river maps.

The only mitigating point is that strainers are usually—though not always—fairly easy to see. They generally take the form of trees and other large objects. An old sunken log with a lot of limbs intact, however, is something else. Fortunately these usually rot fairly fast. Fallen trees tend to occur on the outside banks in curves because the current undercuts the banks. Since the centrifugal force of the current can push you into them, it's wise to stay toward the inside of the curve. And never, never enter a willow thicket or other strainer-type situation if you cannot see a clear path through to the other side. I have been very close to death in such a cul-de-sac, twice, and I do not recommend the experience, though it does make you appreciate life.

Slalom Kayaker using the eddy below a big rock. Such spots can be used to rest or scout in midstream.

Sweepers are a less murderous variant: These hang down over the water and can comb you out of the boat if you don't watch out. Or rather, they'll comb you out of an open boat. We don't come out of our boats so easily, remember? When you get a low-hanging limb across the face in fast water, the current takes the kayak on out from under you and next thing you know you're upside-down. Capsizing on a simple little Class I creek just because you did not notice that drooping branch can be very embarrassing, so watch out.

In some really horrible situations, a sweeper may knock you over and set you up to be grabbed by a strainer. May this never happen to you. Unfortunately, there are no tricks for dealing with sweepers and strainers. You do this by not going into them, and you do that by watching where you're going.

Wire fences are extremely dangerous and hard to spot; they may occur in cattle country. In some states, luckily, it's illegal to put a fence across a navigable river or stream, including those used for recreation. Keep your eyes peeled if they're legal in your state.

Eddies are poorly understood by many boaters. Weird as it sounds, not all the water in a rapid is going downstream. Along the banks, downstream from big rocks and islands, or behind bars and points, you'll find places where the water curls back on itself and forms calm pockets or even runs back upstream.

Eddies can be very useful rest points in the middle of a long rapid to get your breath or check out the course downstream or watch the next boat come through. A bank eddy also makes a natural place to load up and launch.

But eddies can be trouble, too. Along the boundary between the eddy and the main current there is a line of turbulent water. Look closely and you'll see a lot of little whirls and swirls where the countercurrents are brushing past each other. Stick your kayak's nose carelessly across this boundary and you may get a surprise. In a minor riffle you'll probably just get yanked off course and maybe finish the run backwards. In more powerful water, the sudden crossing of an eddy line can cause an upset. And some eddies are unpleasant places to be because the turbulence can toss you around in a teeth-rattling way.

The best way to enter an eddy is at about a 45-degree angle pointing downstream. Hit the eddy line with enough speed to punch through and use a sweep stroke to turn with the eddy so you end up with your bow pointing upstream. Turning will be easy because the opposite forces on bow and stern will spin you right around.

A really classy-looking and efficient way to turn into an eddy, if you've worked on your brace strokes a bit, is to reach out next to your bow and hang a high brace in the water of the eddy, well past the eddy line. If you angle the paddle blade about 45 degrees so that it acts as a kind of rudder, your bow will whip around very smartly. You can also turn the brace into a bow draw stroke as the boat slides into the eddy for an even snappier turn. This maneuver is the famous Duffek turn, named for a Czech who popularized it.

Leaving an eddy in a fast current requires a little more technique than just blundering out into the mainstream. In fact, this is one of the most common causes of upsets on the part of beginning kayakers. As you bow comes across the eddy line and suddenly enters the main current, the water rushing past will try to grab the kayak by the edge of the deck and roll it over. You can get upside down this way so fast you never know what happened.

The trick is to lean downstream as you leave the eddy. In anything but a very strong current you will not have to hang one of those extreme, armpit-soaking braces; just use knee and hip action to tip the kayak downstream enough that the force of the current comes against the rounded bottom of the boat. This gives it nothing to grab and you can come around safely. In a fast rapid you'll have to brace downstream. In easier stuff you may be able to keep paddling and just hold the lean with body action alone. The faster the current, the more you'll have to lean. This is something you learn by experience, like learning how far to lean into a turn on a motorcycle.

Leaving an eddy, paddle hard while you're heading for the eddy line because there usually is not enough room to build up much momentum; you need to be moving pretty briskly when you hit the main current.

These maneuvers are unnecessary on Class I and most Class II streams—though I have occasionally seen fairly ticklish eddies on Class II water—but if you expect to go on Class III runs you will need them, and they are absolutely mandatory on IV water. Practice on an easy stream first. Go on a daytrip, or camp beside a fast stretch, and spend some time just entering and leaving an eddy—doing peel-offs, as the whitewater cowboys call it. It's rather fun and helps you learn a useful skill.

Reversals are like eddies in that part of the water is flowing back upstream, but in this case the action is vertical. Water flows over a ledge or other sudden drop in the riverbed. Falling, it pulls the water immediately downstream back onto itself in a rolling, recirculating motion. To some extent this phenomenon occurs at the base of any drop, but in cases the hydraulic forces can be strong enough to grab a boat and hold or capsize it. This is what we call a "hole" and you can recognize it, after you've seen a

few, by the peculiar, glassy, unnaturally flat, sliding look of it—
a flat slick patch in the middle of a lot of heavy turbulence.
Unfortunately, the worst holes lie below drops and may be in-
visible from upstream.

Whitewater players like to fool around in small holes. You can
poke the kayak's nose in just right and get tossed around in a
fascinating way, doing pop-ups and endos and so on. A reliable
roll is essential, though, because you will definitely capsize doing
this. Personally I do not go in for these tricks, which are hard on
the boat and serve no practical purpose, so if you want to learn
how to do them, get some hotdogger to teach you.

For the loaded tourer, a hole is an obstacle to be avoided if
possible. If you do hit one, usually you can paddle hard and punch
through. A big touring kayak had an advantage here due to its
higher buoyancy. If the hole tries to stop you, reach out beyond
the hole and plant your paddle in the solid water below it and
haul yourself out. If you get sideways in a hole, go into your best
high brace, planting the paddle blade in that water below the hole
and then paddle out or let the hole spit you out. If you try to
brace in the hole itself, the highly aerated water will not support
you.

Bigger holes can gobble and hold a boat. This is what is called
a "keeper" hole, and you definitely do not want to get caught in
one. Unless you can hang an instant and rock-solid brace on firm
downstream water, you'll flip in a second, and the rolling motion
of the water will spin your 'yak like an axle. Relax. Most of the
time the hole will spit you out, boat and all, after gnawing on
you for a few seconds. Most holes are rather irregular in their
operation, and you need only hang on until the right fluctuation
sets you free. If at all possible, *stay in the boat,* even if you can't
roll. (A paddler who can't roll shouldn't get onto rivers with
keeper holes, however.) Your kayak is a big object and essentially
buoyant, and therefore the hole will spit it out faster than it will
release a human body. People have bailed out in holes and been
held and drowned while their kayaks emerged downstream. Just
hold your breath, stay bent low over the foredeck, don't let go
of your paddle, and the instant you feel the hole letting you go,
you can begin your roll or wet exit.

A few—very few—holes are so powerful they simply will not release anything. These horrors are the kind of thing you run into on Class V water; you will probably never even see one. The only real hope, a thin one, is to bail out, remove the life jacket, and dive for the bottom, in the rather forlorn hope that the water down there will be flowing downstream and you can make your escape. This information is given purely for your academic interest. Stay away from keeper holes if you are still reading books; to run this kind of water, you ought to have enough experience to write the books.

A peculiarly nasty reversal is found at the bottom of a certain type of vertical drop. Vertical falls are funny things; some quite high ones are safe to run and some very low ones are killers. It seems to be a matter of the shape of the riverbed at the bottom of the drop. Natural falls in soft rock country (limestone and the like) usually carve out plunge pools where the reversal effect is negligible. Man-made drops are the worst, being very regular in configuration. To give you an idea, on the Spring River on the Arkansas-Missouri border there are drops of up to 8 feet which are regularly and safely run by total beginners in rented canoes. But back in 1973, on a river in Ohio, four paddlers drowned in the reversal below a man-made drop of *six inches*. Stay very far away from any man-made drop—low diversion dams used in irrigation have killed many people on Western rivers, and dams are hard to spot from upstream. Be almost equally shy of very straight, regular natural drops of more than 45 degrees if there is no obvious runout. If you see a straight line across the river ahead of you—a kind of abrupt discontinuity in the surface—get out of the water and go have a look at it before you get carried over something you might not want to run. Dams should be marked, of course, but vandals love to destroy such signs, so you can't depend on it.

In some rural areas there are low-water bridges—concrete slabs, with a few culvert pipes to let the water through—where dirt roads cross the river, and some nasty reversals can develop below these at certain levels, while at low water you might be sucked into the culvert pipes. It is dangerous either way, so carry around these things.

If you're unsure about the advisability of running any drop—even a relatively small one—it's better to err on the side of caution and carry around.

MAKING THE RUN

Now you've come to your rapid. You're a little nervous about the sound of this one and you can't see where it goes, so you get out and walk down the bank to scout it. Good. It never hurts to scout and you can learn a lot. Anyway, it's a chance to stretch your legs and rest your arms.

Scouting is something of an art in itself. You have to be able to figure out the correct route, which is usually fairly easy, and then predict how it's going to look from your kayak, which is something else. Almost certainly everything will look totally different from the two angles. Reference points along the bank—unusual trees, rock formations, and the like—will help; if there's something you're absolutely going to have to miss, or a turn you must make, pick something you know you can see easily and make a mental note of it—"Hang a hard right when I get even with that red rock," for example. It may be useful to follow the mental rehearsal trick used by some gymnasts and divers, in which you mentally go over the whole run before you begin, picturing yourself making all the right moves. This is better than going into the rapid with half-formed ideas and forgetting them when it gets bumpy.

If you can read water well, though, there is no need to scout every rapid; most of the simpler ones can be sight-read as you go through. This is the real danger of faster water—you get less time to plan and execute your responses. Remember these principles:

(1) A V-shaped or U-shaped pattern, pointing <u>upstream,</u> will have some kind of obstruction at the point.
(2) All else being equal, the biggest standing waves mark the deepest and clearest part of the channel.
(3) Take sharp curves closer to the inside bank than the outside. The centrifugal force will try to push you toward the outer bank, and this is a likely spot for fallen trees and rocks.

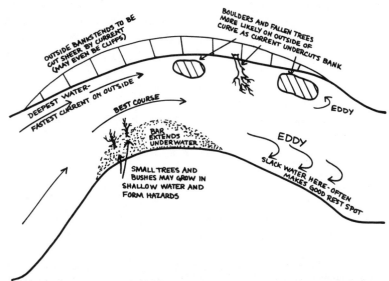

What Happens In A Curve. Stream bends are a common trouble spot for novice paddlers; this diagram illustrates some typical phenomena. Obviously outside of curve is more dangerous, but current tends to carry boat toward outer bank through centrifugal force, so paddler must consciously resist this. Water may be too shallow close to inside, and eddies can cause loss of control and even upsets if paddler is unready. In high-water conditions river may come up over lower ground along inside bank; if trees are present this may create an extremely dangerous situation. This spot would rate Class I or perhaps II depending on gradient and speed of current.

(4) Anything that doesn't fit the pattern—a big wave outside the main concentration, a slick glassy-looking patch amid turbulent water, a sharp, dark line across the river ahead—is probably trouble and should be avoided and scouted if there is any problem about missing it.

If you will bear in mind those four principles, they alone will help you avoid the great majority of whitewater accidents and show you the best course down most rapids.

Remember, most of the time the water wants to go where you want to go—downstream by the simplest route. Usually it will take you there if you let it.

In all but the simplest rapids you will from time to time have occasion to move the boat laterally across the current to miss

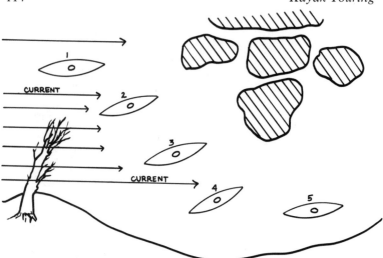

Back Ferry. Kayaker approaches at (1), giving wide berth to fallen tree (which could have branches extending further underwater, and at (2) turns kayak until stern is angled to right, while simultaneously using a strong backstroke. Current pushes kayak to right at (3) and (4) while backstroke keeps kayak from being carried downstream into boulder; at (5) kayaker straightens out, safely past. A skilled and knowledgeable kayaker will have already begun backpaddling to slow kayak well before reaching (1). (Diagram is somewhat simplistic for purposes of demonstration; in actuality current would be more complex.)

various obstacles or negotiate zigzags and S-turns. The technique of maneuvering across a moving stream is called ferrying.

In its crudest form ferrying can be done simply by turning the boat to point across the current and paddling briskly. This is adequate on slow water, but in a fast current ferrying takes a little more thought; turning broadside to the current is not always a good move.

On fairly broad, straight, big-wave rivers, as found in the West, it is indeed possible to drift sideways down the rapid, using forward and backward strokes to avoid obstacles and holes. Some Western kayakers, notably Walt Blackadar, have developed this into a whole school of whitewater running. You drift sideways and use your paddle in a downstream brace to keep the current from turning you over. It is possible to run even quite big waves this way by reaching over the top of each wave and quickly

Big Western rivers are tremendously powerful but usually leave lots of room—good country for large touring kayaks. *Courtesy Old Town*

bracing on the downstream side. Walt Blackadar used to float down appalling water this way, relaxed and calm, just reaching out and patting the back side of each wave with his big flat Iliad paddle. If the river is big enough to let you get away with it, this is a good technique for large touring kayaks, as it does not call for sudden turns and puts a premium on stability.

But on some small, narrow, winding streams, or where the course is choked with boulders, there may not be room for a boat to go through crosswise and have any maneuvering space. Then you have to resort to more conventional ways of ferrying.

You can, of course, simply point the kayak at some point to the side of the obstruction and accelerate to miss it. But you're still moving with the current, and if you don't time your moves just right, you may be swept broadside-on into the obstacle, which is more dangerous than hitting it bow-on. So when using this approach—and it is still the most effective technique in most situations—make your turn well upstream of the obstacle, make

Narrow, rocky streams demand precise handling. *John Gephart*

sure you are lined up to miss it before straightening out, and plan your moves so that as you pass the obstacle you're already getting lined up to miss the <u>next</u> hazard downstream. Don't try to do this at the last instant.

In some situations you can set the kayak at about a 45-degree angle to the current and paddle *upstream,* against the current. The force of the water will push you across the stream. If you can paddle just hard enough to counteract the current's force, you can slide straight across the river.

You can do this in two ways. You can point the kayak upstream, angled in the direction you want to go, and use a normal forward stroke; this is the front or upstream ferry. It takes less strength and works well against strong currents, but then you have to turn around completely in the middle of fast water, which is an unnerving business. Or, you can made a back ferry, by pointing the stern at the desired angle and using a strong backstroke; this is physically harder and less efficient but much quicker to execute.

Both front and back ferries have their uses and should be learned by any serious fast-water kayaker. However, they are difficult to execute in the middle of a rapid. The foamy water offers little for the paddle to grip, and turbulence makes it hard to hold the right angle. These ferries are usually better for lining up in preparation for entering the rough stuff. Still, with practice and strong arms they can sometimes be used in very tight spots. Work on them.

Finally, you can use a draw stroke to yank a kayak sideways in a hurry if you only need to move it a foot or so—fine for missing something you only saw at the last moment, but not really a strong technique if you've got time and space for anything more efficient.

Leaving out the unorthodox lateral-drift approach, there are two basic ways to maintain control or steerage way with a boat in moving water: move faster, or slower, than the current. Generally speaking, if the obstacles are hydraulic in nature—holes, waves and the like—it's better to accelerate and power through unless you intend to hang around and play. If the main hazards are solid ones such as rocks or logs, and particularly if the passage is very restricted, it's wiser to slow down and use techniques such as the reverse sweep and back ferry. Then, if you do hit something the impact is reduced. This is the main reason Western and Eastern kayakers operate so differently, even to using different boats. Western whitewater kayakers tend to go for big-volume 'yaks compared to Easterners—Western rivers tend to be big and open but full of huge hydraulics, while Eastern streams are little and rocky.

STAYIN' ALIVE

Safety rules for whitewater kayaking are mostly the same as those for operating any small boat:

(1) Don't run alone; a three-boat group is minimum. Sure, *I* go alone, and if you know the risks and deliberately decide to accept them, I am with you; the right to risk your own life is a sacred one. But you ought to know it's dangerous.
(2) Wear your life jacket and helmet in any kind of whitewater.
(3) Know your abilities and weaknesses, be honest with yourself and others, and never be too proud to admit a run is too much

for you—or try to persuade anyone else to attempt something he or she feels unable to handle.

(4) Scout any rapid you aren't sure of. Mistrust guidebooks and maps. Many are inaccurate, and rivers change.

(5) Outfit your boat properly with full flotation bow and stern, correct-sized grabloops (but no loose lines), and properly-adjusted spray skirt. Keep the boat and paddle in good condition and don't put off important repairs.

(6) In a group, maintain safe intervals between boats, and never start down a chute if there is any chance another boat ahead of you may be in trouble—unless you can clearly see a way to help without endangering anyone.

(7) If the water is cold, wear a wet suit.

You may have noticed that I have not repeated one common rule given by various authorities—that you must be a competent swimmer. I don't understand this rule. No matter how well you swim, you can't stay afloat in real whitewater without a life jacket, whereas if you do wear your life jacket, anybody can swim well enough to get through. And the high bobbing position created by a life jacket makes it impossible to swim in the usual manner anyway. For the record, I can't swim a stroke, and I've put in more time going down rapids without my boat than a lot of people have in theirs. Of course, a non-swimmer should spend some time in a pool or shallow pond, floating around in the life jacket, in order to become accustomed to the sensation and to learn how to use hands and feet for control and propulsion. Non-swimmers need life jackets with very high flotation.

The swimmer's real advantage is psychological; he or she is more used to being immersed in the water. But I've seen plenty of skilled pool and beach swimmers come completely unglued when suddenly dumped in a rapid, and I've seen plenty of non-swimmers keep their cool and float through fast chutes with no problems. That's why I'm very skeptical of the rule that kayakers must be able to swim.

Speaking of swimming, what if you do eat the river and dump the boat?

The first thing to remember as you make your wet exit is *stay upstream from the kayak* (or any other boat). If you get down-

Running the Colorado River in the Grand Canyon—some of the toughest whitewater in the world, definitely not for novices. Even this big-volume Easy Rider Augsburg II is almost submerged by the power of the river. *Courtesy Easy Rider*

stream from your boat it could run you down or pin you against a rock, cliff, or snag. If at all possible, hang onto the boat by a grabloop, and hold your paddle too, but let go immediately if necessary to keep from being taken somewhere you don't want to go. In a rescue operation, the rescuer has the right to order the swimmer to let go of a boat, paddle, or anything else if this is hindering the rescue or endangering others. The swimmer should obey without argument; the rescuer has a better view and may see hazards the swimmer can't.

If you find yourself swimming through a rapid, *keep your feet up* and point them downstream. Many people have drowned by having their feet caught by submerged logs, cracks between rocks on the bottom, and the like. If your foot is trapped, the current will push your head under with terrible force, even though the water may not be over your head. Keeping your feet downstream lets you use your leg muscles to absorb the shock of any impact with rocks and so on. Float on your back—many life jackets give you no choice anyway—and watch where you're going. After you flush through the rapid into the calm water below, you can adopt a simple backstroke and work your way to shore.

Don't be too eager to get to the bank if the water is still moving fast. Instinct says to make for land, but in the rapid itself you're better off in the water unless there's something lethal downstream, like a big waterfall or a wire fence. As long as the passage is clear, swim it out. Trying to scramble up a bank in the middle of the rapid could get you mixed up with fallen trees or other snags. In a turn, the shallower water will be toward the inside bank, but that is also a likely place for willows and other strainers, so watch out. Keep your head, don't fight it, and you'll probably be fine.

If you have to rescue a swimmer, paddle near enough for him to grab your stern grabloop. Then you can play tugboat until you get to shore. Don't let the swimmer get within clutching distance of any other part of the boat; he may be so shaken up and frightened that he may grab wildly at anything that comes by, including your paddle or the side of your cockpit, which might flip you over.

Do not engage in pointless heroics—paddling, swimming, or wading in to rescue someone—unless there is clearly something you can do to help. In many cases the rescuer simply muddles up the situation and gives the victim something else to dodge. Adhere to this rule: *rescue people first, then equipment.*

I hope the last few pages, with their unavoidable emphasis on the negative possibilities in kayaking, haven't scared you off. As I've said, running whitewater up through Class III difficulty is not a high-risk sport, and if you observe the rules just given, plus some simple common sense, there's no reason you should be afraid to run the average whitewater stream once you master the basic strokes. The vast majority of the rivers of North America are no harder than Class II over most of their length, while the really hard stuff is so unusual that people travel thousands of miles just to see it. The keys are to use your head and know your own limitations as well as those of your boat.

7

Open Water

Open-water cruising is a glorious experience, and far too many
kayakers miss out on it. For one thing, the scenery is usually
outstanding. Everybody seems to agree that a clear blue lake is
one of the finest sights in nature; think how many paintings have
this theme. In good weather you can relax and enjoy the view
without having to worry about rapids ahead, and even when things
do get rough there is usually plenty of time to plan your responses.

There is a great feeling of self-sufficiency in paddling on broad
expanses of water. On a narrow mountain stream, you tend to be
just another wilderness traveler, with the current constantly re-
minding you of the river's power and your own insignificance.
But out on open water a mile or more from shore, you can be
the captain of your own sleek, seaworthy little ship. Somehow,
open-water kayaking has more of a feeling of, well, boatness about
it.

Large comfortable boats like this Klepper single are fine for open-water cruising.
Courtesy Klepper America

There are more practical arguments as well. Beginners ought to do a fair amount of flatwater paddling before venturing onto rivers with strong currents. The demands on technique and strength are nowhere near as great. People who own large flatwater touring 'yaks, especially two-seaters, will have a much better time on open water, where maneuverability isn't particularly important and the extra stability is nice to have. And, because you can use a larger boat on open water, you can also carry more supplies and camp in a bit more luxury.

The strongest argument, however, is simply that there's more open water around. Good whitewater streams are getting hard to find. Most of the best fast rivers in the U.S. have already been murdered to provide power for such vital necessities as lights for Las Vegas casinos. Many of the streams that remain are crowded, with litter an increasing problem, and in some cases the authorities are requiring permits in order to hold down human traffic.

But there are lakes all over the country, to say nothing of miles of seacoast, and you can do a good deal of paddling on protected coastal waters without getting into the hairy business of deep-sea kayaking. Also, there is plenty of room for everybody. Big open rivers are likely to be polluted in this insane age, but there are still stretches which retain their charm. And, unlike many white-water streams, large bodies of water remain usable all year round.

It may be noted that I use the term <u>open water</u> rather than the more common <u>flatwater</u>. I've always felt that the latter word is an unfortunate one. For one thing, open water doesn't necessarily stay flat—get a good wind up and you'll see that it gets very bumpy indeed. Three-foot waves are no real threat to a competent kayaker, but I wouldn't call them flat either. Anyway, this whole concept of dividing every stream into either whitewater or flat-water seems questionable. The lower Mississippi, for example, certainly isn't a whitewater stream by any accepted definition, yet its surface is a constantly changing whirl of boils, violent eddies, and murderously powerful currents. It seems silly to call it flatwater. For that matter, my own term isn't all that great. The Okenfenokee Swamp offers some of the most fascinating paddle touring in the country, and the water is as flat as you will ever see, but there's no way you could call it open. I suppose we need to work out some new terminology. Meanwhile, you know what I'm talking about. . . .

Open-water paddling demands no special boat-handling skills. All you need is the basic propulsion-and-control strokes—the forward stroke, the backstroke, and the sweep for turning. The draw will also be useful for sidling up to docks and bringing two kayaks together for lunch or to consult the map.

A roll may or may not be needed depending on what sort of boat you have and where you intend to go. With the larger, stabler cruising kayaks, you shouldn't need a roll—they're very hard to roll anyway—and if you're operating in shallow water or near the shore you can swim or wade out. But if you've got a narrow, tippy boat and expect to cross big, open water, it's a good idea to master some sort of roll; you don't want to have to swim a couple of miles through waves and chop. The extended-paddle roll is probably adequate here. With no current, you should have plenty of time to get set.

The skills needed for successful open-water cruising are peripheral to the business of actually managing the boat. You need to be able to read a map and use a compass, and you definitely need a grasp of weather signs and principles. You maneuver a whitewater stream through fast reactions, water-reading skill, and good boat handling. You stay out of trouble on open water by planning and judgment.

The basic fact of moving water is the current; the basic fact on open water, usually, is wind. Large stretches of water are nearly always windy. In fact, under some conditions they generate their own weather, as glider pilots know.

Now a kayak is far less wind-sensitive than any other type of boat. It lies so low in the water, and presents such smooth and rounded surfaces to the air, that the wind simply can't get much hold on it. Paddling into a strong wind is tiring, but much less so than in the traditional canoe, with its high, saillike ends. Nor does the wind shove you off course as it does in a canoe.

But it's not so much the wind itself that causes problems; it's the waves. If the wind is blowing over a long, open stretch, the waves can build up quite a head of steam; if they run into a narrow channel or a shallow patch, they can get big and scary looking.

Books on canoeing tell you to be careful crossing lakes and to stay off if the wind and waves get up. It takes very little to swamp a small canoe, and even three-foot waves can be very dangerous. Kayakers, relax; very few inland lakes are big enough to crank up waves capable of endangering a decent kayak with a competent paddler. A three-foot running chop, taken head-on, can be unpleasant on a cool day; you get a bucket of water in the face every few seconds, and if your spray skirt has any leaks you'll get a wet crotch; but otherwise, it's no big deal. A good kayaker can negotiate waves a great deal larger than this.

The canoe books, again, tell you to take waves on your quarter, zigzagging if necessary to avoid taking waves bows-on. This is simply to avoid swamping. You don't have to worry about swamping, unless you are stupid enough to try and cross a big windy lake without your spray skirt, so you can take the waves straight on. If you hit them hard you will probably go right through them like a submarine, which is fun on a warm day. If it's cool and you don't want to get that wet, take it easy and you will probably ride right over the swells.

Of course, you may have to quarter across a wave pattern, if that's the direction you need to go. This is a fatiguing business; the waves push your bow around, and you have to paddle twice as hard on the downwind side of the boat, or take extra paddle strokes, to stay on course. Your rhythm goes totally to pieces, and you'll probably curse copiously. Here is where a rudder comes in handy.

This brings up an important safety point. Although a good paddler in a well-designed touring kayak with spray skirt in place should be able to survive in very big waves, this assumes the paddler has enough energy to keep controlling the boat. Over extended periods of wave busting, even a strong man can become fatigued, and in rough weather this might be dangerous. Be conservative about making long open-water runs in rough weather. Maybe you can use an island or promontory for a rest. Remember, there is calm water on the downwind side of any bit of land, and even a weed bed will reduce the force of the waves.

Running before the wind is enjoyable; you can surf along with minimum effort. Normally the waves on inland lakes are not large enough to create the problems sometimes encountered by kayaks in ocean surf.

If you have to cross a wave pattern, with the wind on your beam, you've got a bit of a problem. Most stable touring kayaks won't actually flip in such conditions—though the narrow-beamed sea kayaks may tend to do so—but it's certainly hard to paddle straight and the wallowing sensation is unpleasant. To get through, work out a zigzag course, tacking like a sailboat, or quarter across the waves to a point upwind of your destination and then drift down onto it.

If you have to turn sharply in the middle of a wave pattern, time yourself so you make the turn on top of a crest, not down in the trough.

Remember, wind-driven waves in some ways act like the current on a river, so don't lean toward them any more than you would lean upstream. It is possible to do bracing strokes on open water to prevent a capsize—you might be suddenly hit by a motorboat's wake, for example—but be sure to brace downstream away from the waves. The sculling brace is good here.

Stay well clear of the downwind shoreline; the wind and waves could force you onto rocks or snags. Oldtime sailors rightly feared lee shores.

Regardless of wave conditions, stay off open lakes during obviously stormy weather. The big danger is lightning. Out there on the water you make the ultimate lightning target. If it starts rumbling, head for shore—period.

All this talk about lakes, by the way, refers strictly to the normal sort of medium-sized, sheltered inland lakes—the giant variety are another story. The Great Lakes, in particular, should be treated exactly like the ocean, and kayaking on them should be regarded as a branch of sea kayaking. Conditions on Lake Superior can be far more dangerous and demanding than, say, most of the Gulf Coast in summer. If you live near the Great Lakes, you can certainly kayak on them if you've got good equipment and know what you're doing—but don't let that lake title fool you into taking them lightly.

Actually, the biggest danger on many bodies of water isn't a natural one at all. I refer, of course, to motorboats manned by the irresponsible or the incompetent and the two types are not always mutually exclusive. This shouldn't be surprising; consider how the average American operates an automobile and you have to shudder at the thought of the same person behind the wheel of a speeding motorboat. Nor do boating laws require an operator's license or impose a minimum age.

The only effective safety measure is to stay away from waters frequented by these people. Wearing bright clothing, carrying signal flares and lights, and other warning measures are largely ineffective, since they assume that the motorboat operator (1) is looking where he is going and (2) cares whether or not he runs over you. Neither is necessarily true. In fact, not a few of these louts will deliberately run as close to a kayaker as possible in order to watch you capsize. Just go somewhere else.

Be particularly wary of water skiers; the towboat operator tends to look back and watch the skier rather than the water ahead. And while fishermen are, on the whole, thoughtful and pleasant boaters, stay away from any lake where they are holding one of those fishing tournaments. Those guys go crazy; it's like being in the woods in deer season.

Even relatively considerate motorboat operators can generate enough wake to toss a kayak around a bit, and sometimes you have to pass through a marina area to reach your destination. The best way to deal with this is to pivot the boat sharply around and take the wake on your bow, exactly as you would take a big wave. You also could brace on the side away from the wake and take it on the kayak's bottom.

Commercial towboats on large rivers can be very dangerous. They can't stop in any reasonable distance, so it's up to you to stay out of the way. Don't get too close to the bank, though, or the wake may toss you up and leave you stranded. Along large rivers, the banks may be covered with rock, pilings, and other stabilizing structures, so this can be bad news. I once damaged a kayak on the Mississippi when a passing towboat's wake slammed me against a concrete-reinforced embankment.

Be especially watchful under foggy conditions. Try to wait for the wind to blow the fog away. Usually it does this once the sun warms the air. And carry a big flashlight if you have to run late into the evening. I've paddled open water by moonlight, and it's one of the most fantastic sensations on earth, but it does demand caution.

If you should capsize in open water and cannot roll back up, *hang onto your boat.* If it gets away from you, a capsized kayak may be blown by the wind faster than you can swim after it. Hang onto your paddle if you have no spare and no one around. If you're drifting down on a rocky shore, or even a sloping beach with waves coming in, remember to stay upstream of your boat.

A valuable open-water skill is the deep-water remount. Many find this easier than rolling, though it is easy only with the kind of beamy, stable boat that does not roll well anyway. A fairly large cockpit is also helpful.

Secure your paddle temporarily to a bow or stern line. Now turn the kayak upright; hoist yourself across the bottom, grab the far gunwale (or reach under and grab the cockpit coaming), and slide back, pulling it over with you. If the water isn't cold, try to bail the boat out as much as possible from your position in the water.

Now crawl up over the rear deck, letting your legs hang down on either side to help balance you and keeping your body low. When you reach the cockpit, sit or crouch cautiously, working yourself forward until you straddle the cockpit, feet hanging into the water on either side. Let your rear end drop into the seat and swing your legs up and in. Finish bailing out.

With a big beamy boat such as a Klepper, this isn't a very hard trick to master, even on rough water. With a large double, where one crew member can help stabilize the boat while the other gets aboard, it's easier yet. It's a bit harder with normal-sized kayaks—not impossible, just harder. You can do it, with some practice, in most medium-sized general-purpose touring and flatwater cruising boats. Really small kayaks are another story. I've seen it done with a regular slalom kayak, but the guy who did it was an absolute master with superb balance. Of course, the Aleuts regularly practiced the deep-water remount in various forms—but did not use the roll—with their sea kayaks that often were as narrow as 20 inches, but I don't think I'd want to try it. This is not a viable substitute for a whitewater roll—it requires more time than you usually have on the rivers—except on pool-and-drop streams.

There is also a technique in which two kayaks lift a third out of the water to empty it, but I am skeptical about its effectiveness except in a swimming pool, maybe.

It is very important to have some grasp of self-rescue technique even if you run in groups. Kayakers can easily get separated on open water in rough weather or fog, and once you turn over they may be unable to find you.

One unusual travel and camping possibility, curiously ignored by most kayakers, is the lowland swamp or bayou. With its shallow draft and narrow beam, a kayak is a great craft for negotiating the narrow channels through a swamp. You can also forget about snakes dropping into the boat—something they unaccountably like to do with open craft. It's a far cry from foaming whitewater and mountain gorges, but the swamp has a fascination of its own. The incredible abundance of life—bugs, birds, snakes, turtles, fish, plants of every kind—is almost enough to make you dizzy. You feel as if you've paddled through a time warp into some earlier age before man.

When kayaking and camping in the swamps, carry plenty of insect repellent and watch your step if you get out to walk around— if you can. Military jungle boots are by far the best footgear, and the enclosed jungle hammock, which normally I do not care for, is probably the best bed and shelter for swamp camping, where dry ground is hard to find. Above all, make sure you have an accurate map and a good compass because a swamp is the easiest place on earth to become lost once you leave the main channel.

Of course, if we're talking about open water, we can't ignore the most open water of all.

8

Down to the Sea in Kayaks

Sea kayakers are the astronauts, the argonauts, and the Vikings of the paddling world—the probers at the edge of the possible. Time was when whitewater jocks regarded themselves, with justice, as the elite. No more; today's kayakers have come to realize that the ocean is a far mightier antagonist than any river. The power of the sea, the enormous distances involved, the weather that is like nothing found anywhere else, the complex tides and currents—all make sea kayaking at the top levels a game for experts with nerves of brass.

At less extreme levels, any reasonably experienced kayaker can do a fair amount of cruising along coastal waters, exploring bays, inlets, and harbors, without needing expedition-grade gear or expertise. All that is really needed is an intelligent awareness of the dangers—particularly weather and tides, and, in some areas, surf—and a high level of caution. The ocean must be approached much more conservatively than inland waters as the consequences of error are too high. On a river, even if you dump it, lose your boat, and get kicked around by half a mile of heavy rapids, chances are you'll eventually get ashore; dry land just isn't that far away. Obviously it doesn't work that way on the sea.

Beginners should stay away from the ocean until they have some experience on less demanding waters. Lakes are good basic-training grounds for this purpose. In some areas, particularly the Pacific Northwest, there are commercial outfits that will take you on group tours and teach you the basics, and I strongly recommend joining one of these tours or hooking up with a club rather than trying to teach yourself.

There is one possible exception. People who regularly sail small boats on coastal waters probably have enough background in winds, tides, and the like that they can pick up the basics of sea kayaking as soon as they get the hang of operating the boat itself. In some areas, especially New England, there are people who go in for rowing in dories and the like—it has become an authentic subculture—and such a person could no doubt master a kayak quite easily.

For everybody else, sea kayaking has to be regarded as an advanced-level sport. If you're still having trouble keeping the boat moving in a straight line, give yourself more time before tackling the salty stuff.

This book is too short to try to give you a full course in sea kayaking, even if I felt qualified to write it. The subject deserves a book to itself. Such books exist—check the reading list—and if you're seriously interested in taking a 'yak to sea, you ought to read them until you wear the letters off the pages. All we will do in this chapter will be to take a very brief, general look at what sea kayaking is and what it involves, in case you think you might want to give it a try.

SEA KAYAKS

Sea kayaks are very specialized boats designed to meet the unique demands of ocean paddling. They are, I think, the most beautiful of all kayaks, and a great deal of thought goes into their

Sea kayaking is not as simple as it looks. Be wary of off-shore winds and currents which can take you out to sea despite your best efforts. *Courtesy John Gephart.*

design. Not all of the thinkers come to the same conclusions. In fact, there is much more variation among sea kayak designs than among whitewater boats, most of which seem to be clones of the same banana-shaped original.

Certain requirements are basic and everybody agrees on them: a sea 'yak should track extremely well, with maneuverability a negligible factor—one nice thing about sea kayaking, you've usually got plenty of room to turn—and it must be very strongly built to withstand the powerful forces acting on it, including possible landings in rocky surf. Beyond these basics, there is quite a bit of disagreement over just what constitutes the ideal sea kayak.

One popular movement, favored by young Englishmen of a macho bent, is for very long, narrow kayaks patterned after the Greenland Inuit boats. These are quite commonly as long as 17 feet, and may be as little as 18 inches in the beam. As you'd expect, such boats are very fast indeed, track beautifully, and turn over if you don't part your hair exactly in the middle. A

The Easy Rider Eskimo, a new sea kayak designed along traditional Inuit lines but made wider for stability and comfort. *Courtesy Easy Rider*

reliable roll is a necessity with boats of this type, and you'll get plenty of chances to practice.

The best-known kayak of this type is the Nordkapp, designed by Frank Goodman and manufactured by several different concerns. Nordkapps have been used by several successful expeditions in the waters around New Zealand, Greenland, Norway, and the British Isles, among others. Nordkapps are 17 feet long, 21 inches wide, fast as the devil, and very tippy.

Another designer, Derek Hutchinson, author of the book *Sea Canoeing,* has turned out several boats of this general type, at least one even narrower—20 inches—than the Nordkapp. And if you're really feeling brave, Country Ways has a kit for a Greenland-style 'yak with a length of 18 feet, 8 inches—at least a foot of which is above the waterline in the form of a protruding bow— and a 19-inch beam. They call it the Angmagssalik, and if you can pronounce it I suppose learning to keep it upright will be a lesser challenge.

Most of the modern sea kayaks designed by people like Goodman and Hutchinson incorporate watertight bulkheads, turning the bow and stern into large flotation chambers and reducing the volume that can be flooded in a capsize. There are watertight access hatches to allow you to stow your gear in these compartments. Theoretically, you should be able to dispense with dry-stowage bags, provided you have considerable faith in man-made gadgets. (There are a very few, but very convincing, horror stories about leaks.) A pump is standard equipment in any true sea kayak as, in heavy waves, you dare not pop the spray cover to bail in the usual way. Some sea kayakers fit a foot-operated pump so they can pump without stopping paddling, a very valuable feature.

Sea kayakers who go in for the narrow Greenland-style boats usually defend their tender craft with fierce and fanatical devotion. To the charge of instability they reply that any kayak can be capsized by large waves (which is true if the waves are big enough) and their boats are much easier to roll back upright. They point to greater speed, easier handling, and light weight. Quite often they will tell you that a kayaker who can't handle a Nordkapp isn't skilled enough to be out on the ocean at all.

Other people see it differently. They point out that the Greenland-style 'yaks have very limited cargo capacity—a serious drawback for extended touring—and that they are very uncomfortable to sit in for long periods.

A more telling point is made by John Dowd in his excellent book *Sea Kayaking*. In a Greenland-style boat, Dowd observes, a sick, injured, or fatigued paddler is in grave danger because it takes constant attention to keep the tender boat stabilized. As Dowd says, you can't really relax in a Nordkapp. On day trips or cruises along the coast this may not be too serious, but on a long trip, far from land, it would seem very serious indeed. Who can guarantee that a paddler will not become sick or tired, or sprain a wrist bracing on a sudden big wave?

My own sea kayaking expertise is far below the expert level, but I must say I find this last point very convincing. Once I was on a long lake cruise, camping on islands, when a sudden attack of pleurisy took me down. In great pain, desperate to get to a doctor, I launched *Foxfire* in the middle of a violent windstorm—gusts over 30 miles per hour were recorded, and the waves were enormous by lake standards—and more or less let her drift. My left arm was useless. I could do no more than trail the paddle over the side one-handed as a kind of rudder. Yet *Foxfire* took me safely across twelve miles of open water, through a Force Six wind, and didn't take on a drop or even give me any scary moments. Now lake kayaking isn't sea kayaking, of course, but my point is this: a less stable kayak (*Foxfire* has a 24-inch beam and a round bottom) would never have made it. I can see how this could happen on a sea trip just as easily, and I, for one, tend to agree with Mr. Dowd.

For whatever reason—safety, comfort, cargo capacity—other sea kayakers favor larger, stabler, more capacious boats. Many people still like the good old Kleppers, which are indeed excellent sea craft and almost uncapsizable, except in the most extreme conditions. Others prefer something a bit handier, somewhere between the beamy, yachtlike folders and the tiddly Greenlanders, and this is the idea most American seaboat builders favor at this time. One very fine craft is the Sea Otter, designed by Lee Moyer of Pacific Water Sports in Seattle—16 feet long and 24 inches wide, with a very fast, straight-tracking hull and a single large watertight compartment in the stern. The hatch is considerably larger and easier to use than the tiny holes on some of the

Greenland boats. This is one of the finest all-round sea kayaks in the world and it would also make an excellent touring boat for cruising on lakes and the like.

Most river kayaks are no good for sea kayaking, being too short and too low in volume to be really seaworthy. A large touring boat might work out all right for paddling around sheltered bays, fjords, coastal marshes and so on, however.

Many sea kayakers like to have a rudder—a great aid in paddling through quartering swells or running before the wind. With the big doubles such as Klepper, it is common to fit a simple sailing rig. The eccentric visionary George Dyson, builder of giant multi-seat kayaks, has invented unusual sails which turn into neat little tents for camping on shore at night.

ALL AT SEA

The actual paddle techniques used in sea kayaking are rather basic—just the standard open-water strokes, with a roll of some sort useful and even vital in any but the beamiest kayaks. The specialized demands lie mostly in understanding the complex environment of the sea and being able to plan ahead and use sound judgment.

The sea moves in many ways—winds, tides, various currents. A successful small-boat seaman has to understand how these things work and what he must do to cope with them. He must also be able to predict the action of the sea. On a river the water will always move in the same direction at any given spot, and only water levels which usually change gradually, except on dam-controlled streams, cause any significant variation. The ocean changes from hour to hour and conditions are different in all areas. The Gulf Coast is a whole different world from the cold archipelagoes of the Pacific Northwest, which in turn is different from New England. Different problems arise in different areas, calling for different skills and techniques.

This is why you can't learn real sea kayaking—as distinguished from merely paddling around in sheltered coastal waters—from this or any other book. You can only pick up some general principles. You'll need a good experienced companion who can explain the particular hazards and problems of the waters in which you intend to kayak. Even an experienced sea kayaker should seek out such advice in waters with which he is unfamiliar.

It might seem that even a beginner could simply paddle along the coast, keeping land close at hand, and get away with it. You can certainly do this sort of thing in some places—the coasts of Florida and Texas, for example—if the weather is good and you have unimpeachable information that it is going to stay that way. But it's not as simple as it looks. You'll have to be wary of offshore winds, which can blow you right out to sea despite your best efforts. In areas with powerful tides, you may find yourself fighting surf if you get too close to shore, and either wind or tide, or a combination, might force you onto rocks. Vicious tidal rapids occur where rivers enter the sea under certain conditions. In other situations, river mouths make sheltered refuges. And so on; you see the point. All these things fit together into a complex pattern, and you have to understand the various forces, both separately and in the way they affect each other.

Mark Billington paddled this Easy Rider Dolphin from Seattle to Ketchikan, Alaska. *Courtesy Easy Rider*

There would be no sense in trying to go into all these complicated matters in a single chapter like this. Such subjects as ocean
weather, tides, navigation, and the like have been the topics of
enough excellent books to fill a small library. A worthwhile understanding of these things requires considerable study and experience, as any small boat sailor knows. How far you want to
get into such knowledge will depend on how ambitious your sea
kayaking plans are. If you just want to fool around in deep protected bays and inlets, or cruise along sheltered inshore waters
such as the Intracoastal Waterway, or poke around in saltwater
marshes in Florida or Louisiana, you can get along with little
more than a basic knowledge of weather patterns so you will know
when to get off the water. If you have in mind making the first
solo kayak run from the Aleutians to Tierra del Fuego, you had
better learn enough to qualify yourself to write a book on weather,
tides, and navigation. Anywhere in between, figure it out for
yourself and be conservative. It's better to know more than you
need than to know less.

It might be added here that the traffic problem is even worse
in popular coastal waters. Sailing people are usually pretty considerate, and in any case you ought to be able to outmaneuver
and outrun a yacht, but powerboat skippers can be impossible.
Harbors are particularly dangerous places. Try to find somewhere
else to launch and recover.

You'd think the wake from a big oceangoing ship would be a
horrible thing, but actually it just slides under you as a big swell,
lifting and dropping you, and passes on. Tugboats and naval vessels have steeper wakes; the smaller Coast Guard cutters, in particular, have rather nasty wakes. Turn and take them bows-on.

Launching and landing in heavy waves is a science in itself.
The usual procedure on shallow, sandy beaches is to put the kayak
at the edge of the surf, just within reach of the incoming waves.
As the waves recede, hop in, snap the spray skirt quickly in place,
and let the next wave lift you and take you out. If you don't have
too big a kayak, you can reach down with your hands on either

side and push off against the sandy bottom, using your knuckles like a gorilla walking. You can also push off with your paddle, but this is a good way to damage it. Or you can simply carry a short stick along for this purpose; you may be able to use it as part of a simple sailing rig as well.

Coming in through surf is considerably trickier. In big surf, a loaded touring kayak tends to dig its nose in and may even go end-over-end. You can come in sideways, using a brace to stabilize you. Bracing in surf is opposite the usual river technique, as you brace upstream; that is, out to sea, into the wave. You always lean seaward in this situation, never landward, or you can even turn around and come in backwards, if the waves aren't too huge, using your paddle to slow you down. Usually, if you look around, there is some relatively sheltered area where a bar, point, jetty, or even a big kelp bed breaks some of the force of the waves.

Man-made obstacles are a major hazard in coastal surf. Pilings can destroy your boat and trap you besides, so give them a wide berth. On public beaches, watch out for swimmers, and don't mingle with surfers. They tend to resent kayakers—understandably, in view of the dangers of a collision—and the type of water they like is no place for a loaded touring 'yak anyway.

All this assumes a sloping, sandy beach. Surf on rocky shores is horribly dangerous. If you paddle such areas, you must stay well clear of the shore until you can find a sheltered inlet, usually common on rocky coasts, and a safe landing beach. Make sure there is a landing spot inside before you enter a deep blind inlet or fjord. You might find it's completely walled with sheer cliffs, and then you'll have to fight back out to open water against the surf. How do you find out what's in there? By using your topographic maps, of course; you have to have maps of sea *and* land. (And, of course, know how to read them.)

Big ocean waves, as long as you're clear of shoal waters, are surprisingly easy to handle; the long swells just slide under you and you rise and fall in a rather enjoyable way. It's only in special conditions that the waves get rough over deep water, usually when the wind pushes them up so high that they begin to collapse and break, falling down their own fronts onto you. The best way to deal with this situation is to be somewhere on land—well before the weather gets that heavy.

This is why I keep stressing the need to understand and be able to predict weather patterns. A good radio in a waterproof container is worth anything on a sea cruise—I even take one on long trips on big lakes—because it can warn you of approaching storm fronts.

However, if a kayaker does get caught out on the sea by a storm, it is not necessarily best to turn and run for land; a storm on open water is still less dangerous than a landing through storm-driven surf. Usually it should be possible to find a sheltered spot to land—the lee side of an island or point, for example—but if all else fails, an experienced kayaker will simply ride out the blow, or try to. A drogue or sea anchor will hold the kayak's bow into the wind so that the kayaker doesn't have to depend on constant paddling to avoid broaching. A drogue is something like a parachute, streamed out astern at the end of a long line. But no one except an expert should be out there in that sort of situation in the first place.

Tidal currents are a whole separate ball game; in some areas, notably among the islands of the Pacific Northwest, they can be extremely complex. Accurate charts and tide tables are essential, as is a practical knowledge of conditions based on experience and personal input. Fishermen and yachtsmen are good sources of information on such matters. The Coast Guard, in my opinion, is likely to exaggerate dangers and try to talk you out of going at all. Best of all is another sea kayaker who knows the area. Fortunately clubs are springing up in various places, with talk of a national or international organization to keep everyone in touch, and this will help the information situation a great deal.

As for living hazards, the non-human kind, that is, sharks have been reported to attack a few kayaks, but it seems to be a rare phenomenon. Killer whales have been proved to be good-natured buffoons where humans are concerned, and several groups studying whales have found kayaks ideal for getting in among the pods without disturbing the great beautiful beasts.

There is a vogue—no other word applies—for whale-watching

nowadays, and along the West Coast some people have taken to paddling out to look at whales close up. I would advise caution. No doubt the whales wouldn't deliberately harm you—they seem unbelievably patient considering what they've had to put up with—but an accidental brush or a swipe from a tail would turn you over at least, and I wouldn't discount the possibility of a youngster playing with you. Have somebody else along, at least, and maintain a little distance.

The incredible Mr. Dowd informs us that walruses may attack without provocation, but personally I can't believe I am likely to need this information. If you go paddling in walrus country, you should be so experienced you shouldn't need to read books any more.

9

Camping Gear

Day trips are great fun, and you can certainly cover many enjoyable miles in your kayak without ever spending a night outside hard walls. All the same, camping out on rivers, lakes, islands, and beaches is an important part of kayak touring. Indeed, many would say this is the point of the whole business, with the kayak just an unusually pleasant way to get there. If nothing else, camping out definitely extends your range of operations and makes you smugly independent of things like motel rates.

Kayak camping differs radically from the traditional North American style of canoe camping. Glance through the average canoe book and you'll see huge army tents, cast iron Dutch ovens, wooden food boxes, ice chests, even folding chairs. Granted, most of this literature goes back to the Heroic Age of North Woods Canoeing; later generations are taking a lighter, lower-impact approach. All the same, the relatively enormous capacity of an open canoe tends to encourage a much more luxurious outdoor lifestyle than is possible with a kayak. The same is true of Western-style river rafting, where ice chests are virtually part of the boat.

Some authorities suggest that kayakers should imitate backpacking practice. This gets us a good deal closer—onto the same river, anyway—since the hiker has many of the same problems and has to adopt somewhat the same go-light, when-in-doubt-leave-it-at-home attitude. But in many respects the packer's problems are not the same as ours. For one thing, while we all have to watch the weight, backpackers can tolerate much more bulk, and, for another, few hikers have as much cause to worry about gear getting soaked.

No, kayak camping is a separate and demanding little science in its own right. But it does have its advantages. The unyielding loadspace limits take a lot of pressure off your self-control. If you're the insecure type, always catching yourself taking things along you don't really need or cramming last-minute extras into a bulging backpack—or, worse, tying them on the outside—you'll get over that fast when you try to load a kayak. You can get just so much under the decks and that's all. Incidentally, this saves you lots of money, because now you won't be tempted to let some fast-talking salesman or glossy ad get you to buy a lot of junk you don't really need. If you go in for any other form of camping, such as backpacking, you'll be amazed at how much you've learned to reduce your load.

Nor is this Spartan style of camping harsh and unpleasant. Most of that junk you have to leave at home is more trouble than it's worth anyway. The less stuff you carry, the less you have to keep dry, pack and unpack, and so on. This gives you fewer worries and more time to enjoy yourself. You may even find yourself getting very philosophical about how little people actually need, compared to the mountain range of possessions they think they have to have.

The key points in selecting kayak tripping equipment are lightness and compactness—not necessarily in that order.

You must keep the weight down because a kayak already sits low in the water, and if you overload your boat you're asking for trouble. She'll wallow like a pig in waves and go down rapids with the maneuverability of a telephone pole, and if you hit anything—and you probably will—she may crack wide open.

But at the same time, bulk is, if anything, more important than weight. Under the deck of a kayak, cubic inches are even more critical than ounces. Even the big folders, which have great load-space compared to regular 'yaks, are not bottomless wells. As for going on long, self-supported trips in a slalom kayak, you can do it, but it takes some cramming.

One more factor that will influence certain choices: remember that wet stuff under the boat? We try to keep it outside the boat, and even after an accident has admitted it to the interior of our Noble Vessel, we have various clever arrangements to keep water from actually making contact with our priceless goods and chattels. Only life isn't always so perfect, and now and then despite our best efforts our gear gets wet. Wet, my wet suit. Every now and then it gets soaked.

Now some things, like food, simply have to be kept dry or be ruined, so we make elaborate double-bagging efforts and pray a lot. Other things, like cookpots, get as wet as you like with no harm done. But where there is a choice between something that can stand getting a little wet and something else that will be ruined by the damp, it is logical to choose the more amphibious alternative.

THE BEDROOM

On warm weather trips you may be able to get by with only a light covering. I've spent a lot of summer nights outdoors under a G.I. blanket. One memorably hot summer I spent several weeks paddling around the bayous down near where the White and Arkansas rivers empty into the Mississippi, and I carried only an old cotton sheet and sweated copiously at that. Usually, though, you need a sleeping bag.

For generations, waterfowl down has been considered the only worthwhile insulating material for first-class sleeping bags. Good down, in a bag of proper construction, is undeniably the most efficient fill of all for weight and bulk. Being light and supremely compressible, down bags are the first choice of most backpackers and bicycle campers, and theoretically ought to be perfect for kayak camping—except for one little drawback. A down bag works only as long as it is as dry as a Coast Guard weather report. Get it wet and it is transformed into something so wretched a dog wouldn't curl up on it. Not only does it lose its insulating value, it takes a long time to dry out and can be ruined by rough handling while wet.

Here I feel justified in being doctrinaire: down bags, in my opinion, are a very poor choice for any sort of waterborne camping. A few diehards echo the old cry, "There's no excuse for a real outdoorsman to get his bag wet!" Ridiculous. Under sufficiently humid conditions, such as the ground fogs common along rivers and lakes, a down bag will soak up water out of the air. And the need to keep your bag absolutely dry forces you to carry a more sophisticated, heavy, bulky tent, thereby eliminating any advantage obtained from the down bag's undeniable virtues.

Nearly all modern American river runners now use bags filled with the modern hollow-fiber synthetics, usually Hollofil II or Polarguard. Unlike down, these fibers retain quite a bit of insulating value even when wet and will dry rapidly. (Usually body heat alone will dry out damp spots.) Under some circumstances this difference could save your life. It has saved mine, I can testify. At the very least, it can help prevent much discomfort.

The great beauty of all this is that this is one case in which the best choice isn't the most expensive. Bags made with synthetic fibers are quite a bit cheaper than down bags of equal temperature rating, yet they are entirely valid bags. The military forces have tested synthetics in Arctic conditions, and many off-the-edge expeditions have successfully used them.

Now the fill must be stabilized so it doesn't migrate around, form clumps, and leave cold spots. Down requires a lot of complex internal baffling, but the synthetics come in batts and can merely be stitched to the nylon shell of the bag. The cheapest procedure is to run a single line of stitching clear through the batting and the inner and outer shells; this is called "sewn-through" construction and is quite poor for anything but warm-weather use, as it leaves a cold spot all along the stitched line.

Better bags employ two layers of fill—one stitched to the outer shell of the bag, the other to the lining—and these are offset so there are no cold spots. The difference is well worth paying for.

The most efficient type of bag is called a mummy. This type takes up less room, and weighs less, for a given temperature rating. However, in really hot weather a mummy can be pretty confining, so I'd get the kind with the full-length zipper rather than the down-to-the-waist pull-on type. Then on hot nights you can unzip it and just lie on top of it.

But we don't want to get too fancy here. Most kayak touring is done in relatively mild weather. Deep winter kayak travel, while fascinating, is very challenging and requires heavy-duty gear, extra clothing, and a big kayak to hold it all (as well as much experience). An Arctic-grade bag is massive overkill for the average kayak tripper, being unnecessarily bulky, heavy, costly, and too hot for warmer weather.

Most kayak cruisers will be best served by a so-called "three-season" bag. It will be rated down to about freezing, though not really comfortable much below 40° F or so; you can get through a cold snap by sleeping in your sweater. This bag will weigh four to five pounds, depending on your height. It is a bit heavier than the equivalent down bag, but not prohibitively so. It will also be a little bit bulkier. But the difference has been blown all out of proportion, sometimes by the down lobby, sometimes by snobbish outdoor-chic types. For what it's worth, I often go camping in *Lady Mary,* my old Mark I slalom boat, and I've done my share of backpacking and bicycle camping—even wrote a book on the latter—so I think I know something about weight and bulk. I use synthetic bags exclusively and have never found them excessively hefty or hard to pack.

A bag of this type, with double-layered offset fill, will cost about half to two-thirds the price of the equivalent down bag. Such bags are made by L. L. Bean, North Face, Eastern Mountain Sports, and Eddie Bauer, among others. Beware of super-cheap bargain bags; the stitching tends to be very poor and the fill may be a no-name mess of mill floor sweepings.

As for what goes under you, most modern lightweight campers use closed-cell foam pads. Besides providing some ground insulation, these are light and cannot be damaged. They are also wretchedly uncomfortable—I would just as soon sleep on the bare ground as far as useful padding goes—but today's wilderness wanderers are nothing if not trendy, so the old air mattress is on the way out.

Except for kayaking. Foam is absolutely out for our purposes;

light as it is, it is just too bulky to go under a kayak deck without sacrificing space needed for other things. A few Klepper jocks have been seen lashing foam pads to their afterdecks, which is probably a workable idea, but the rest of us have to give the fat, puffy things a wide miss.

Don't be upset by all the propaganda; modern air mattresses are neither heavy nor particularly unreliable, if you'll take a little care with how you handle them. They are less likely to be punctured by sharp objects than to succumb to flying sparks, dropped cigarettes, and the like. Get a three-quarter length model rather than the head-to-toe kind, and be sure to get the modern coated nylon kind with the separate air chambers. Then if you do get a puncture it isn't the end of your night's sleep. Mine came from Bean's, weighs eight ounces, and rolls up into a bundle the size of a wadded-up tee shirt.

SHELTER

Most people think of tents when they think of camping. You certainly need something to keep the rain off, and it does tend to rain a lot around bodies of water. But shelter from the weather doesn't necessarily mean a tent. In fact, plenty of people dislike tents and never use them. If an occasional shower is the only problem, you can cope quite well with a tarp. Nylon tarps are available for not too much, or you can simply acquire a sheet of the tough translucent plastic called Visqueen which the construction industry uses by the running mile. Any building supply store will sell you a roll. A sheet of Visqueen, say, ten feet square, is by far the cheapest effective shelter you can get and one of the simplest.

A tarp can be rigged in many different ways, which is part of its charm. Most people normally rig it in a kind of lean-to shed roof fashion, with one side open; this is very pleasant in mild weather, as you have a feeling of being outdoors, yet the wind and rain are kept off. In cooler weather a small fire (where permissible) will reflect heat onto the occupant of such a shelter— an extraordinarily comfortable and cozy arrangement. In hard, driving rain, it may be better to rig the tarp like a pup tent. Either way, it's a good idea to have a tarp large enough to let you tuck one fold under you to protect you and your bag from dirt and ground water; this saves carrying a separate ground sheet.

Nylon tarps have grommeted holes for attaching lines. Cord can be tied to Visqueen by bunching the plastic up around a small rock and tying the line around the resulting protuberance.

One problem with tarps: they require some form of support. In the woods you can simply use trees, but on open beaches and gravel bars trees are few and, literally, far between. A couple of kayak paddles, tied crosswise, make a good support for one end of the shelter if you can find something for the other—say, a stick of driftwood or a bush.

A few people favor the tube tent—essentially a body-length tube of plastic into which one crawls for the night. A line between two trees holds it off the occupant. There is no ventilation unless you rig it so the wind blows straight through it (in which case there's little point in having it) so the moisture given off by your sleeping body condenses and drips all over you. In such a close space there is no headroom and no way to avoid contact with the

Light nylon tarp provides shelter from rain or sun with less weight and bulk than tent. *William Sanders*

wet walls. This is why a tube tent is probably the most wretched excuse for a shelter yet devised. Its only value is in survival kits because an injured person can sometimes rig a tube tent when unable to erect anything more complicated. For real camping, forget it.

On the whole, a simple tarp is the best answer to the rain problem, unless you're going into the heavy rain country of the Pacific Northwest. If your only need for shelter is measured against occasional rainfall, then don't bother with a tent; save yourself the weight, bulk, and expense. A sheet of Visqueen is of course cheaper, but a nylon tarp will make up into a more compact bundle and is therefore better if you're using a smallish kayak. Take some ordinary tent stakes anyway; don't depend on tying things to bushes, which have a bad habit of not growing where you want them.

Having said all this in favor of tarps, let's back up and consider another aspect of the shelter situation: bugs.

In many parts of the U.S. and Canada, during the warm season, insects are not only a nuisance but also a serious threat to health and sanity. They are particularly bad around water, where mosquitoes breed, and worst of all near still water. Along mountain whitewater streams, where the water is too turbulent for mosquitoes, things may be bearable, but in the summer, especially anywhere in the South or the lake country of the U.S.–Canada borderlands, you'd better be ready for screaming squadrons of whining bloodsuckers every night.

Some people manage all right with an open tarp shelter and liberal applications of strong insect repellents, but most of us find it necessary to get some kind of physical barrier between our skins and the things that go buzzz in the night. It is possible to rig a simple mosquito net over the bed area, under the tarp, and this still adds up to less bulk and weight than a tent. However, it leaves you exposed while you're eating, reading, or whatever.

Despite the problems involved in carrying any sort of effective tent in a kayak, I usually take one whenever the weather is warm enough for the bugs to come out in force. (This is one reason I favor cool-weather camping over the usual summer trips.) On balance, it seems to be worth the added hassle. Your own decision on the matter will rest somewhat on your personal tolerance for bugs and they for you—they home in on some people and virtually ignore others—and where and when you're going. For instance, the lake country of the North in fly season demands a tent, as does Alaska.

The smallest, lightest, most compact form of tent is a bivvy sack—essentially just a waterproof sack to cover the sleeping bag, with an enlarged area around the head and shoulders. In one of these you can only lie down; you can get up onto your elbows after a fashion, but that's about it. So a bivvy sack is fine for sleeping and not much else. You can't cook, eat, play cards or do much of anything else in a bivvy sack. You can't even rig up a lantern and read unless you want to burn the claustrophobic thing down (which may occur to you after two days of steady pelting rain). It keeps the bugs off fine, but if the bugs are that bad then you'll probably want to get under cover well before bedtime, which means some boring hours. Some people like bivvy sacks, though. I certainly advise trying one out before buying it; they are expensive.

At the other end of the spectrum, large dome-shaped tents, complex mountain tents meant for expeditions, and all canvas tents are too big and bulky for normal kayak camping. Some of the smaller domes will fit fairly well into a big touring boat or a folder, but on the whole it's best to stick with small, simple designs, if only because all those long heavy fiberglass wands are hard to stow.

A major problem in small tents is condensation. The human body gives off mind-boggling quantities of water vapor in a night, and this tends to condense on the inside of the tent and drip down to form puddles or make damp spots on your bag. If the tent is well ventilated, with plenty of door and window area covered by mosquito netting, and if there is any air movement at all, this vapor will, for the most part, dissipate harmlessly. But if it's a still night, or the door and window flaps have to be tied shut against blowing rain, the moisture can really build up.

The usual answer is to build the tent itself out of uncoated breathable nylon, which in theory allows the water vapor to pass through the tiny pores in the fabric. Then, to keep rain out, rig a secondary roof or fly—essentially a small tarp which covers but does not touch the main tent. (By the way, a rain fly for a three-man wedge tent makes a pretty good light tarp by itself—try J.C. Penney.) The fly adds some bulk and weight, of course, and so some small tents are made with roof and walls of coated material. This makes a light, compact tent, and in dry or windy campsites it will be adequate, but the condensation becomes much worse in a tent of this type.

I used to say that these single-layer tents were unacceptable, but now I am less certain. I've used both a good deal and have come to the reluctant conclusion that breathability is not all it's cracked up to be. Under some conditions almost anything will drip. A heavy dew will condense on the inside of any tent—camp in a grassy meadow and you'll get the full effect—and a thick fog will do the same, even if you aren't inside.

These things are not all that serious in warm weather, and when it turns cold enough for wet surroundings to be a health hazard, I go over to a tarp anyway. The problem can be reduced considerably by camping on open, windy beaches, gravel bars, and the like, but to a certain extent it seems to go with the territory. If you've got room for it, I still recommend the breathable tent with separate fly, but if you're crowded for space, the single-wall variety shouldn't be too bad for most climates.

The most elegant solution to the problem is to make the main tent body out of mosquito netting. This will allow any level of moisture to escape without condensing, and you can lie there on clear nights and look at the stars without getting nibbled to death. Yet a fly makes the tent waterproof. Being made of netting, such a tent makes a light, compact bundle. I am a great admirer of this concept for warm-weather use; however, these tents are usually pretty expensive.

Among current commercial tent designs, I favor the Moss Solus (a solo model), the Sierra Starflight, or the Eastern Mountain Sports One Night Stand. All are light, compact, and beautifully made. All are expensive. So it goes.

I do not understand why some of the most expensive tents are so big and heavy. Five pounds is plenty for a two-person tent and four is entirely possible with modern technology. A lot of weight is added by providing various accessories and features that are not really needed but look great in the shop.

The typical kayak camper has no real requirement for an elaborate tent. We're talking here about mild-weather, low-altitude camping for the most part. You don't climb mountains with a kayak, and few of us have to deal with snow, so why does everybody assume you need an expensive expedition-grade tent?

Discount and surplus stores are full of cheap orange nylon doghouses, usually of Oriental origin, for relatively trifling prices. Nearly all established authorities will assure you that these creations are worthless junk, inadequate even for overnight use, and probably linked to cancer in laboratory mice. My own highly heretical opinion is that they represent adequate housing for most mild-weather camping and quite decent value for the money. Because they are made of thin material with no fancy features, they are often quite a bit lighter and more compact than the more expensive models. I own a couple of these things; one weighs 4½ pounds and the other weighs a couple of ounces less, with poles and stakes.

Sure, they flap in the wind. If a little flapping keeps you awake, you must not have spent the day paddling very hard. Sure, they're flimsy and wear out. At these prices you could replace one every year and still be ahead. I have one I've used, hard, since the winter of 1976; it's been through rain and wind and a couple of hailstorms and never failed me. New, it cost thirty bucks. In the final analysis, they will keep the rain off your face and the bugs out of your space, and all else is vanity.

All the same, I do suggest you stick with a separate-fly design in this price range. Single-wall tents have to be pretty solid because one leak and you're in trouble; with a separate fly you get twice the protection, and if the fly leaks, the water will just run down the inside, still clear of the tent.

A kind of tent, I suppose, is the jungle hammock—a heavy-duty hammock with a small roof and mosquito-net walls. These devices are useful for swamp camping, where there may be no solid or dry ground to pitch a tent. Most people can't sleep comfortably in them, but you may be an exception. They do reduce the load, being tent and groundsheet and mattress in one. If you use any type of hammock you should carry some rags and wrap them around the tree before lashing the support ropes in place. Otherwise, the ropes can chew through the bark, which may permit the entry of fungi and boring insects.

ODDS AND ENDS

Some kind of light is a necessity; if nothing else, carry one of those little Mallory flashlights for finding things after dark and checking out any crunching noises behind the tent at the edge of the woods. (That is, if you're sure you really want to know. . . .) Carry spare batteries and tape the switch so it doesn't exhaust itself inside the pack. In winter, when nights are long, it's worthwhile to carry a bigger flashlight. If you're going to be crossing open water where powerboats or commercial traffic are common, you definitely need to carry a good big waterproof flashlight in case you get caught after dark.

Coleman lanterns are too big and heavy, of course, but there are candle lanterns which work well for kayaking. The light isn't too great, but they take up little room and the candle stubs make neat fire starters. The flat folding kind is more compact and less trouble than the spring-fed type. Get the special stearene candles, which burn longer and brighter.

Knives are handy, but don't go wild; you can spend a fortune on knives nowadays. All you really need are a simple good-quality pocketknife with a couple of blades—keep the small blade razor sharp and don't use it much so you have it ready for things like removing splinters—a smallish sheath knife, mostly for preparing food. A folding knife is bad for kitchen work because the hinges get so full of crud. Those Finnish fishing knives are especially good for this and they are cheap.

Some people denounce large sheath knives as useless encumbrances. Many even say that nobody but a greenhorn would carry a belt knife over three inches long. Well, it depends. I carry a rather large belt knife on the river. I run a lot of streams where willows and fallen logs present a certain risk of snagging clothing in an upset; several people have been drowned in this way and on one occasion I came extremely close to joining them when a willow stub held me under for what felt like hours. I have taken to carrying the big knife with the idea that I might be able to cut myself free in such a situation. The willow stub in question broke just in time, but the next one might not be so considerate.

The big knife also comes in marvelously handy around camp. I've used it to split chunks of driftwood after a rain to get at the dry wood inside; I've chopped myself a walking stick after spraining an ankle; and once, having lost my spoon, I cut a piece from a lightning-blasted walnut tree and carved myself a wooden spoon that I still have. And there have been those times when I've been glad to have a potential weapon. I don't say you ought to get a knife like this (actually you can't—I made mine) or carry anything heavy; I'm just saying that it isn't necessarily a mark of incompetence when a person fails to follow so-called Expert Opinion.

A little G.I. can opener in your wallet may be worth a lot one day. Canned food is not kayaking food, but you might stop at a store. Pocketknives with can openers and other gadgets can be more trouble than they are worth on the river if all those hinges get full of sand and jam. You ever see a Swiss colonel in a kayak?

THREADS

Clothing for wear around camp should be similar to what you wear in the boat—then, you can wear one outfit while the other is drying. There should certainly be no need for more than one change of clothing unless the weather is really bad. In summer, shorts and T-shirts are adequate; however, those alligator shirts dry fast and don't stick to you when wet the way T-shirts do. But even in warm weather it's a good idea to take a warmer long-sleeved shirt along in case it gets cool in the evenings. A sweat shirt, in particular, is comfortable and easy to pack.

In cooler weather, wool is preferable because it retains some warmth when wet. Good sturdy wool trousers can be found in military surplus stores; my warmest wool pants, for bottom-of-winter use, are German Army issue (modern, not Wehrmacht) but U.S. Air Force uniform trousers are good for most conditions. You can also get good wool pants from old wool suits sold in thrift shops. A sweater is nice and warm but less versatile than a wool shirt because you can't leave it open if it gets a little too warm. Still, I usually take an old wool sweater when nights are cold. In such conditions you'll be wearing your wet suit for paddling, so you don't need a change. Wool clothes are bulky, but then by this time of year the bugs are pretty well gone and you can carry a light tarp for shelter, saving you enough loadspace to accommodate the extra clothing. See how it all hangs together?

A pair of moccasins will be so nice to have around camp that you will probably find some way to take them; you don't want to wear your wet boat shoes all evening. If you plan to hike around the area, you might want to carry a pair of boots, if your load space permits.

A light, unlined windbreaker over a sweater or wool shirt is better than a heavy coat and more versatile. But you'll want some kind of jacket for paddling and rain protection anyway as we discussed in an earlier chapter so you can simply use your paddle jacket as a windbreaker if you're hard up for space.

If nights are cool, be sure to take a warm cap, such as a knit Navy watch cap. Your head is an enormous heat sink, And don't forget a bandanna. An ordinary bandanna can be used for so many things—scarf, hat, headband, towel, water filter, bandage, sling, patch material, distress signal—that I usually wear one and carry a second.

KEEPING IT ALL DRY

Above all, your outfit has to stay dry. Half-measures won't do here. In case of an upset, your kayak will be filled with water <u>under pressure</u>—not just splash and spray—and if there is any way it can get into the cargo, it will. Garbage bags are for garbage, or for turning two weeks' worth of food into garbage. You've got to have reliable waterproof containers for everything. I can't over-emphasize this point; it is a corner that beginners often, and very unwisely, try to cut.

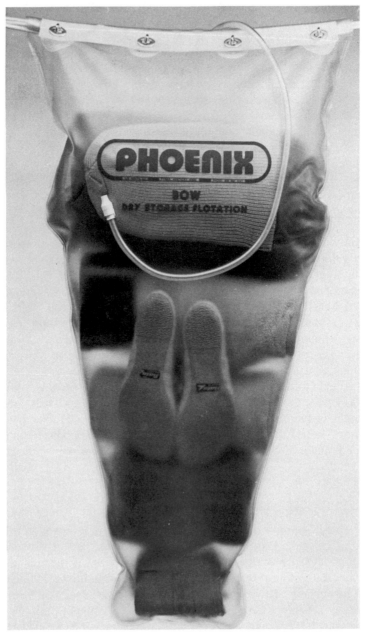

Waterproof sto-float bag keeps gear dry while adding flotation. *Courtesy Phoenix Products*

There really isn't much choice here. The only waterproof bags that will work in most kayaks are the sto-float bags made by various companies such as Phoenix. These are simply your standard kayak flotation bags, fitted with watertight flap-and-snap arrangements that let you stuff your gear inside and then inflate them. You could, no doubt, get a regular soft waterproof bag of appropriate size into the boat by partially deflating the rear float bag, but you have the float bags anyway, so why buy and carry two different containers? And a lot of commercial wetpacks won't fit inside a normal kayak.

There are bags with sliding closures along the side, and these are very reliable and secure, though rough to operate with cold wet fingers and hard to get open during a lunch break or other short stop. I prefer the kind with the roll-over-and-snap closure, even though it has to be fastened more carefully.

Whatever you get, be sure it's good material, 20-gauge PVC at least, and that the seams are solid. This is a very, very bad area in which to try to economize. Remember: in kayak camping, *your outfit is only as good as your provisions for keeping it dry*. A cheap sleeping bag in a good wetpack is a far better bet than a fine bag in an unreliable or leaky wetpack. So buy your sto-float bags first and then see how much you've got left for the other stuff.

If you're careful in selecting your equipment, you shouldn't need a bow sto-float. They're hard to get at anyway, and don't offer much additional space. Most makers will sell the bags individually so you don't have to buy a set.

Now we've got you all outfitted, you're ready to—excuse me? Oh, yeah, almost forgot. Going to have to eat now and then, aren't you?

Let's move into the kitchen and have a look around—

10

Fuel

The Edwardian wit Jerome K. Jerome wrote, "People who have tried it, tell me that a clear conscience makes you very happy and contented; but a full stomach does the business quite as well, and is cheaper, and more easily obtained." Right. If you can manage to eat well and regularly, you can tolerate a good deal of discomfort and frustration. In fact, nothing tastes as good as a hot meal at the end of a rainy, tiring day. If you botch the culinary end of things, however, the best trip can be spoiled by hunger pangs.

Unfortunately for the would-be camp gourmet, the special requirements of kayak camping place some serious limitations on the possible menu. We can't just toss some groceries into the boat; if the trip is going to last longer than a weekend, we've got to do some careful planning.

Foods for kayak camping have to meet the following requirements.

Nutrition. A precise balance of vitamins and the like is unimportant for anything shorter than a couple of weeks; even considerably longer trips can be made without too much worry over dietary requirements if the paddlers are in good shape to begin with. If they aren't, they shouldn't go at all. It takes the body longer than just a few weeks to start developing serious malnutrition.

What is needed is energy. Paddling all day is hard work, and you use up a lot of calories. In cold weather you also use up calories staying warm. So the main thing is to provide yourself with high-energy foods. Fats and carbohydrates are the fuels your "engine" burns; fats are relatively inefficient, slow to digest, and pose problems in packing, while sugar burns too fast for serious work. This leaves mostly starches—rice, noodles, potatoes, breadstuffs, and the like. The main meal in most camp menus is built around a starchy food. Don't worry about gaining weight; paddling hard will take it off again. In fact, a long wilderness paddle trip will require a daily calorie intake that would get you lynched at a Weight Watchers meeting.

Palatability. There is an old army saying: "It doesn't matter what food you give a man if he won't eat it." Nobody expects Cordon Bleu meals on the river—though some camp cooks are very talented—but most of us want the food to at least taste like food. Unfortunately, most of the starchy bases just mentioned are in themselves pretty bland, so we usually include some sort of sauce or flavoring to be added to the base. One good medium for many sauces is butter; you can eat nearly anything if you add enough butter, and the bonus is that butter is a tremendously effective energy food in its own right. Other condiments such as salt, pepper, curry powder, and the like will go far to improve otherwise bland and boring fare.

Many people feel it's not a meal if it doesn't include at least a little meat in some form. The actual protein needs over the average camping trip are so low that the body doesn't actually require meat, but a psychological need is as important as a physical one sometimes, so the meat, when carried, is in small quantities, dried or canned, and serves as a condiment more than a major dietary component.

Packability. We're back to that limited loadspace again. We can not carry bulky or heavy food items in any but the biggest kayaks, and even then only for short trips. The food must be easy to pack without fear of damage—no fresh eggs, for example, or soft fruits—and, because we can't carry ice or refrigeration, it must not be perishable. That leaves us pretty much confined to dried foods of some kind. Cans would be all right except for the weight; why carry all that water, which is what cans mostly contain, when it's all around you? (Sea kayakers, however, have to carry their own water supplies anyway, so they may as well carry some of it in the form of canned food.)

Ease of preparation. Usually when you fix a meal on a cruise you've been paddling for hours and don't want to wait a long time to eat or do a lot of extra work. And, when using a stove, you don't want to have to cook anything a long time and use up a lot of fuel.

Basically, this nearly always comes down to foods you can prepare by adding boiling water or boiling for a reasonably short time, which takes us back to rice and noodles and such. Dried beans are impractical except on a rest day or when working out of a fixed base camp as they take too much soaking.

You can do a certain amount of crude baking over a well-built bed of coals, so if there is a reliable supply of firewood it may be worthwhile to carry breadstuffs as well. Frying, however, is impracticable; a skillet heavy enough for efficient frying is hefty enough to make a good small-boat anchor, and food sticks and burns in those light aluminum frying pans.

Put all these requirements together, and you see why the most common main meal dish on most camping trips works out to be some sort of starchy base prepared by boiling—rice, noodles, pasta—with a flavoring sauce, often based on butter or margarine, and sometimes some bits of canned or dried meat as well. Such a dish satisfies all the above requirements and can be made in numerous ways to avoid monotony and boredom. Some typical examples are macaroni and cheese, curried rice, spaghetti, scalloped potatoes, and the egg-noodle dishes produced by companies such as Kraft or Lipton.

There are special freeze-dried dinners sold in outdoor shops which are very light and compact, and some people even claim to enjoy the flavor. Well, beavers like the taste of trees, too. If you've got the money, these dinners are a big help in the loadspace battle, but ignore the serving information listed on the package—

the usual "serves three" freeze-dried dinner generally serves one, if that one isn't very hungry, and I can polish off two and still want dessert.

Personally I never take anything but regular supermarket dried foods, which are almost as light and compact and far cheaper. In fact, I've figured out that I eat cheaper in the woods and on the rivers than in town! You can make up various dishes around instant rice, or those Kraft macaroni dinners. If you are sure firewood will be abundant and that you will be allowed to build fires there are longer-cooking but otherwise good dishes such as Rice-a-Roni. Most supermarket instant dinners will benefit from careful repacking in plastic bags—the boxes always contain huge amounts of airspace—but be sure to include the directions for preparation if you don't have them memorized because often the amount of water, for example, is quite critical.

Butter, or rather margarine, is best carried in the bottled liquid form available in supermarkets. Margarine is actually nutritionally superior to butter as it contains no cholesterol and doesn't go rancid as quickly.

Get some 35mm film containers—the plastic kind—and package up some condiments such as black pepper, curry powder, garlic salt—whatever you like. Just a little variation in the seasoning can go far to break the monotony on a long trip.

At the risk of blowing my whole go-light dried foods creed, I must admit that in cooler weather, when I'm paddling *Foxfire,* I usually toss a good-sized onion into the boat somewhere. A few slices of fresh onion do wonders to liven up camp fare, and the onion usually lasts about a week; I've never had any problems with spoilage because I finish the onion off too quickly. But never put an onion in a wetpack! A couple of times I've even taken a few whole potatoes. The weight isn't so bad, and they taste great when baked in foil, but I wouldn't do it on a long trip.

As for other meals, there are many instant breakfast cereals such as instant oatmeal; choose what you like. For lunch most people prefer something they don't have to cook—dried fruit, sausage (the kind you don't have to refrigerate—though these usually leave a greasy taste), cheese, various peanut-and-raisin concoctions and so on. I believe I must be a little unusual; I prefer to fix a hot meal at noon, though I usually make something simple and light such as ramen noodles or instant soup. This is mostly to force myself to take a break; I've found that I cover more ground in a day if I rest a bit at noon, and I can't seem to make myself stop very long for anything but a cooked meal.

Snacks of various kinds are very much worth taking. Paddling, as we noted, takes plenty of energy fuels, and it helps if you stoke the furnace now and then. In fact, if you're paddling steadily and trying to cover a lot of miles, it's not a bad idea to make a routine of taking a break each hour, drinking some water, and nibbling a little high-energy food.

If you want desserts, and most people do, you can get instant puddings which require no cooking, though they don't set well in hot weather. You may be surprised at your lack of enthusiasm for sweets; people often find their appetites change on camping trips.

Bread is impractical to carry. The best answer, if you want bread, is to carry some Bisquick and bake it in a wrapping of aluminum foil in a bed of coals. Reflector ovens are too heavy and bulky to carry in small kayaks, though okay in bigger boats. I have had some success with a small aluminum dish—part of one of those Boy Scout mess kits—which I grease and fill with a stiff dough mix, then prop up in front of the coals. Takes practice, but the results can be pretty good; I've even made simple cakes this way.

What about the old trick of wrapping dough around a green stick, I hear you cry—didn't I read the Boy Scout manual? Sure. You try it; don't blame me when the charred mess falls off into your fire.

POTS AND PANS

The easiest and cheapest way to outfit your kayak kitchen is to pick up a couple of inexpensive aluminum saucepans from a grocery or variety store and remove the handles. A solo camper needs nothing bigger than a two-quart pot, but two or more people should have at least one four- or six-quart pot between them. One pot is enough for basic cooking, but a second pot, which should fit inside the other, is very useful for fixing coffee and the like and doesn't add much weight. There is a legend that aluminum pots poison the food, but no scientific proof, and millions of people seem to be surviving the experience.

If you're hard up for money—as you may well be after paying for all that other stuff—you can get excellent pots at a Goodwill or Salvation Army store for next to nothing, and you'll be helping a good cause too. You can even cook in coffee cans, for that matter; I certainly have done it often enough.

The steel Sierra-type cup is very durable but rather heavy. I usually carry one of these clipped to my belt or life jacket strap— it makes a handy emergency bailer—but also take a light plastic cup graduated in various increments for measuring in cooking. A big spoon is the only utensil needed; forks are effete flatlander gadgets, and you've already got a knife.

As I've already remarked, frying pans are rarely worth taking, unless fishing is the major purpose of the trip and you are willing to tote the extra weight in order to experience pan-fried trout or whatever. Actually you can fix most fish quite well by wrapping them in several layers of aluminum foil and baking them in the coals of a good hardwood fire. You can't fry anything very well in an aluminum frying pan, and an iron skillet is too heavy. Nor can you fry anything over the average camp stove without burning it.

Take lots of aluminum foil; it weighs little and has many, many uses.

FIRES

The first thing to remember about fires is that you may not be allowed to build them; this is the rule rather than the exception on some heavy-use streams, especially in dry season, and in other areas fire permits are required. Check the regulations, if any, before going.

The second point is that, even when fires are legally permitted, they may not be ethically or environmentally justifiable. Obviously you don't build a fire if there is any danger of it spreading, but even when safely managed, fires can leave ugly black scars on otherwise beautiful beaches and gravel bars. A few of these can really ruin the looks of a good campsite, especially if some-

body has thrown cans and foil wrappers into the fire to blacken
and lie there for years.

If a stream is subject to frequent flooding, building a fire below
the high-water mark will help. The floods will wash any traces
away or bury them under sand and gravel. But the best policy is
to keep the impact small in the first place. Make the fire no bigger
than necessary and break or chop wood to short lengths that will
burn up completely rather than leaving blackened sticks and stubs.
Elaborate fireplaces are unnecessary. If you build a fire ring (and
this is pointless on an open gravel or sand beach), take it apart
and obliterate the traces by throwing the blackened rocks into
deep water.

In an area that is used heavily, you may wish to use existing
fire rings. People *will* build the things, so at least help hold down
the proliferation. If you're feeling really conscientious, you can
go around demolishing the extra ones and cleaning up the sites.

There's no great trick to building a fire along a river or lake in
dry weather; look along any exposed beach or bar and you'll
surely find more than enough sun-dried billets of driftwood. If
you're on a river that floods often, look around the bases of willow
trees where flood debris washes up. (Watch out for snakes!) Beavers are very thoughtful about leaving neatly cut sticks with all
the bark stripped off, ready for the fire. In fact, it takes a real
pessimist to tote an axe in beaver country.

Actually, you don't need an axe at all. Dry firewood can be
snapped to length over your knee. If it's too big for that, it's
unnecessarily big anyway. In wet weather it can be helpful to be
able to split damp wood open to expose the dry interior, but this
can be done with a big belt knife or a machete. I sometimes like
to carry a machete, fastened down on *Foxfire*'s deck, in cold
weather when I may want an all-night fire.

The main secret of fire building is to get enough smaller sticks—
pencil size—to kindle the larger fuel. Get about twice as much
as you think you need. For starting purposes, scraps of paper are
good. I used to carry a paperback book and tear out the pages
for starters as I finished reading them. A candle stub is also very
good, especially in wet weather.

In really cold, rainy weather, with all the wood wet and a real
need for a fire for warmth and drying clothes, I will confess to

having used stove gasoline as the ultimate persuader. This is contrary to all safety rules but it isn't too bad *if* you measure out just a little bit of fuel—a couple of teaspoons are plenty—and then carefully close the fuel container and put it well away from the fire before striking your match. If the ground is wet enough to justify such an extreme procedure in the first place, the fire shouldn't spread. Then get a safe distance away and toss in a match. Do this only when hypothermia is the alternative.

STOVES

If you can possibly afford it, consider getting a small stove. I know, I know—it's something else to carry and fool with, but in this case I think the benefits justify the added load.

Most authorities cite environmental values in advocating stoves; fires use up wood that should be enriching the soil, leave ugly black spots, spread to the forest, and so on. That's all very true, but river and lake driftwood isn't going to become part of the soil to any useful degree anyway, and usually there is plenty to go around. The other arguments can be dealt with by following correct procedures in building fires and breaking camp. The bottom line is: Stoves are convenient. You can get a stove going and have your meal cooked in the time it takes to gather firewood, let alone get it burning, and you can do this in any weather conditions or in the dark. You can operate a stove even while sick or injured, when it might be impossible to gather firewood. And in cold weather, or on cold water, a stove will let you get a hot drink into a hypothermia victim much faster than is possible with open fires. And, after all, you can still build an occasional small fire if the mood strikes you and you've got the time; the stove can be just a backup.

There are various types of stoves on the market, each with its advocates (except for the Taiwanese copies of the Swedish stoves— I've never heard *any* good words for them). Basically, you can choose a stove which burns some form of unleaded "white gas"— actually, you should only burn the special fuel sold by companies such as Coleman—or you can get a butane model. White gas burns more efficiently, especially in cold weather—for real winter camping it's the only valid choice—while the butane stoves, on the whole, are relatively simpler to operate. Butane is also a bit handier to carry as it comes in pressurized containers.

There are various stoves of each type. The little SVEA is popular, and I like the Optimus 8R, made by the same company and in many ways similar mechanically; it lies flat in its metal box and thus does not tip over easily. The Coleman Peak 1 single-burner stove is becoming very popular and in many ways is considerably more sophisticated and efficient than the Swedish stoves; its ported burner is much quieter and runs far better at low simmer settings, and it has a huge fuel tank. All these stoves burn white gas.

In butane stoves, the Bleuet is the best known, and its canisters, the well-known blue "camping gaz" cylinders, are the most widely obtainable. The tiny Hank Roberts Mini is marvelously compact and light, making it a natural choice for minimum-space kayak campers—it's the only stove I've ever been able to carry handily in my slalom boat—but its cartridges are a bit harder to find. This is a big problem with butane stoves, whereas Coleman fuel can be bought anywhere in the U.S. or Canada.

The Bleuet is the easiest stove of all to operate—just turn it on and light it with a match, like a kitchen range. However, it loses efficiency badly as it nears the last quarter of its contents, and you can not remove the cartridge until it's empty, resulting in irritating delays as you burn off the last dregs of an exhausted canister. The Mini has a liquid-feed cartridge which overcomes this and can be removed at any stage; in fact you have to remove it to pack the stove away. But the Mini is a very cranky little stove, given to sudden flare-ups until it has warmed up. It takes much patience to master and is an exception to the rule that butane stoves are handier than liquid fuel models.

Which one to get? If you just want convenience and will be using the stove mostly as backup in case of rain, the Bleuet is okay. If space and weight are at a premium, get the Mini and experiment with it at home before taking off. For more serious work, on the whole, I think the Coleman is the best product on the market.

A few people like kerosene stoves. I don't really know why; the stuff stinks and the stoves are hard to get going. But the fuel

Small butane stove saves work and eases impact on environment. *Phyllis Sanders*

is easier to obtain than proper white gas stove fuels in many countries; in Latin America, a kerosene stove is the logical choice.

MSR makes a very small, light, efficient unit which burns a wide variety of fuels—Coleman, kerosene, diesel fuel, probably even moonshine. If you're really going off the edge—Alaska, Mexico, or Africa—you ought to consider one of these. For normal U.S. conditions it is overkill, it is extremely expensive, and is very complicated to use.

Alcohol stoves are ridiculous, in my view. The fuel costs like human blood and you don't even get all that much heat for your buck; in fact, alcohol is the least efficient fuel of all for camp stoves. Sterno, which is really jellied alcohol, for all practical purposes simply does not work. Propane stoves used to be popular and worked very well indeed, but the long, heavy fuel bottles were too much trouble to pack around. Too bad.

One more thing: if you get any liquid fuel stove, be sure to get proper fuel containers, such as the aluminum bottles made by Sigg. Keep them tightly closed and well clear of all fires.

DRINK

Nutritionally, you don't need anything but water to drink, but many of us feel a profound non-nutritional need for coffee at certain times. Instant coffee is readily obtainable at any store. If you find a brand that tastes in any way superior to old crankcase drippings, please let me know.

Really, tea is a vastly superior drink for boondocking, and I find myself using it more and more as the years go by. Unlike coffee, it can be made just as well in a pot over a fire or camp stove as anywhere else, unless you are too snobbish to use tea bags, and there are really fine teas available in bags, including Chinese blends. Tea seems to pick me up more than coffee. It warms better in cold weather and yet doesn't overheat you in warm weather. It seems to clear my head and it doesn't upset the stomach the way strong coffee can. There is even a link with kayak traditions, as the Inuit love nothing more than a good cup of tea after a successful hunt or a long paddle. Tea bags are handier to pack than loose coffee crystals or powder, too, and you can carry lump sugar for sweetening. If you don't like caffeine, you can always get those herb teas and depress yourself reading the fatuous profundities and philosophical cliches on the package.

In cold weather hot chocolate is outstanding. I would never go out in the winter without a good supply of those packets of Swiss Miss with the little marshmallows. Funny, I don't care much for chocolate in town and hardly ever drink tea, preferring strong black coffee. As I say, your tastes may change out in the wilds.

As for cooling drinks, most lemonade powders and the like are more trouble than they're worth. Puncture a packet and they make a horrible sticky mess. But in really hot weather I strongly recommend carrying lots of Gatorade powder. Mix it to half the strength recommended and it will get into your system faster; the sugar content tends to slow absorption at full-strength levels. Gatorade helps replace important minerals lost through heavy sweating. It's much more effective than salt tablets.

Alcoholic drinks are unnecessary but a comfort at times. A

small flask of whisky is all right if you don't want more than an occasional shot. I've tried a wineskin with satisfactory results; when empty (sigh) it made a handy secondary water container. Beer is mostly too heavy to carry, though when Lindemann crossed the Atlantic in his Klepper he drank a can of beer per day as part of his basic menu. A real German there! Anyway, do your drinking only *after* the day's paddling is done. There are already too many drunken louts paddling around, shouting and throwing beer cans and ramming other people's boats. Don't join them.

Actually, the biggest beverage problem may be plain water. There are very few places left where you can safely drink the water from under your boat without some form of treatment. Unless you absolutely know the water to be safe, take precautions. There are little tablets available, or you can simply carry a couple of bottles of ordinary drugstore tincture of iodine, adding eight drops to the quart, double that if the water is really dubious. Iodine is what I use, and contrary to popular legend, it doesn't taste bad at all. But there are a few people who should not use this, pregnant women especially, although it's hard to imagine a very pregnant woman getting into a kayak.

It's not just pollution from human settlements that you have to worry about. Some very nasty parasites are spread by the common beaver, for example. So even wild streams, far from civilization, may be suspect. Only deep natural springs are really trustworthy.

Let the tablets or the iodine act for half an hour before drinking the water. Make sure you slosh some of the treated water onto the screw threads of your water bottle, where parasitic cysts and bacteria can lodge. You can wash pots and utensils in untreated water if you give them a thorough rinsing in treated water afterwards or boil them out. Boiling will purify even very bad water and sterilize the container as well. Don't brush your teeth in untreated water. There are portable filtration units, but they all cost a fortune.

On some rivers the water is so muddy it can not be effectively rendered potable. The lower Colorado is a classic example; boil that water long enough and you wind up with a pot of nice, clean hot sand. Other rivers, such as the lower Arkansas, contain too much salt. On such streams you'll have to carry your own drinking water. This is enormously heavy, so plan your trip carefully to put you near a good source of drinking water—a tributary stream or a public campground with water—each afternoon at or just before time to make camp. Of course sea kayakers have to carry fresh water too.

Even on fresh, clear water, you'll want some sort of water container to carry in the cockpit for frequent sipping. A one-quart plastic bottle is about right; anything bigger is unwieldy and anything smaller is inadequate. Metal canteens are needlessly heavy. A big folding plastic jug is very useful for maintaining a supply of treated water in camp, saving you trips back and forth with the pots; empty and rolled up, it takes up little space.

Kayak, paddle, life jacket, sleeping bag, tent, food, stove—will you look at all this stuff we've got here?

Let's *go* somewhere.

11

Getting Ready

You can certainly have a great deal of fun with your kayak—
more than enough to justify the expense and trouble of getting it
and learning to operate it—without ever going on overnight trips
at all. I know quite a few good kayakers who have no interest in
camping out or spending long periods away from home—they like
their comforts—or who simply don't have the time because of
other commitments. And some whitewater enthusiasts don't like
to carry equipment and supplies because it makes the boat heavy
and interferes with doing advanced maneuvers and playing in
rapids.

There's nothing wrong with these people, or with their approach
to kayaking, but personally I can't help feeling they're missing
out on something. Then again, they probably don't understand a
lot of things I do, either. But most people who get into kayaking
eventually get the urge to at least try an extended trip, and a lot

of them buy the kayak primarily for this purpose. In fact, there are those for whom the kayak is essentially a means for getting out into the wild country, rather than an end in itself.

Despite the efforts of developers, polluters, and other horrors of our time, there is still quite a bit of spectacularly beautiful country out there, and much of it lies along rivers. In fact, some of the best and wildest places are almost inaccessible except by water. A strong hiker can go nearly anywhere, but backpacking—and I speak from a great deal of long-range backpacking experience—is still at best a hard, sweaty, exhausting business, and sometimes it's hard to appreciate the scenery when your back, hips, and feet are killing you. A kayak doesn't chew up the ground like wheels or lugsole boots, or leave any "track" at all. And on big lakes and coastal waters, you can sometimes experience the Robinson Crusoe euphoria of island camping, something forever out of reach for those who travel by foot, hoof, or wheel.

WHERE TO GO

Obviously you have to have some idea where you're going and how to get there. Maybe you already had a particular stream, lake, or region in mind when you first got the kayak. Or maybe you've got a chance to join a group going somewhere. I imagine, in fact, that a sizeable number of readers can bypass this section simply because they already know where they want to go. If you're still casting about, though, or trying to choose among several alternatives, there are several factors worth considering.

The most obvious and important criterion is to make sure your own skills are equal to the projected trip. If you have whitewater in mind, refer to the International Scale and find out what rating has been assigned to the stream in question. Be honest with yourself: is this something you can handle? If you still have to read books like this, forget it with the Class IV and V stuff; if you can run Class IV and (gulp) up, you know it and you don't need me to tell you where it is. Even Class III water should be approached with great caution by the inexperienced, and even then only in company with more advanced boaters of a helpful and watchful disposition.

Touring puts higher demands on skill and knowledge than does short-range daytripping. Just because you've managed to wallow down a couple of Class III rapids with an empty boat and several experienced buddies on hand in case of trouble, don't get the idea you're ready for an extended tour on an overall Class III river. More likely you're about equal to Class II with perhaps an occasional easy Class III rapid. And while your first Class IV run is a big moment and just grounds for pride, it doesn't qualify you for a long trip in wild country on solid Class IV water, and if you try it you may not live to regret your foolishness. Similarly, a couple of paddles in sheltered coastal waters is not adequate preparation for a long run on the open sea.

The International Scale does not tell the whole story; many factors can affect the difficulty and risk of a run. Any trip should be rated about one class higher if it passes through remote country where the chance of rescue or walkout is poor, and the same is true of all cold weather runs. Most river ratings are given at normal levels, but spring or summer floods can turn a mild little Class I creek into a raging brown monster. (One of the worst moments I've had on any river came during the big flood of '79 on, of all things, the lower Buffalo in the Ozarks, which normally barely qualifies as a whitewater river at all. Weeks later, there were dead deer in the tops of the trees along the bank.) On the other hand, low water will reduce the force of the current and make a run less dangerous, though finer control will be required to avoid damage to the boat.

Simple numerical ratings lack detail. Get more information if you think you might be operating close to the top of your skills. For example, a guidebook might list a run as "Class III with a little IV"—meaning, probably, an overall III with two or three IV rapids. Now even if you can't handle Class IV rapids yet, you might still be able to make this run, if you can determine definitely that it is possible to (a) spot the tough rapids early enough, (b) get out of the water in time (not always possible, especially in canyons), and (c) carry around them.

Similarly, gradient figures can be misleading. A river might have a listed drop of 40 feet to the mile; this would indicate fairly reasonable Class III or II + water if the gradient is uniform, but on a "pool and drop" river that 40 feet may actually work out to an easy 30-foot drop with one unrunnable 10-foot waterfall. Or a run with a 30-foot gradient may go through a lot of willow jungles, or there may be unstable banks which frequently drop trees across the stream, creating very dangerous strainers. In my own state of Arkansas, the Mulberry River kills people with dreadful regularity, even though it wouldn't rate above II+ by the usual standards. There are willows like tank traps, and things like that don't show up on maps. Don't forget the statistician who drowned in a river with an average depth of two feet.

Open water is a simpler proposition, but you still need information before you get wet. In particular, try to find out the prevailing wind patterns for the area. And if the body of water in question gets a lot of powerboat traffic, find out where the marinas and launch ramps are so you can stay clear of them.

Where do you find out these things? Check the reading list in the back of this book, as well as your library shelves and bookstores. Remember, however, that books go out of date very rapidly, so check more current sources as well. (Thousands of people flock to the Buffalo River, drawn by published descriptions of the "wild, lonely, deserted" Buffalo country, forgetting that those books were written years ago. As a result, the Buffalo is about as lonely and deserted as Times Square.

More reprehensibly, some hacks have cashed in on the current interest in wildwater sports by writing exciting descriptions based largely on imagination, hearsay, or material cribbed from other books. One widely sold whitewater book I have examined contained authoritative-looking descriptions of most of the major whitewater streams of the United States. Based on the streams that I happen to know personally and intimately, the only conclusion I could draw was that the author had never even seen the rivers in question! Another book purported to give detailed information on various rivers; in a chapter on the aforementioned Buffalo, one of the best-known rivers in the country, the author referred to small dams—of which there are none anywhere on the river.

So get plenty of input and cross-check it. If you can, talk to experienced kayakers who have made the run; canoeists or rafters are helpful but may give misleading impressions. Open canoeists tend to overrate rapids by kayakers' standards; rafters are more likely to underrate them. Make sure your informant has no financial or personal stake in impressing you; commercial guides in some places have been known to exaggerate dangers in order to discourage private operators, while of course some people will blow up any run they've made just to make themselves look good.

Information may be had from various public agencies such as state tourism or game-and-fish offices, National Park ranger stations, and the like. Kentucky has an amazingly complete free booklet listing its whitewater streams with ratings and descriptions; some other states have similar publications. The Corps of Engineers has very detailed maps of rivers and lakes under its management.

No matter how detailed your information, never forget: *when in doubt, scout.* All the guidebooks and maps in the world are worth less than one good intelligent look.

PLANNING THE TRIP

Planning is a very individual matter. Some people are insecure and nervous if they don't work everything out down to the last detail before they make a move. Others find that any serious planning ruins the fun for them. Most of us need to try for something midway between these extremes. Some planning is necessary, but keep it flexible. Things like rain, accidents, and sore muscles can throw a tight schedule into chaos. Leave yourself a generous "botch factor" so a minor delay isn't a disaster.

How far can you expect to travel in an average day? This is a meaningless question; there's no way to provide a definite answer without knowing such variables as paddler's strength and endurance, type of kayak and paddle, current speed if any, wind, number and type of rapids, even time of year—to give just a few examples. Only experience will let you predict your daily mileage, so be careful to estimate on the low side at first.

Be conservative anyway, It's far better to make your day's goal sooner than expected, which, after all, just leaves more time to make camp and fish and swim and poke around the countryside, than to have to paddle your brains out and make camp with night falling and all your muscles sore.

A moderately fit paddler ought to be able to average ten or fifteen miles a day on a Class I or II stream. With no headwinds, the same is about right on open water. A strong paddler with a fast boat and good skills can do much more. Twenty miles a day is nothing for a fit flatwater paddler with a fast, long-hulled 'yak and no headwinds.

But don't let yourself get hung up on mileage totals. You can get so compulsive about this that you lose track of the whole reason for being there. Anyway, there aren't many really long stretches of good wild water left in this country any more. If you take it easy, you can make it last longer and get more of a feeling of the country.

As for planning what to take along, we have discussed this in other chapters, and I've included a typical equipment list in the back of this book.

PREPARATION

You don't have to train for a tour the way you would for racing, but getting into shape will pay off in improved control of the boat and reduced fatigue.

Various calisthenics such as pushups and situps are helpful, as is running or cycling to build up the wind. An inexpensive set of weights is a good investment; give special attention to strengthening your wrists, which figure strongly in braces and rolls.

Go over your outfit and patch rips, replace frayed lines, repair holes in wetpacks, and whatever else needs attention. This is obviously important with gear that has seen hard use, but check over new stuff too because sometimes brand new equipment turns out to need work. Make sure you know how to use all your equipment. This may sound like obvious advice, but astonishing numbers of people go camping with new stoves they've never tried to light at home, or new tents they've never tried to erect in the yard.

I can't overemphasize the importance of starting with short overnight trips before trying longer cruises. You can learn a great deal on overnighters, and if you mess things up the consequences are not so severe. A restless night in a damp sleeping bag is unpleasant but seldom catastrophic if you'll be at home the following night. But if you find out that your tent or wetpack leaks halfway through a two-week wilderness cruise, things could get grim.

You won't have to pack several days' worth of supplies, so use the space thus saved to carry some heavy or bulky luxuries—canned food, a bottle of wine, a big air mattress—so you get the feel of how the boat handles when heavily loaded. If several of you go together and can find a place to camp beside a quiet, clear pool or slow stretch, or even a small easy rapid, you can spend some time practicing your braces and rolls under field conditions. This is also a good opportunity to check out people you're thinking about asking along on a longer trip—or who have asked you.

These overnighters are fun in their own right. If you are like most people, you can't get out for long trips any time you feel like it. Chances are you'll have a lot more weekends than week-long vacations. In fact it's a lucky person who gets in two extended trips a year, but almost anyone can get away for a weekender now and then. Some of my best memories are of moments on these short cruises. If you want to become a skilled and confident kayaker, spend as much time as you can out there doing it, and you'll rack up more hours if you don't pass up the weekend runs.

GROUPS

Most kayakers and other river runners do their cruising in groups, and not just for safety. (In fact, some of the least safety-conscious cowboys I've known have paddled exclusively in large groups.) Many people enjoy the company of others; indeed, there are plenty of experienced outdoors types who find the idea of solo wilderness travel distinctly disturbing. One former Sierra Club leader and nationally known wilderness activist once confessed that he had only once in his life spent a night outdoors alone and hadn't liked it at all.

But putting together a group for an extended cruise isn't just a matter of calling up the first people who come to mind, or putting a note on the bulletin board at the outdoor shop. Almost any bunch of reasonably matched paddlers can get through a daytrip or overnighter without great risk of anything worse than a resolve never to go paddling with so-and-so again. But over a period of several days, frictions can build and authentically ugly scenes develop.

How many in the group? Three boats is considered the minimum for whitewater, but this is an imprecise rule. Much depends on the difficulty of the water and the expertise of the paddlers. A group of three novices, or six or nine for that matter, is in far more danger in a rapid of any difficulty than two experienced paddlers. In fact, I feel safer alone than with a bunch of beginners. They don't know enough to be able to help me if I get in trouble, but I usually end up having to risk my boat and body rescuing them. That minimum of three (three boats, not three people, a canoe with two paddlers counts as one) refers strictly to paddlers competent to run any level of whitewater that will be encountered without any special guidance or coaching. Numbers alone are meaningless.

How many is too many? This comes down to personal taste and environmental responsibility. For myself, there's no way I'd travel in one of those huge paddle navies one sometimes sees, like Aleut war parties. Others may not mind or may even enjoy the crowds. But large groups have far too much impact on campsites for most wild rivers and lakeshores. Any group of more than six people should either stick with developed campgrounds or split up at camp time.

Evaluating and matching skill levels is difficult if you've never paddled together, and otherwise honest people may give exaggerated impressions of their skills, perhaps through sincere misevaluation. At best, personal answers to questions like, ''Think you can handle it?'' tend to be imprecise.

Many have proposed, convincingly, a rating system for river runners, keyed to the International Scale of river difficulty. A Class III paddler, for example, could be expected to be able to handle Class III rapids with reasonable hope of success. The following criteria should apply fairly well:

CLASS I: Novice. Able to get in and out of kayak, paddle in a straight line, do basic turns, and perform backstroke and simple draw. Has practiced wet exit wearing spray skirt, life jacket, and helmet, and knows basic rules for floating down rapids and recovering boat. Has paddled kayak on still water.

CLASS II: Experienced beginner. Can do above techniques, plus forward and backward ferries, effective backstroke in moving water, and low brace. Able to leave and enter simple eddies safely and reliably. Knows how to read simple rapids and can recognize obvious hazards and obstacles. Some experience running Class I rapids; confident in moving water.

CLASS III: Intermediate. Good control of kayak in fast water. Can do all techniques listed in this book, including high brace, ferrying in strong current, and brace turns, and can enter and leave eddies in fast water. Has practiced Eskimo roll (effective variety, not extended-paddle roll) and can perform it with fair reliability in calm water, occasionally in moving water. Good water reading skills; can sight-read way through Class II rapids and can scout intelligently. Considerable experience in II + water; can rescue self and at least help rescue others in Class II conditions.

CLASS IV: Advanced. Can perform all techniques, including reliable roll to either side and from position of unreadiness, in very turbulent water. Excellent control of kayak in rough water. Knows how to cope with holes and big waves. Reads water instantly and accurately and responds appropriately. Extensive Class III + experience. Can lead rescue operations. Qualified to teach beginning kayak classes.

CLASS V: Expert. If you're one, you know it. Outstanding control of boat in any water, superb judgment and water reading skills, personality virtually impervious to panic. Expedition material.

Since longer trips impose extra stress due to such things as fatigue, a kayaker should participate in trips slightly below his or her maximum level. That is, a Class IV paddler can definitely handle a Class III+ tour with an occasional Class IV rapid but might find it a little rough to run solid IV water day after day, though rivers on which you can do this are very rare. As mentioned earlier, cold weather or remote country should raise the effective level of danger by about one notch, and this should be taken into account in choosing group members.

Experienced paddlers may occasionally be able to take a strong and intelligent learner on a trip slightly above his or her level, if they are willing to be patient and do a lot of explaining and supervising, and if their less experienced companion is receptive to guidance and instruction. This sort of thing calls for a lot of diplomacy and understanding all around, so not all personalities are suited to it.

Generally it's better to operate in groups of roughly equal skills or with one or more advanced paddlers willing to run below their maximum levels. In sizing up a prospective group member for a tour, then, it would be better to pass up the meaningless and vague questions and instead ask detailed questions based on the points listed above. For a long and possibly dangerous or difficult run, it may even be wise to ask a candidate to demonstrate his or her mastery of the appropriate techniques on some local stream.

All this is speaking purely of kayaking and water reading skills. But other skills are involved here; an expert kayaker may not be much use in camp. Actually, many experienced group leaders say they prefer so-so paddlers with backgrounds in other outdoor activities—backpacking, bicycle camping, and the like—to hotshot boat handlers who have done little camping. In particular, a good camp cook is worth any number of paddle geniuses and should be treated with special consideration. The ideal goal, of course, is for everyone—expert campers and top paddlers—to learn from each other.

Kayakers usually hang out together, but sometimes it is necessary or desirable to mix kayaks with other boats. This is okay as long as everyone understands each other's limitations. People in open canoes often have to carry around rapids which kayakers find rather simple, so the kayakers should be patient and refrain

from making disparaging remarks and should even give the canoeists a hand on their portage. On the other hand, kayakers have
a lousy view downstream and sometimes have to scout where
canoeists can sight-read their way through.

Rafts and other inflatables pose special problems. They should
bring up the rear in any group; if a rafter or inflatable boater gets
in trouble in a rapid, he doesn't need a pointy kayak piling down
the chute towards those inflated air chambers. Rafts make ideal
rescue boats, being stable and easy to board in rough water, so
they are naturals for the sweep position. Yet because they are so
much slower than canoes or kayaks, they tend to get dropped off
the back. This can lead to great resentment, so pay attention and
wait for the blow-up boat when necessary.

It is common to have the raft carry everyone's gear. In fact,
this is the standard procedure in much Western kayak touring,
though to me it is contrary to what kayak tripping is all about.
But make sure the rafters are genuinely agreeable to this arrangement; don't just take it for granted that they're eager to carry
everybody's junk. At the very least the rafters should get some
kind of extra benefits in return—exemption from camp chores
and first crack at meals.

Kayakers often display an irritating and wholly unjustified con-
viction that they represent something of an elite. This leads other
river runners to regard them as a lot of egotistical showoffs. If
you're going to run in a mixed group, cool it.

If mixing boats is tricky, mixing personalities can be downright
explosive. Personality conflicts you'd hardly notice in town become homicidal obsessions after a few days in the boondocks.
There are people I like, good friends, with whom I will not paddle
under any circumstances—I've tried it. And there are others, I
have no doubt, who will not paddle with me.

Consider the hypothetical characters mentioned earlier—the
laid-back type and the compulsive organizer. It doesn't take much
imagination to see a potential conflict when these two travel in
the same group. Or take what we said about different approaches
to whitewater kayaking. The guy who likes to play for hours in

rapids is going to have to work out his differences with his friend who just wants to get through and move on down the river, or they may not stay friends very long.

These conflicts can be avoided if everyone will sit down ahead of time and talk about them in a mature and intelligent way. Problems won't go away because you try to ignore them; they'll simply run submerged and then explode into real trouble after you're too far into the trip to do anything about it.

Of course, some people have abrasive or disagreeable personalities and nobody can stand to paddle very long with them. This is another reason I recommend those daytrips and overnighters together before going on that long cruise; you get to spot the whiners, the bullies, and the showoffs before it's too late.

There also are otherwise normal people who genuinely and sincerely cannot adjust to the outdoor life. For whatever reason, they are permanently and hopelessly wedded to civilized urban life in its most artificial forms, and extended contact with even semi-wild surroundings fills them with horror and disgust. They may occasionally get daring enough to go camping in a big motorized affair with electricity and so on, but that's the limit. The only way they can endure the outdoors requires a lot of gadgetry that could never fit into a kayak. Watch out for these people; don't make the mistake of thinking you're going to convert them by dragging them into the bush. I've seen such people bloated with cramps because they were simply incapable of relieving themselves without a regular toilet to sit on. Others I've seen go into conniptions at the sight of an ordinary harmless snake or an inoffensive buzzard. One English author even motorboated clear down the Mississippi and kept the wilds at bay by coming ashore and staying in motels each night! After awhile this isn't funny. People have been known to go into shock and have to be evacuated.

There are still others, comfortable enough with the outdoors, who are afraid of water; in a rapid, or out on open water far from shore, they may get so hysterical as to endanger themselves and others. They may keep it bottled up until a minor crisis arises, then go completely bananas; trying to rescue such a person after an upset is one of the nastiest experiences around. These types rarely turn up in kayaks on their own but may be a problem in mixed-boat groups, especially in canoes or rafts with family members. All too often, a child or spouse or friend is coerced or wheedled into coming along, only to go to pieces the second day out; then you get bad scenes and guilt trips. Never take a completely inexperienced person on any trip longer than an overnighter, if you value your stomach lining. You cannot predict how any individual is going to react. Of course, you can take into account closely related experience. A person who does a lot of surfing or sailing can be assumed to be comfortable with the water, and a fisherman or hunter presumably is not put off by the rawer facts of nature. You should also not expect to turn such people around or straighten them out; these problems usually relate to more basic psychological insecurities which only a professional can diagnose. Insist that the tenderfoot try at least one or two shorter runs first. It should be possible to do this diplomatically; just drop an invitation to join "some of us on a little run this weekend." You don't have to tell the person he or she is on trial.

Children can pose particular problems. The ones who get scared and cry, or whine endlessly, are relatively rare on the river—most kids love it—but nowadays parental authority is virtually an extinct concept, and children who accept no rules or discipline are a grave threat to themselves and the people who eventually have to rescue them. It is also hard to get some kids to refrain from littering or making a lot of loud noise in wild areas. I'd be leery of family groups unless you know them well.

As for children in kayaks, few of them under 14 or 15 have the strength to really control a full-sized kayak, but those little Kiwis ought to work well. In my experience, the best beginner boat for a child is one of those small, inflatable canoes such as a Sea Eagle 290; they are very stable and easy to handle, and they use a standard kayak paddle and the basic kayak strokes so the youth gets some good training. This is how my daughter started.

One more area we ought to cover here: the male-female hassle. There are absolutely no grounds for assuming that men function better in the outdoors than women. Some men childishly assume they outrank women in the overall scheme of things, and especially on the river. It never occurs to them to let a woman run lead boat, even though she may be a skilled kayaker who has been down this stream more times than any other group member, or to ask an expert female kayaker to teach them how to roll. (On the other hand, some women will resent any advice or instruction from a man, which is just as silly.) Actually, there are some superbly talented women kayakers around—some of them can definitely out-kayak me any day—and skill should be recognized regardless of gender.

SOLO

Any book on river running will tell you it's dangerous to go alone. This book will be no exception. On open water it's one thing; except for sea kayaking, or in cold weather or remote regions, the risk isn't all that great, though having another boat along is certainly good insurance. A competent whitewater kayaker on a simple Class I stream shouldn't be in enough danger to need a rescue team, though it never hurts to be careful.

But on whitewater of any difficulty, running solo definitely raises the danger factor by a major degree. "Never go alone" is usually cited first in any list of whitewater safety rules and with sound reason.

Now it should be added that this essentially sensible rule has been twisted by a few authorities who are guided more by emotion than logic. One book includes the statement, "Running *any* level of whitewater alone is suicidal." Now really. Taking this at face value, it doesn't matter if you're a Class V expert who routinely runs stuff like the upper Owyhee or Lava Falls in the Canyon— you're fishbait if you enter a two-foot-deep Class I riffle alone!

Actually, serious risk of death, let alone anything suicidal, is very rare in Class I and II whitewater, even if the paddler does everything wrong. The worst that usually happens is a wrecked boat and a scary swim, with perhaps a few bruises. Even in Class III rapids, a competent paddler in a good life jacket and helmet is seldom in mortal danger. The one big exception is where there are strainers, but when a person gets trapped by one of these, there is really nothing anyone can do to help anyway. Several expert kayakers of my acquaintance have had the dreadful experience of watching helplessly while a companion drowned in a willow jungle.

An inexperienced paddler running Class IV or higher is indeed asking for trouble of the terminal kind, but then this is true with or without other people around. Beginners simply don't belong in that kind of water–period. But the principle remains: running serious rapids alone is more dangerous than running them with competent companions. And if you go on extended trips in wild country alone, on streams with real rapids, or across big open water in windy weather, there is an undeniable possibility that you will one day be killed under circumstances which might not have proved fatal if someone else had been along.

Even this statement needs qualifying. As I said earlier, this rule assumes that the others are competent to help in an emergency and will do so in a useful way rather than becoming hysterical or engaging in pointless heroics. I knew one otherwise decent kayaker who went into a kind of depressive paralysis in any crisis and became incapable of helping anyone, even himself. Moreover, some people are worse than no one at all—nothing like dumping in a rapid and then having your "rescuer" crack your bones with a paddle.

The nature of the problem may not be obvious. It isn't primarily a question of rescuing someone from drowning; in fact, this seldom comes up. Usually, a ditched kayaker can float safely down a rapid and swim to shore in the calm pool below. If the water is so rough that this is dangerous or difficult, it is unlikely anyone will bring off a kayak-borne rescue either, though a line thrower on the bank may be of value. Towing a swimmer behind a kayak is hard and awkward and usually possible only in calm water; you do it to prevent an exhausted person from drifting into the next drop downstream, or to get a victim ashore fast in cold water.

This is where the other people should come in—after the accident. If the water and/or air is cold, the victim may be too chilled to be able to light a fire, change clothes, or otherwise take care of himself, and if the dry clothes and food just disappeared down the river in a flipped kayak, the danger of terminal hypothermia is very serious. In remote country, having somebody to retrieve your boat and gear can be a lifesaver.

Having agreed that going alone is dangerous—flagrantly so in some situations—I will upset a lot of you by stating that, in my opinion, you still have a right to do it if you want to.

There is today a widely-held attitude that safety is some kind of absolute moral principle, and that society has a right, even a duty, to impose it on everyone. There are even organized movements to prohibit various activities entirely and, failing that, to impose a maximum of regulations calculated to save us from ourselves. Some of this probably originates with self-seeking bureaucrats or politicians, but many people sincerely believe that the ultimate good is the avoidance of injury and the prolongation of life, and that people who feel otherwise are irresponsible neurotics who should be restrained for their own good.

Running rivers alone is dangerous. Running rivers at all is dangerous; water is dangerous. We cannot breathe under it or walk on it. If safety is an absolute goal, stay out of kayaks and all other boats; don't even go to the beach. Of course, I don't know where you'll go instead. Stay in town and you might be murdered, stay indoors and the house could catch fire, go outside and the pollution will get you, and who knows what may prove to cause cancer. Your safest bet, I suppose, is an oblong box, hermetically sealed and padded inside; for extra protection, have it covered with six feet of earth. I mean, where else do you go when you've decided not to live?

Some authorities, including several I respect, have argued that you have a right to risk your own safety but not that of those who may have to rescue you. This sounds convincing at first, and in some situations it is valid enough—in places like the Grand Canyon or along parts of the Salmon, there are public employees who will be required by their jobs to go after you, and they have every right to refuse to let you stick your neck out and make trouble for them. But these same officers almost always require permits before they'll let you on the river at all, and they will not issue them to solo runners, so the question is largely theoretical.

Except for these special situations, I find the above argument unconvincing. What exactly are these people supposed to rescue you from, and how will it endanger them? It's your immediate companions who are likely to take chances getting you out of the river. On a solo run, by the time anybody misses you and comes looking for you, you're either on dry land or you're dead and your rescue has become a pointless effort.

Realistically, the only situation in which outside help is possible is one in which you're stranded somewhere along the river with a wrecked or lost boat, or with some injury or illness, and for some reason can't get out on your own. Unless you're at the bottom of a sheer-walled canyon—a rather rare situation—rescue operations may be expensive and troublesome and the authorities may make you pay the bill later. Still, I can't see why anyone ought to get hurt. Modern helicopters and four-wheel-drive vehicles have pretty much made this sort of thing routine today.

For the record, I go alone a great deal. I go out for the solitude and accept any added danger as a reasonable tradeoff. If I am killed one day, it will be a fair price for the good times I've had. I've had my share of very close shaves, including a couple that nearly finished me, and I haven't changed my mind. Moreover, not so incidentally, I can't think of a single time when having other people around would have made any difference at all.

None of this is meant to persuade anyone to take up solo river running. On the contrary, I advise against it for the average person and definitely discourage it for beginners. The only person who should even consider going alone is one who has enough experience to evaluate the risks and make a deliberate decision in full knowledge of the possibilities. Among other things, this person really ought to have at least one genuinely scary fast water bailout under his belt to have some idea of the power of the river, and a reliable roll becomes far more important for the solo kayaker than for anyone else.

I like the way Moms Mabley put it: "Do what you want—but *know what you do.*"

12

Doing It

Hey ho. Let's go get wet.

TAKING THE SHUTTLE

On a lake or the sea, it's usually possible to lay out a circular tour if that's compatible with your other ambitions. You can just come back to the starting point, and the only real problem is making sure you have a safe place to leave the cars or trucks where thieves and vandals won't get at them. But on a river, you have to figure out some way to hook up your put-in point with your take-out. This is called the shuttle and is the subject of much discussion and river rat lore. In fact, there are people, often relatively mediocre paddlers, who are recognized masters of the shuttle, and any group that can acquire such a member is lucky indeed.

There are several possible approaches to the shuttle problem. One of the most common answers is to travel in two or more vehicles and go by the take-out first, where one of the vehicles is dropped off. Everybody piles into the remaining machines and goes to the starting point; then at the end of the trip the waiting car is used to go collect the others. This is complicated and wasteful of time and gas, but it has the advantage of requiring no outside participants; everyone involved gets to paddle and nobody has to be hired to drive. It usually gets very crowded going to the put-in, though. Generally, this technique is best reserved for relatively short trips; it isn't very much fun if the put-in and take-out are a couple of hundred miles apart.

Another approach, popular with young guys, is to wing it—just leave the cars and go on down river and rely on thumbing a ride back or paying some local to drive you back to the cars. I don't recommend this one, though I have to admit to having done it. I quit after a man was hurt on the river and we wasted hours finding a farmer to drive us back to the put-in to get the trucks—too chancy.

Probably the best way, if you can foot the bill and find the people, is to hire locals to drive the vehicles down to the take-out while you make the run. Up in the mountains where I come from, this has become a welcome source of extra cash for a lot of hardscrabble farmers and struggling crossroads store proprietors. The main drawback, aside from the added expense—which is no worse than the gas you waste with the more complicated shuttles—is that it depends on the availability of reliable shuttle drivers. Along a river that gets a lot of float traffic, there's no trouble getting taken care of, only that is exactly the kind of stream most of us prefer to avoid. If you are lucky enough to find a relatively unspoiled stream with few paddlers around, you may not be able to find shuttle drivers. Still, try asking around at the nearest store and you'll probably locate someone who needs the money.

Of course, if you have a friend or spouse who will do the shuttle for you, or drop you off and then come meet you at a scheduled rendezvous, this is ideal, but not everyone is that fortunate or has such accommodating friends.

One interesting alternative is to use a light motorcycle, or even a bicycle, as the shuttle vehicle on shorter runs. This lets you make the run with only one car or truck; you carry the motorcyle, perhaps on a small trailer, and drop it off at the take-out, where someone can ride it back to get the vehicle after you arrive. The chief problem here lies in finding a place you can leave a two-wheeler with any serious hope of finding it there when you return. Often, a rural gas station proprietor will help.

It is important to work all this out ahead of time, not just "think about it when we get there;" otherwise, you'll waste a whole day. It is also vital to settle questions of sharing gas and other expenses before you go if you want to keep your relationships friendly. Sharing the gas money all around is standard practice, but a driver may want some money for things like wear and tear on tires, especially on rough roads. Even if you think the driver is being a little out of line, ask yourself whether an otherwise good relationship, or having a reliable person to paddle with, isn't worth a few extra bucks now and then.

Get the terms settled before you go, not afterward. This also applies to things like shared food items and equipment. A couple of people can save space by sharing certain things, but you'd better be sure you don't get into situations that go, "I thought *you* had it," or, even worse, "Why didn't you bring your own?"

GETTING WET

Finding a good access point in the first place may not be simple. A road may cross a river on the map, but the bridge may be so high above the water that you can not get the boats and gear down to the bank. Landowners are seldom eager to have strangers driving across the back forty, leaving gates open and scaring the cows; at least, you may be asked to pay for launching privileges. Launch areas at public parks and reservoirs tend to be crowded and noisy. Here we get back to advance information again, as discussed in the previous chapter.

Loading a kayak takes some thinking; you don't just start cramming things in. Because of basic rules of physics, any weight added out near the ends of the boat makes it hard to turn and, once turning, hard to straighten out. The load must be arranged with heavy objects near the cockpit—right behind the paddler—

and lighter things like sleeping bags farther from you. Weight should also be kept low for stability. Finally, weight must be balanced laterally so the kayak doesn't tend to tilt to one side. Once it's all loaded, ease the kayak into the water and see if it rides level, and if not, repack the gear. A slightly unbalanced load, too close to be obvious to the paddler, will, over a long day, fatigue the whole body from that constant unconscious strain of equalizing that imbalance.

With standard sto-float wetpacks, you have to put the bags into the boat and then stuff the gear in—an awkward but unavoidable job. Most of the load will go into the stern bag; the bow bag is too far forward to hold much useful kit, and anything heavy there will be bad for handling. (A slightly stern-heavy boat is far less troublesome than a bow-heavy one; a distinctly bow-heavy kayak is very dangerous in heavy water.) The bow is a good place to stash your repair kit since the resin odors cannot then get into your food; other than that, unless you really have to pack a maximum load, I'd leave the bow bag for flotation only. It's hard to get at, anyway, especially with fixed foot braces.

Remember, the rule is: bulky and light to the rear, dense and heavy at the front, and weight concentrated as much as possible near the bottom and centerline. This would mean you'd probably cram your sleeping bag in first, shoving it all the way to the back, and follow it with light clothing such as insulated vest, parka, or whatever you're carrying. Clothes—the few you carry—would go in next, and then things like food, stove, and various tools. Books are very heavy for their size and go on the bottom, in the middle. Things like socks and your rolled-up air mattress can go along the sides or anywhere there's space.

Tents are hard to fit in; this is one reason kayakers try not to carry them unless they're really needed. Small, backpack-type tents will usually fit in somewhere between the sleeping bag and the clothes, but the poles should be stowed separately. I usually duct tape or rubber band them in a bundle and tie them solidly alongside the seat in the cockpit behind the hip braces.

You really learn a lot about packing when you load a kayak. Watch for ways to save space; for example, fill your cookpots with food packets and other small items and tuck extra matches inside your stove's windscreen.

Sometimes access has to take precedence over other factors. The first-aid kit is a pretty light item, but put it up close to the opening where you can get at it fast. Mostly, though, access and weight requirements coincide: the sleeping bag is about the last thing you'll want to unpack. If it's raining you won't even want it out until you've got the tent or tarp up, so it's fine back there. I suggest putting your clothes in a plastic bag of their own so you can take them out while getting at the tent in a rainstorm, without having to get them wet.

There will be some things you want to be able to get at without opening the main wetpacks, even some things you need to be able to reach while in the boat. Paddle jackets usually have handy pockets, of course, and some paddlers seal maps in clear plastic and tape them to the deck for easy reading; I tuck mine into the top of my life jacket, but then most of the rivers I run are as familiar to me as my own yard, and those more dependent on maps need to be more careful. A waterproof pouch in the cockpit is a handy place for a camera or binoculars if you can secure it in place without the use of any sort of strap or lashing that might be loose enough to trap a foot or interfere with a bailout.

One thing: you can forget the hassle of lashing things down, which rafters and open canoeists have to face. Once you get those wetpacks in place and full, they aren't going anywhere no matter what, short of a completely wrecked boat.

But loose stuff in the boat—that's another story. If you keep fooling around with kayaks and other small craft, sooner or later you will find yourself tossing something into the bottom of the boat without securing it in any way because you can't take the time or figure out where to put it. Or you're just going a little way, and then before you know it, you're bobbing along next to your overturned boat with your binoculars, box of fishing lures, or best pipe at the bottom of the river astonishing the fish. I've lost more good gear that way.

It's really bad to have anything loose in the cockpit anyway because it could interfere with an emergency exit, but at least fasten it all down somehow. This includes your litter bag. You may not mind losing it, but the rest of us mind looking at a week's worth of your garbage along the banks, as if there weren't enough already.

The temptation to load unsecured gear is greater in a big boat like a Klepper and must be resisted. In any frame boat, there are plenty of wooden members to which things can be tied, so there's no real excuse. The greater capacity of these boats makes them far easier to load, incidentally, and you can use standard canoe wetpacks since they don't need flotation bags. Watch out for the abrasive effects of wooden frame members on wetpacks, though. As noted, some sea kayaks have special watertight compartments which presumably eliminate the need for wetpacks, but I can't see myself trusting them that far. I think I'd at least use some plastic bags just in case.

At some point, especially if you're new at this, you will probably realize that all this stuff simply isn't going to go in; you've over-equipped yourself. Be cool and reexamine your outfit; what did you stick in at the last minute that you can really do without? Almost certainly there's something. If you can't get a week's worth of food and supplies, and gear for camping in any but cold weather into a standard kayak—even a high-volume slalom boat—then you're carrying something you can do without because plenty of us have done it.

Those soft plastic 'yaks such as Hollowform have to be fitted with hard foam pillars fore and aft so they don't collapse and trap a paddler in a pileup. Consequently, they require special split flotation bags. Such bags are made in the storage-combination style as well, but it's very hard to do a decent job packing them. None of the half-bags is really big enough to hold a sleeping bag without forcing you to put a lot of heavy gear into the other half, so it's nearly impossible to get the boat properly trimmed, and total loadspace is dreadfully bad—just another reason a lot of us don't like these boats. Still, some people do manage to go on quite long tours with them. Determination and imagination are more important than equipment anyway.

Once your boat is loaded, you'll be horrified at how it handles. Your dancing, agile lovely will feel like a heavy, clumsy, wallowing barge, hard to turn and harder to stop, slow on open water and virtually impossible to back-ferry. Once you get used to it, you'll find things aren't that bad, though you'll never have the monkey agility you had with the empty boat. But the weight, if properly loaded, does add stability; if you kept the heavy stuff low, the 'yak will not capsize as readily. Rolling will take more effort in the initial stages, but once you get her up on her beam ends, the added weight will help you slap her on over. In fact, I've seen an empty kayak right itself, from the weight in the bottom, (though that one was a weird boat in many ways).

Don't try to lift a loaded kayak. Load it in shallow water and when you want to beach it, raise one end slightly and slide it up on the bank. Don't let it drop onto rocks, either, a kayak isn't a wheelbarrow.

So now you've got it all aboard, got the wetpacks sealed and inflated, and clambered in and pushed off—what now? On open water, everybody can move out at will, merely taking care to stay within sight of each other. On a whitewater stream, more formal arrangements may be in order, particularly if not everyone is at the same level of skill development.

Going through a rapid, the lead boat should be operated by an experienced and genuinely skilled paddler—in difficult water, ideally the most expert kayaker in the group, though this may not always be the case. The leader should preferably be a mature person with good judgment, both of water and of the abilities of the others in the group; whatever line he or she takes through a rapid, the others will tend to follow, so the leader has a real responsibility here. Sometimes more than one line is possible through a given rapid, and in such cases the leader must have sense enough to pick the line everybody can handle or else have everyone pull out above the rapid to scout it and discuss the run, always a valid idea. In this area, it may be noted that the operator of a decked C-1 whitewater canoe has a distinct advantage in the lead position, being able to see downstream much better than a kayaker, and being in turn easier to see up ahead. C-1 paddlers also tend to be good river hands because very few people get started in one of these tricky boats, almost all C-1 jocks have a great deal of kayak and/or canoe experience.

Once the lead position has been established, the lead boat should not be passed. If you are still learning, and you get into a group being led by a good experienced kayaker or other river runner, don't charge off on your own; several novices have been killed unnecessarily when they passed the lead boat and got into things they couldn't handle.

Another skilled paddler should bring up the rear. This is called the sweep position. If one of the party members has special knowledge of first aid or medicine, that person should run sweep. This is the boat that will be in the best position to begin rescues, so sweep is a very important post and, all things being equal, should be run by a mature, panic-resistant type. As noted before, in a mixed-boat group, inflatables are good in this position. A raft with several people aboard, rowed by a skilled operator (paddle rafts, in my opinion, are worthless toys), can ease past a swimmer while the passengers reach out and pull the victim aboard. You can even begin artificial-resuscitation procedures, or treat for hypothermia, while on a big raft, saving valuable seconds. But a good-sized inflatable canoe is a pretty good rescue and sweep boat, too. I've used my own big Sea Eagle 380 this way, rigged with ropes around the top to give a swimmer a handhold. The better inflatable canoes can keep up with kayakers far better than any raft and are better at sliding into narrow places.

Just as no one is to pass the lead boat, neither should anyone fall behind the sweep boat. If the sweep paddler sees someone doing so, he or she should stop and find out why before proceeding and, if necessary, wait until he moves on.

Maintain good intervals when going through rapids. There's nothing more infuriating and unnecessary than another boat coming down the chute at you just as you get stuck. In a difficult and narrow rapid, the leader may want to go first, get out, and walk back to a vantage point—perhaps with a throw line—and signal the others through, one by one. Once everyone is through, you can resume order. Everyone should wait until the last boat is through before proceeding, though. On the long stretches, try to stay in sight of each other.

A simple set of signals should be worked out in advance because the roar of a rapid usually drowns out shouted words. These should be made with a paddle, not a hand, and should not be easily confused with operating strokes. Agree on signals for such things as "Pull in and we'll scout it" or "Get out of the water—

danger ahead'' and so on. Some have proposed a universal signal code for paddlers, and several suggested codes have appeared in magazines, but so far none has gained general acceptance.

Less experienced paddlers should be sandwiched in between more advanced members of the group. If they are pretty close to their limit on this run, everyone should keep an eye on them. A certain degree of diplomacy may be necessary; sometimes advanced paddlers should quietly carry around something they privately know they could run because an overeager beginner is sure to insist on trying it in emulation of the veterans.

All these rules apply primarily to groups which include relatively inexperienced paddlers, since I assume that is the largest group of potential readers for a book of this kind. Genuinely experienced and skilled kayakers may feel free to dispense with things like designated lead and sweep boats—though these things never hurt on a really tough run—and just wing it. All the same, make sure two of you don't go for the same chute simultaneously, and if you want to play in the rapid, wait until everyone is through if there's any chance you could get in the way. There's nothing like roaring down a fast chute to find the only passage blocked by some exhibitionist showing off his pop-up technique.

CAMP

If you've made this run before, you may already have your pet campsites. If not, you'd better start looking before the last minute or you might find yourself spending the night in a loathsome spot.

It's fairly easy to list the desirable features of a campsite: a flat space to put up tents or lay out bedding, trees or a hill to break the wind, a source of drinking water if the main stream is muddy or otherwise undrinkable, shade if it's a hot day, plenty of firewood, no bugs or other pests, privacy, and, if possible, a scenic view and/or extra recreational possibilities such as a pool for swimming or a likely fishing spot. To these may be added a practical point—some way of getting in and out of the water. Sometimes an otherwise nice spot has vertical banks or mud flats at the water's edge, making it difficult, unpleasant, or even dangerous to disembark and carry the gear up to the site. And of course you want a clean site with a minimum of litter.

It is less simple to actually find such a spot in real life. Usually we have to compromise in some area or other. How this is arrived at depends on personal priorities. Personally, I will accept some awkwardness of access if I can get a secluded spot that hasn't seen much use, but I have little interest in splashing around in the water. Others may have opposite preferences.

Certain problem spots should be avoided by everyone. If the stream has any tendency at all to rise rapidly, get well up above the high-water line. Many campers have been flooded right out in the middle of the night, with some even drowning in their tents. Dam-controlled rivers are particularly prone to such fluctuations. In rainy weather, a rise is more likely, but remember that it may be raining far up on the headwaters while remaining clear where you are, and a head rise will still get to you. Even when you're pretty sure you're up far enough, try to leave yourself an escape route; avoid camping at the base of cliffs or on sandbar islands.

An examination of the ground will give you an idea. Any gravel bar or sandbar has been formed by flood waters and therefore can be flooded again. This isn't to say you shouldn't camp on gravel bars, which are otherwise ideal campsites—just that you ought to be cautious in rainy weather or flood season.

This brings up the question of ground surfaces. Gravel, as I said, is great because it's clean, drains fast in a shower, harbors no bugs, and you don't lose your gear easily. Sand looks pretty and can be fun, but it gets into everything and everything disappears into it, and in wet weather you'll track the stuff into the tent and all over everything, though it does feel so good under your bare feet. It also harbors sand fleas in some places.

Grassy meadows are beautiful, but I suggest admiring them from afar; they are frequently the homes of hordes of ticks and chiggers, particularly in the South. If you camp on a grassy area, the problem of condensation inside a tent becomes much, much worse. Grass gives off amazing quantities of water vapor during the night and you'll wake up with everything soggy.

Beware of dead trees, which can fall on you in the night. Statistically, falling limbs account for a surprising proportion of the outdoor deaths in a given year. Also, don't camp at the base of unstable cliffs or other rock formations that may dump boulders on you. Generally, you are better off in the open, even if it is windier.

If you want privacy like most of us do, check the surrounding area for tracks and roads; often an apparently secluded spot turns out to be a popular local fishin' hole and may even be the favorite spot of local teenagers. Or this may be the launching point for some commercial guide or outfitter.

All this assumes you will be allowed to camp where you like. In some areas there are Federal or state regulations requiring you to camp in officially designated campsites. In others, landowners will have something to say about where you come ashore.

Stream side landowners represent a major and growing problem nowadays; many of them have begun to resent the incursions from the city, and it's hard to blame them after seeing the behavior of some river runners. If you do find a pleasant, open-minded landowner who lets you camp on his property, be especially careful to clean up the site in the morning, close any gates you open, and otherwise go out of your way to respond with courtesy because such people are becoming hard to find.

Some landowners can be downright vicious. If you are ordered off someone's land, even if you think he's overreacting, shut up and go. Country sheriffs tend to side with landowners, who usually represent important support at election, and you could be arrested for trespassing or worse. There is *no* state in the country where it is legal to shoot trespassers, but a great many people firmly and unshakeably believe the law gives them the right to do this, and you'd better not argue with the open end of a shotgun. Just get off the guy's land and go somewhere else.

Every now and then you run into somebody who tries to order you off land that isn't his. Sometimes the land is in dispute with a neighbor, or the government took it but he's never admitted they had the right, or he just has delusions. We've had some very ugly incidents in the Ozarks; Arkansas law provides that a landowner can't block your passage down the river even when it crosses his property, but a few recalcitrant types decided to write their own law with firearms and barbed wire, and it took major legal action to settle the matter. What you do about this sort of situation is entirely up to you depending on your own judgment, personal taste for armed conflict, weapons if any, and mood of the moment. Ninety-nine paddlers out of a hundred will do better to go quietly away.

These situations are rare. Contrary to an impression that a few soreheads have created, most country people are friendly and helpful. Actually, some of the worst offenders are retired city people who buy land out in the country and bring their urban attitudes with them.

There is one distinctly dangerous situation you just might encounter in some areas these days. Certain people have discovered it is possible to cultivate highly illegal herbs in wild and mountainous regions, and such people have been known to get very jumpy when strangers begin poking around. The stuff doesn't grow well right along streams, so you're unlikely to have this problem on the river, but if you go walking around to explore the area and stumble across a patch, get out of there and stay away or you could get shot. Right now the problem seems to be greatest in Arkansas and Hawaii.

One of the most common and annoying problems for campers in many places is that of livestock. Frankly, I hate cows. They foul up your drinking water, knock down your tent, step on your paddle and break it, trample the ground into a muddy morass, and carry ticks like crazy. They can turn ugly and stomp you every now and then. They have no sense; you can't scare them away without a fifty-fifty chance they'll stampede right over you. This isn't just a problem you encounter on private land. Some landowners think nothing of letting their cattle wander all over National Forest or Park land where they can be fairly sure they won't get caught, and the havoc on the ecology is enormous. If you see cow sign around a campsite, and it looks fresh—you don't have to be Daniel Boone to find it—go away.

I suppose I ought to pause, somewhere along about here, for a few words about environmental responsibility and no-impact camping. Never throw tin cans, butane canisters, and foil wrappers on the ground and just leave them there. Put out all fires before you leave, and on beaches, clean up those ugly black fire rings. Always dig a latrine and cover it up when you're through, paper and all. Don't wash dishes or yourself in clear water and get it all full of soapsuds. Never cut living trees or bushes except to save your life. Foreget about building permanent or semi-permanent structures of rocks or poles; leave the place natural. Pack all your trash out with you, <u>all</u> of it. And so on and so forth.

Did I really have to tell you any of that? Obviously some people don't follow these rules, but I find it hard to believe it's because they don't know any better. People who go off and leave piles of cans and trash on the beach know perfectly well that they aren't supposed to do it. They just flat out don't care—about the land, about other people, about the regulations, about anything or anyone but themselves. What we need, of course, is better enforcement and some stiff penalties, but these problems are beyond the scope of this book, except that I <u>do</u> encourage readers to report these people whenever they see them making a mess. Or, if you're big enough to bring it off, go over and make them clean up before they go. A couple of us once confiscated a canoe and informed its owner that he would get it back when he picked up his trash.

But we're talking about you and frankly I don't believe anyone who reads this book has to be told these things. I think the mere fact that you bought this book indicates that you're the kind of person who wants to know how to do things right, and that means you've already heard about environmental responsibility, in the woods and out, and could probably recite the rules from memory. Besides, what intelligent adult has to be told not to throw stuff on the ground and go off and leave it, anyway? I'm going to assume you've got enough brains and common sensitivity to behave with consideration toward the land and the other people who follow you, and leave it at that.

One other point that should perhaps be raised; people who go back to the earlier days of American camping will remember how it used to be standard to erect all sorts of neat little structures—benches to sit on, elaborate rock fireplaces, and so on—and to dig ditches around the tent to carry off rainwater, and other feats of engineering. Such things have long been discredited, and replaced by the modern no-impact, no-trace ethic, but occasionally an older camper still succumbs. Worse, some youth groups such as Scout troops are still led by people who learned such things in their own youth, and are being taught these absurd and unsightly practices. Gently dissuade any group members who want to build such structures, and if you find any on public land, demolish them and scatter the components.

In some cases you may be required to use officially designated or developed campgrounds. This isn't just bureaucracy at work, necessarily; often there is a real need to reduce human impact on the river, or the land along the banks may be privately owned and closed to campers.

Public campgrounds don't have to be so bad; some of them are pretty tolerable when they aren't too crowded. Sometimes you can use the primitive variety—just a cleared place with a couple of fiberglass outhouses and maybe a pump for drinking water and a dumpster for the trash. No doubt most of us would prefer to find our own completely natural campsites, but I, for one, am willing to live with this sort of minimal human structuring if it will help reduce the wear and tear on the rest of the country— and you don't have to worry about a landowner running you off. Anyway, on most of the more popular float streams these days, you're not likely to find a wholly virginal campsite; most likely you'll discover at least one ugly fire ring and some cans and fish bones, maybe something much worse. I don't see how a spot like that is any more natural or unspoiled than a small simple public campground, with no solid structures beyond a couple of toilets and maybe a picnic table or so, that has been kept scrupulously clean by conscientious rangers.

Of course, it's possible the water you're paddling on isn't entirely natural; chances are there's a dam somewhere upstream, affecting the flow. In such a case it seems a bit precious to quibble about the campsites. You may even be cruising on a man-made lake. Don't be too quick to dismiss the big artificial impoundments, by the way. Some of them have been around long enough to develop their own ecologies and offer very enjoyable cruising. Personally, I'd be happier if nobody had ever dammed a stream anywhere, but now that we have the lakes, I don't see why we should be too good to get some use out of them.

On a few of the big impoundments there are small islands, the tops of hills where the valley was flooded by the dam, and sometimes you can camp on them quite legally. The island-camping experience has to be one of the all-time highs, and it offers something unique in the middle of the continent, far from the sea or the islands of northern lakes.

13

Trouble

I always worry when I write things like this chapter. It seems that when we have to talk about a lot of negative possibilities, somebody may get scared off, and I'd hate to think that anything I wrote had caused anyone to shy away from kayaking. It really isn't a particularly dangerous activity if a reasonable degree of caution and judgment is applied. It is considerably less dangerous than riding a motorcycle, or even riding a bicycle in city traffic, as I can personally attest, having been nearly killed a couple of times by crazy drivers. Your kayak might be a safer vehicle than your car. Nobody ever got trapped in a burning kayak.

So, don't let this chapter turn you off. Just let it make you careful. I know, I know, this is the guy who ranted one chapter back about risks and your right to take them. However, it's one thing to accept a given risk because you've thought it over and decided it's worth it, and quite another to blunder along in careless ignorance. Courage has nothing to do with stupidity.

Most of the rules of safety, whether in a kayak, on a job, or anywhere else, boil down to the same basic principles: pay attention to what you're doing, wear any protective clothing or gear the situation calls for, don't try to operate beyond the limitations of your skill/strength/equipment, and never be in too much of a hurry to take the time to do a thing *right*. This last point is very important and often neglected; many injuries begin with failure to secure, adjust, repair, or go around something or just to stop and look. Haste doesn't just make waste—it makes fractures, too.

Remember this: on any extended trip into remote country, these rules become far more stringent. A very good summation of wilderness safety was attributed to a Rio Grande river guide: "We're going into some wild country. If anybody breaks a leg there's no way we can get him out and it's an awful rough ride on downstream in the bottom of a boat. So *don't break no legs*." Good point. "First aid" is all very well but they should call it "second aid"; the first cure for injuries is to stay alert and use common sense to prevent them. The best medical kit is between your ears.

This book will not attempt to provide comprehensive medical information. A good working knowledge of first aid is a basic part of becoming a qualified kayaker, and every paddle group should have at least one member who has studied the subject. Check the reading list, in which I have made specific recommendations. I would also urge you to take a Red Cross or other class, particularly in resuscitation techniques, which you cannot learn from a book.

All we will do in this chapter is look at some of the most common problems encountered on paddle trips and how to cope with them.

TOO COLD

Hypothermia is one of the nastiest of all hazards encountered in any form of water travel. Whitewater runners, who in the nature of things paddle a lot of chilly water, rank it near the top of the horror list—second only to getting trapped by a strainer. Most hazards will usually leave you battered and gasping, with perhaps a smashed boat, but still alive; hypothermia is one of the few that can very easily kill you.

Don't get the idea that only cold-weather kayakers have to worry about hypothermia. I've been into the first stages myself in mid-August, in the South. The problem lies in the nature of water, which conducts heat several times more efficiently than air. If you've ever slept on a water bed, you know that they can be very uncomfortable if not heated in some way. Your car's engine uses water to carry away heat, and so on. So when a human body is immersed in water, that body will lose heat much more rapidly than it would in air of the same temperature. To give you an idea, 50°F isn't very cold; most people would consider a 50-degree day reasonably comfortable, a bit cool perhaps but not really unpleasant. However, two men died in Texas in 1979 on Toledo Bend Reservoir, killed by hypothermia in water registering 50°F. Both men, when found, were still floating in their life jackets, heads clear of the water. This is merely a random example; similar cases occur every year, all over the country. In fact, the problem may actually be worse in southern latitudes or mild weather. People who know they're facing genuinely frigid waters with ice floes and the like will usually have sense enough to take all possible precautions. Boaters who aren't aware of the danger, feeling comfortable and safe on a sunny lake with air temperatures in the fifties, may not be prepared.

The danger is not confined to the simple effects of chill on the human metabolism; there's a wicked little double-catch built in. The body is programmed to protect the vital internal organs at all costs; this is why it will cut off circulation and let your hands and feet die of frostbite if it has to. But in the water, this means that there is a point at which the victim is still alive and conscious and can still be saved but can no longer perform any useful self-rescue actions, such as grasping a thrown rope or the stern loop of a kayak. The hands are among the first things to go. (If you have read Jack London's terrible and memorable "To Build A Fire," you will never forget that poor guy dropping his last matches into the snow.)

Understand this: *any physical effort drastically accelerates the hypothermic process.* It's a nasty choice; you need to get out of the water fast, yet trying to swim or tread water greatly reduces survival time. Even a good swimmer may be unable to cover 200 yards in 40-degree weather.

The key to the problem lies in a concept called "core temperature"—that is, the temperature of the interior of the body. Like any other heat engine, your body has an optimum operating temperature and various mechanisms for maintaining it. When it gets too hot, it triggers sweat glands which wet and cool the skin. When it gets too cold, it generates heat through its own chemical processes—all very elegant. But once this balance is upset, once the metabolism is unable to produce heat as fast as it is being drained from the body, we have hypothermia. This condition has been called the "killer of the unprepared," and it is hard to fault the description because the primary answer to hypothermia is definitely to be prepared. A good wet suit is one of the best investments any boater can make. Even duck hunters are beginning to discover them. Moreover, because the feet represent a key point of heat loss, and tend to lose circulation in a kayak in cold weather, I strongly recommend foam wet suit boots for anything but the warmest conditions. Your life jacket, if of the foam-block type, will also provide some valuable insulation.

I shouldn't have to tell you to be more conservative and cautious when it's cool weather, or when the water's cold. A good, reliable roll is really worth the work you put in learning it. Once the water gets chilly, there's no better way to cut down on that lethal immersion time.

If you do go into the water, you can do much to reduce the chance of hypothermia if you'll keep your movements to a minimum. In cool water, keep still and let your buddies get you ashore—unless you're quite close to the shore, of course, in which case it may be better to go ahead and get out of the water fast. On most mountain streams, the banks are close enough together that you shouldn't have any real problems getting out of the water in time, but on lakes or the ocean you may be in serious trouble. If you can't roll or do a deep-water remount, it is sometimes possible to crawl up onto your overturned kayak's bottom and cling there while being towed to land. A buddy with a big stable kayak may be able to let you crawl up onto the rear deck, lying flat; I've seen this done in practice but I'm not sure the average kayaker could bring it off without causing a second upset. The main thing is to *get out of the water* if at all possible, even if the air is cold. Anything you can do to this end, such as lying atop a capsized boat or scrambling up onto a rock or piling, will prolong life. A life jacket that floats you high in the water will be more valuable than one which barely keeps your face above the surface.

Reduce heat loss by shielding the areas where blood vessels come close to the skin; keep your legs together and your arms down at your sides except when performing some necessary act such as grasping a safety rope. Assume a fetal position. Here is another reason a good life jacket is worth far more than any swimming expertise, and the various drownproofing techniques sometimes taught are lethal in hypothermic conditions as they rapidly accelerate heat loss.

Frankly, if you dump it out on a big lake or the ocean in cool weather and you're alone, your chances of survival are not high. They're not much better on a river; you can usually scuttle ashore after a fashion, but you'll probably be too chilled to get a fire going or get out of those wet clothes. Everything that has been said so far about the dangers of going alone should be multiplied by a large factor if the water temperature is below 60°F.

Once hypothermia has set in, the process accelerates at appalling speeds. In any really advanced case, survival will depend on the efforts of the victim's companions, and they will have to act fast and know what they're doing. Just getting the victim out of the water isn't good enough. The body can no longer generate enough heat on its own to reverse the effects of hypothermia; outside help is needed. It doesn't help either to wrap the victim in a blanket or coat. Insulation does not generate warmth in itself, merely traps it, and the victim no longer has any worthwhile body heat to trap.

The most useful immediate technique is heat transfer. Remove the victim's wet clothes—cut them off if it's faster—and place him in a sleeping bag, preferably a rectangular or barrel bag if one is available. One or two people should then remove their own outer garments and get into the bag too, contributing their own body warmth until the victim's system can recover. If the party has any bags of the type that zip together—a group which includes a married couple may have such a set—these will work well for this technique.

Some people with overactive imaginations, picturing the use of the heat-transfer method with persons of the opposite sex, have conjured up some fairly ribald implications. One of the first people to discuss this technique in print was an attractive female kayaker from the West Coast; from then on, every group she paddled with seemed to include at least one oaf who felt called upon to announce that he intended to capsize in the next rapid. Well, there's no harm in a cheap laugh now and then, if it helps people remember something important. All the same, hypothermia isn't even remotely funny.

Hot drinks such as cocoa are helpful, unless the victim is unconscious or semi-comatose and might choke. *Do not give alcohol in any form.* By dilating the capillaries, alcohol greatly augments the hypothermic effect and is pure poison to a hypothermia victim. Core temperatures must be raised first. There is a very dangerous condition known as "after-cooling"; at the first relief of getting out of the water, the blood vessels dilate and chilled blood from the arms and legs flow back toward the heart. It will kill you like a bullet through the head. To reduce the danger of this effect, *do not* rub or chafe the extremities, or try to walk the victim, or even permit him or her to move about. Do not stand the victim next to a fire until core temperature is up to normal; the fire's heat may dilate the capillaries. Use the fire instead for drying clothes and making a hot drink. Don't waste valuable time and effort on a fire at all if it will interfere with more urgent matters. Incidentally, a thermos of hot coffee or cocoa is well worth carrying in cool conditions—far better than the traditional brandy bottle.

Cold-water shock and immersion may cause the victim to stop breathing, and it may be necessary to apply mouth-to-mouth resuscitation and external heart massage. But at this stage the metabolism has slowed greatly so give artificial respiration at half the normal rate or hyperventilation could result. When the victim begins to recover, high-energy foods such as soup will help.

Less severe levels of hypothermia may result from simply wearing wet clothes or being exposed to a chilly wind and a lot of spray. This kind of hypothermia acts much more slowly and is rarely directly fatal if the victim or his companions stay alert for its symptoms. The danger is in its very slowness; the onset is so gradual that the victim may feel all right up to the moment of losing consciousness. The earlier stages also may affect judgment and coordination, causing an accident of some other sort. Kayakers in particular need to be aware of this form of hypothermia because we stay wet so much. (In case you hadn't noticed.)

The early symptoms of gradual hypothermia are, curiously enough, rather similar to drunkenness—clumsiness, irrationality, and slurred speech. This slowly degenerates into a depressed stupor and eventually into unconsciousness. If your buddy starts exhibiting these symptoms, don't assume he's been hitting a private supply of spirits—get him ashore fast, get him out of those wet clothes, and provide a hot drink. Do this even if you have to be firm; like the drunk, the victim may insist he feels fine. He'll thank you later.

The he in the last sentence wasn't entirely linguistic convenience. Women are considerably less prone to hypothermia than men, owing to their layer of subcutaneous fat. If you've been looking for an excuse to forget that diet, you'll never have a better one. Fat men are also safer in cold water than the marathon runner type. But nobody is immune. You can do a good deal to reduce the risk of low-level hypothermia by stopping occasionally on cool or wet days and walking around a bit to get circulation going, maybe even brewing up a cup of tea or cocoa or coffee. A drink containing sugar will do more good in this respect; cocoa is especially good for warming you up. Eating frequent snacks will also help; fat-based food such as sausage or cheese will do more over the long run than sugars, as fats burn more slowly, but sugar does well for a fast warmup.

If you will just take proper precautions against hypothermia—wear protective clothing such as wet suit and paddle jacket, take warmup breaks on cool days, don't go alone in cold weather or on cold water—and be alert for strainer-type hazards such as willow thickets and fallen trees, you will eliminate a very great proportion of the danger in kayaking.

OTHER COMMON PROBLEMS

You can also get too hot. There's no cabin roof on a kayak, and the sun can really get to you. In really hot weather, especially in desert country, try to arrange your schedule so you can do your paddling in the morning and rest up in the hot afternoon.

Sunburn is a real danger. The sun reflecting off the water makes it worse, and if you have any tendency at all to sunburn, watch it in that kayak. Use plenty of PABA-base sunburn lotion of the strongest kind and cover all exposed skin. Get a helmet that will accept a snap-on eyeshade, if you can, and wear sunglasses. On open water, wear a hat with a big brim and a chin strap. As Mr. John Dowd observes in *Sea Kayaking,* if the choice for you is between looking like a mummy and looking like a broiled lobster, pick the mummy.

Sunburn is an authentically dangerous physical trauma, not a joke. It should be treated exactly like any other expansive first-degree burn. By all means, treat the victim as an injured person, and try to reduce exposure to any more sun as much as possible. A bad sunburn can cause nausea, fever, and other side problems. Don't kid around with it.

Kayakers do have one advantage of sorts here—the deck covers everything from the waist down. You can always spot the kayakers around camp or on the beach—they're the ones with the great tans above the waist and the white legs.

Blistered hands are a common paddler's complaint. If possible, give the victim at least a day's rest. If not, use plenty of tape and don't break the blister. Anyone prone to blisters should consider thoroughly taping the hands before each day's paddling. The control hand is not as likely to blister as the other hand, which has to accept that constant back-and-forth rotation of the paddle shaft. If this hand is really badly blistered, it may be necessary to take a spare breakdown paddle and set it up unfeathered for the time being.

I always wear lightweight leather gloves (buckskin, which doesn't shrivel when wet) on the river; however, most kayakers say this interferes with their paddle control. You might compromise by cutting the fingers off the gloves and leaving the control hand bare.

The hands aren't all that get blistered and raw; you may find your rear end breaking out also. Kayak seats aren't notably comfortable or soft, so try lots of lotion. Another sensitive area is the small of the back, which sometimes gets rubbed raw by the cockpit coaming, especially in extensive rolling or high bracing. There are now a few spray skirts made with padding in this area; I consider this an excellent idea.

If you keep having really bad problems with skin infections and blisters, this may well be indicative of deeper physical difficulties. Be particularly suspicious if you also experience diarrhea, nausea, difficulty in sleeping, irritability, or headaches. Something is lowering your resistance to infection. It may be tension or the change brought on by the different environment, or you may be going too hard and need to let up. A rest day often works wonders. A loose schedule can be a real lifesaver here.

Muscle strains and sprains are not uncommon among kayakers, particularly on the first couple of days out. Improper rolling and bracing can cause shoulder injuries. Elastic bandages should be carried; hot compresses may help. Anyone with a serious injury of this kind should be evacuated, even if you have to send someone to go get help. Permanent damage can be caused by trying to paddle with a weakened shoulder, elbow, or wrist. There are inflatable splints which are well worth carrying; they take up little room, weigh next to nothing, and are worth anything when needed.

Digestive difficulties are very common among urban people who venture out into the wilds. Some people even find they are physically unable to relieve themselves without a toilet to sit on. The change in diet also throws some people off—dried foods tend to be gassy anyway—as does the water in some places. Don't assume you are immune; it can happen to anybody. Carry some Ex-Lax and some kind of anti-diarrhea medication so you'll be ready for either eventuality. If you can, get your doctor to prescribe the latter, as well as an anti-nausea drug.

NATURAL HAZARDS

The danger from snakes and wild beasties has been wildly exaggerated through various folk legends and old-fashioned attitudes. Snakes in particular suffer from a bad press. They are, in fact, very timid and justly terrified of humans—you'd be too if you were nothing but backbone and could be killed by a single light blow. They are also extremely beautiful, the cleanest of all living creatures, and very valuable destroyers of rats and other pests. Do not ever harm a snake—ever.

Snakebite is a rare event, but even when it occurs the victim should not panic; very, very few snakebite cases are fatal. Carry a snakebite kit such as Cutter's and use it according to the directions. But really, there's not much excuse for being bitten in the first place. If you'll wear boots, watch where you put your hands, and be careful to look where you step when walking in low-topped boat shoes (as when scouting a rapid), you shouldn't get bitten.

Water moccasins can be a problem in swampy areas as well as along streams. I used to assume they wouldn't be found in fast water, but a couple of years ago I was running a fast Class III rapid on Big Piney Creek and looked over to see a half-grown moccasin very professionally running the rapid a few feet away! It was something to see; he was lying in an S-curve across the current, drifting laterally, and varying the shape of the curve to control his run as neatly as an expert rafter. He had his head up to look where he was going, and when he reached a willow in midstream, he let himself drift into it and quickly slithered up onto its trunk. It was as slick a whitewater run as I've ever seen. My point is: don't assume, as I erroneously had, that there are no moccasins on whitewater streams. Their bite is painful but rarely fatal to an adult. They can bite underwater, and a friend of mine is currently laid up because he didn't know that.

Water snakes often drop from overhanging trees into open boats, though these are usually the harmless sort as moccasins don't climb very efficiently. If a snake should land on your kayak's deck, just flip him off with the paddle. Watch where you put your hands when gathering firewood or picking up fossils and other interesting rocks. Not only small snakes, but also scorpions, might be under there.

As for spiders, the black widow and brown recluse are mostly inhabitants of dark places and no problem in the wilds. Watch out, though if you get involved exploring old abandoned houses because widows love such places. The hairy tarantula is a fraud and a coward and should be ignored; the bite can hurt a bit but is nothing to get worked up over. Scorpions are authentically dangerous and you want to watch out for them, especially in the Southwest.

Other animals are to admire, not to fear. Grizzly bears can certainly be dangerous—nice to see one endangered species doing a little endangering back; after all, the bears were there first— but probably only a few readers will be so lucky as to get to kayak in grizzly country. Sea kayakers in Alaska, however, have a problem with the huge bears of the coast—the inlets and river mouths where sea kayakers need to camp are precisely the places the bears gather to fish for salmon. I understand it gets really exciting sometimes. Black bears will usually run away if you holler at them—at least all the ones I've met did, though I'm told others have been less successful in out-bearing them. One real danger is present in heavily used areas where people have been dumping garbage or, even worse, feeding the bears; the bears get used to regarding humans as a source of free grub, and may get sore if they decide you're holding out. In such places it's better to keep your food in a wetpack and hang it from a rope in a tree where they can't reach it. Don't stash it in your kayak; a bear is plenty strong enough to damage your boat trying to get at the stuff inside.

Raccoons are harmless to humans, unless you're idiot enough to try to catch one, but they are certainly brilliant burglars and will get into everything you own if given a chance. Zippers and snaps are useless; they can even turn doorknobs.

Moose I know only by reputation, but I understand they can be tough customers if you crowd them, so I'd paddle clear.

On the whole, firearms are a bad idea on the river. Only in serious bear country is there any real likelihood of needing a weapon for defense, and even then many people spend their whole lives in such places and never carry guns. A large Magnum revolver is the traditional choice for these situations, but few people are really good enough shots to use one effectively. If I were going to take a gun on a long cruise in Alaska or Canada, or the coastal waters of these countries, I would take a 12-gauge shotgun. It could be used with light shot as a survival tool to get small game, if you needed to. Loaded with slugs, a 12-gauge will stop any carnivore on earth if you've got the guts to wait till it gets in close. The barrel could be cut off to the legal minimum for easier stowage. A simple single-shot gun would have fewer moving parts to get rusty or full of sand and would weigh and cost less; if you get up against more than one bear or need more than one shot, you're probably dead anyway.

I carried a pistol a few times when we were having some trouble along the Mulberry. A landowner had started threatening paddlers with his rifle; perhaps it worked, since he left me alone. But the gun was nothing but trouble. It got full of sand and water and had to be cleaned and oiled every night, and it got in the way. In many places it also would have been illegal. Except just possibly for the bear problem mentioned above, arming yourself against the Ravening Beasts is silly and causes more problems than it solves.

Domestic animals are much more dangerous than wild ones; I've never been attacked by any wild animal bigger than a copperhead, but I've been charged by bulls and jumped by dogs more times than I could add up. Stay clear of grazing cattle, and if you have to cross a pasture, keep a climbable fence close at hand.

The worst wild animals are the little ones. Ticks are not just a nuisance, they carry some nasty diseases. For some reason, a tick bite at the base of the skull can cause paralysis and coma until the tick is found and removed. Chiggers are less dangerous but very unpleasant. Camp on open gravel or sand and use a good insect repellent if you go wading the brush. Powdered sulfur dusted into your clothes will help keep the chiggers off. After you get back to the river, a quick dip will help get rid of any unwelcome passengers.

Poison ivy might be considered wildlife, and some people get very sick from it. I'm immune, as it happens; I don't know why. It grows all over the place in the Ozarks and many other areas, and it especially likes to grow near water, so watch out for it. Washing with strong soap seems to help remove the oils.

On the whole, the average urbanite has a very distorted view of wild country as being full of dangerous creatures and pervaded by a hostile presence that wants to eat soft-skinned white people for breakfast. On the other hand, some people go to the other extreme. Quite a few sentimental or idealistic types nowadays have convinced themselves that the wilderness loves them and that all they have to do is go out there with a pure and loving spirit and nothing can harm them. They try to feed wild animals and dismiss things like bug spray and boots as paranoia and blithely munch wild plants, berries, and mushrooms with only a vague idea what they're eating.

Both attitudes are foolish if not pathetic. The fact is that the wild world doesn't give a damn one way or another. If you cross its borders, expect to play by its rules; it is neither malevolent nor friendly, merely impartial. Appreciate it; this may be the purest justice you will ever get in this life.

14

Care and Feeding of Kayaks

Modern kayaks are easy to maintain compared to the Inuit hunter's model, which had to be oiled regularly to keep its seams from rotting or leaking and given a new skin every couple of years. Fiberglass boats, in particular, require little attention. If you're the yacht club type who takes pleasure in fussing over a boat, get one of those all-wood jobs instead.

But some people get the idea that absolutely no care is required and that they can treat a fiberglass 'yak any old way with no chance of damage. This simply isn't true, and many fine kayaks have been ruined by owner negligence or ignorance.

The main thing is to treat the boat with reasonable care. You don't have to baby it, but you don't want to subject it to pointless stresses, either. It might seem quick and handy for two of you to carry a loaded kayak by the grabloops up to the campsite so you don't have to make so many trips, but if there is much of a load inside you are subjecting the hull to a lot of strain for which it was never designed. Unload the boat at the water's edge and carry it only when empty. Similarly, if you have to empty out a swamped kayak, lift one end at a time and rock it to get the water out. Don't try to drag a flooded boat ashore, or stand in the shallows and lift the whole end high out of the water with a jerk, or lift it in any way in the rightside-up position—half a ton of water in there, remember?

A fiberglass kayak can take a good deal of rough treatment, but it can still be damaged, especially out of the water. Unloading it from the car, lay it down, don't toss or drop it; a sharp rock could chip the hull. The cockpit coaming lip is especially prone to chipping. Don't let kids jump in it and climb all over it while it's out of the water, either. You may have to get pretty tough with them about this; kayaks fascinate kids.

Early fiberglass boats tended to get brittle if left in the sun too long. Modern resins contain an agent to retard this effect, but it's still better to store the boat under a roof or cover it with a tarp if you're going to be leaving it there for an extended time. Dry out the inside before storing it or it will develop horrible odors. If you have to store it outside—and I don't recommend this because of theft—store it upside down so it doesn't get full of rain. I'm not kidding; I've seen this, more than once. Once I actually saw a kayak with green algae growing inside. Some people don't deserve to own kayaks.

Improper cartopping is a common cause of kayak damage. If you use a rack of the horizontal-bar type, do not load your kayak rightside up. It is designed to sit in this position only in the water, supported evenly over the whole bottom. Lay it across a couple of narrow bars and subject it to the stress of a drive on the highway, and you place a severe strain on the hull and on the deck-hull seam. You can literally ruin your kayak if you do this enough.

If you have to use a straight-bar rack—and it's really a poor choice—at least turn your 'yak upside down. This imposes far less strain on the seam because the deck is more flexible and absorbs shock better. You may well put a dished or warped spot across your deck doing this, but at least you won't harm the boat's performance, though it will look hideous. This procedure is strictly for short-haul use on good roads.

The racks with contoured cradles, like the Yakima, are far better as they distribute the load over a greater area and also hold the boat steadier. If you have an inverted-T rack, however, you're all right; just load the 'yak on its side and lash it to the vertical bar. The oval is basically stronger across the long way—try cracking two eggs, one on the side and one on the end, and see which cracks more easily. Loading this way also lets a group get more kayaks onto a rack.

Kayaks love to take wing at freeway speeds, so you'll have to lash your boat down solidly. You don't want to do this in such a way that you damage the hull. Lash it firmly to the rack and don't spare the ropes. Those flat black rubber shock straps, with the hooks at the ends, are perfect for this. Use them in pairs, crosswise, over the hull at each rack bar. The boat must not be able to pound, vibrate, or slide against the rack of another boat.

It is usual to have lines from bow and stern to the car's bumpers. This is a good practice, as long as you bear in mind that the lashings up at the rack are what hold the kayak down; the bow and stern lines are just insurance. Haul down too enthusiastically on these lines and you impose a tremendous bending stress on the whole hull; you may even crack it. For best results, run the lines in an inverted "V" shape from the ends of the bumpers and use a rubber shock cord from the bow or stern grabloop to keep things taut. On a long drive, check everything at rest stops, just in case.

Wood-frame or all-wood boats require a somewhat different approach. The shape makes it almost impossible to carry most of them any way but rightside up. However, this doesn't seem to do any harm. But the frames should not be subjected to a lot of bending stresses, and the fabric skin should not be chafed by ropes and lines. It's worth the trouble to build a contoured rack for a boat of this type to give it better support, and when you lash it down, put strips of old towel or carpet material over the skin where the ropes and straps will bear the weight. These boats aren't fragile by any means, but they deserve a little extra respect and care, if only because so much careful work goes into them.

Finally, beware of rot; don't store them in damp places or put them away wet.

REPAIRS

Repairing a hole or crack in a fiberglass boat is easier than you might think, though pretty messy. You will need some fiberglass cloth, about 10-ounce weight, and some resin, with the appropriate catalyst. You will also need a coarse woodworking rasp, a cheap paintbrush, something to mix the stuff in—a clean coffee can is fine—some very coarse sandpaper, a pair of throwaway plastic or rubber gloves, and some waxed paper, the kitchen kind.

The first job is to clean up the area around the break, including getting the gel coat off. This is absolutely necessary—failure to do this job right is the most common cause of patch failure—but it's a messy, tiring operation. If you're doing the job at home, use an electric drill with an extra-coarse sanding disc. Work outdoors, with lots of fresh air, and wear a respirator. If you have to work on the boat in the field, use the rasp and sandpaper. Either way, remove the gel coat if your boat has one and roughen up the fiberglass around the break—about an inch all around if it's just a small dent, two inches in all directions if it's a major break. Clean away all the dust from the area to be patched and wipe it clean with a dry rag.

Now you have to cut the patches from the fiberglass cloth. Cut at least two, preferably three, pieces of cloth big enough to cover the area you have just sanded—that is, one to two inches bigger than the damaged area in all directions. Lay these out on a clean surface such as a board or rock.

The resin and catalyst are now mixed according to the proportions given by the manufacturer. Be careful about this; if you mix in too much catalyst, the resin will set up so fast you may not have time to finish the job, but if you don't use enough it will take ages to cure. In the field, if in doubt, go in the direction of too much; go the other way in the shop. Once the reaction begins there is no way to alter its speed, so don't mix anything until you're all set and have your patches and tools laid out to hand. On the outside, if you mixed things right, you've got about twenty minutes.

Take your paintbrush and spread some resin on the damaged area, working it into the break and all over the area you have sanded. Now lay the patches in place. Some people put them all on at once and then apply resin, but I find it easier to lay them on one at a time, using the brush to saturate each layer with catalyzed resin.

You must now smooth everything down. You can simply use the paintbrush handle for this, or a rubber roller if you have one. You must squeeze out all air bubbles—these are a source of serious weakness—and excess resin. Too much resin makes a heavy, brittle patch and may float the cloth up off the hull or get in between layers. Use a squeegee action on the paintbrush handle to get any excess resin out and press the layers firmly together and wipe off any runs and drips with a rag or paper towel. Whitish, fuzzy-looking spots of glass mean the cloth hasn't been sufficiently saturated with resin.

Once the resin starts to gel, you have to stop fooling with it. It should be easy enough to get the job done before the resin starts to cook up, unless you over-catalyzed.

You can get a considerably smoother-looking patch if you take a piece of waxed paper and spread it over the patched area, pressing it smoothly down all over, without wrinkles. Get this done before the resin gels. The paper will peel off easily once the resin has set, giving you a slick surface and also preventing dust and dirt from getting into the wet resin.

Treat wet resin like wet paint or glue. Let it dry in the warm sun, if possible, and let it cure and harden overnight. The warmer it is, the faster the resin will harden; in the summertime, it might be better to wait until after dark if you've got a lighted work area because the heat of the sun can accelerate the gel time and you might find yourself without enough time to do a proper job. With enough experience you can sometimes allow for temperature variations by altering the amount of catalyst, but this is tricky and not recommended for most situations.

Once you get the patch on, though, don't worry about its strength. If you did a good job and used at least three layers of cloth (or even two on a small ding), the patch should be as strong as the rest of the hull.

If the boat has been crunched so badly that there is an actual hole of some size, you'll have to make a kind of putty to fill it or the resin will run through. You can do this by cutting up a scrap of glass cloth into tiny little shreds of thread and mixing these with some resin, or you can use Cab-O-Sil or a similar filler product.

Cleaning up is almost as much work as doing the job itself. Acetone will get resin off your hands if it hasn't hardened yet. Nothing will get it out of your clothes. The brush, gloves, and mixing container are to be considered expended. If you're doing the job in the field, surely I don't have to tell you to pack all this stuff out.

After the patch is hard, take the rasp and sandpaper and go over it to eliminate any hard spikes sticking up; these form where a loose glass thread is saturated with resin. Don't try to paint over a patch to make it match the hull color; it will never look right. Painting a fiberglass kayak is a waste of time and money; the paint job always looks lousy after one season.

You can assemble a repair kit, adequate for field repairs, by putting some resin in a polyethylene bottle from the grocery store, cutting a good-sized piece of glass cloth, and packing them in some kind of absolutely airtight container along with the little tube of catalyst, some sandpaper, one or two pairs of throwaway plastic gloves, a couple of rags, a cheap paintbrush or two, and a couple of waxed paper cups for mixing. Double-bag the resin and the catalyst (separately!) and keep the whole outfit in a sealed heavy-duty plastic bag, well away from the rest of your outfit. This is one of the few valid uses for a bow wetpack; the weight isn't enough to harm performance much, and you've got these smelly, poisonous substances well away from the food. For some reason, some of the chemicals can go right through several layers of plastic bags; if you store food near your fiberglass repair kit, even though both the food and the kit are thoroughly wrapped and sealed, the food may pick up some horrible smells and flavors. Oily or greasy foods are particularly vulnerable.

Get a resin intended for boat use; automotive resins sold in hardware stores are too brittle. How much to carry? It depends on your plans. If you're going down a violent, rocky river where your boat may be badly damaged, you need quite a bit, but if you're just cruising around in easy waters you hardly need anything at all. All this stuff is pretty much whitewater material; deepwater paddlers should have no occasion to make field repairs, unless there is some chance of having to go through rock-studded surf. Many casual paddlers merely take along a couple of pieces of glass cloth and a two-tube set of hardware-store epoxy; this will make an adequate field patch for minor cracks but not for serious repairs.

Above all, take duct tape. You can do a lot of repair work with duct tape alone; plenty of kayakers simply slap a couple of pieces of this marvelous stuff over anything but a really awful hole and do the permanent patching when they get home. People finish runs with 'yaks literally held together with duct tape. It can be used for many other purposes—holding a spare paddle to the deck, patching a hole in the tent, repairing an air mattress—the list is endless. Get a good kind, not that cheap stuff sold in discount stores. You can tie a roll of duct tape to your seat with a bit of cord and shove it behind you out of the way. Don't leave home without it.

Frame boats are easier to repair than fiberglass, the usual type of damage is a rip in the skin. For PVC or Hypalon skins, use the patching materials supplied by the maker and follow the instructions. For home-built, canvas-skinned boats, carry a few pieces of canvas and some liquid rubber, with a curved upholstery needle and a roll of carpet thread. A "baseball" stitch will help hold a long rip together. If you can get at the hole from the inside, put a patch on both sides. And slap some duct tape over it when you're done.

To repair a cracked or broken frame member, carry a few bits of scrap wood of about the same size as the long frame stringers, a hardware store epoxy set, and some brass screws. You can then make a splice by screwing and gluing a short piece to the cracked stringer to bridge the break and pull the member into line. A wrapping of copper wire or nylon line will help.

The skin will last longer if you apply protective strips to the bottom, where the stringers press against the skin, to guard against chafing on rough beaches or in shallows. Klepper and Folbot sell appropriate kits for their boats; home builders can simply use duct tape. Incidentally, duct tape is even more useful with frame or wood boats, so carry a big roll.

15

Gravy

Besides the usual kayaking activities—camping, wilderness travel, or simply playing around—there are various pursuits that fit in well as adjuncts to a kayak trip; indeed, one of these may become so important to you that it becomes the end and the kayak the means.

Here are some of the most popular side activities among kayakers, with a few rather basic tips that might get you started.

PHOTOGRAPHY

A perceptive critic whose name escapes me once observed that photography is the one great modern American folk art. Relatively few people have any background in painting or music, but virtually everyone owns or has owned some sort of camera and has at some time tried to take a picture that would look good.

Certainly, the overwhelming majority of kayakers seem to want photos from their trips, if only because kayak cruises usually pass through such beautiful scenery. And kayaks themselves photograph well, with their bright colors and clean shapes.

The actual mechanics of photography on the water are not particularly different from land technique, except that it is almost impossible to hold a very long lens sufficiently steady in a kayak. The real problem for 'yak-borne photographers is the mundane matter of keeping the camera dry. Obviously it won't do to sling it around your neck, and if you stick it inside a wetpack it will be inaccessible except around camp. This, of course, may be fine with you, but most people like to take at least a few shots from on the water.

There are various special waterproof camera pouches on the market, some more effective than others. The popular "Sports Pouch" sold by various companies isn't too bad for occasional light duty use, but I have had bad luck with them over any real period of heavy field work. I've owned two Sima Sports Pouches and both developed leaks; one caused the death of a treasured zoom lens. The problem lies in the thin material next to the pouch's mouth, which eventually rips. I would not put a camera I cared about in one of these, though it works well for binoculars, pistols, and the like. Aquaterra and Phoenix camera bags are much better. Get a packet of silica gel (most camera stores or gun shops have this) to keep inside the pouch because condensation from moist air is often more of a problem than leakage, and it will get inside a lens and ruin it.

G.I. machine gun ammunition cans are wonderfully watertight, but I for one would never stick something that heavy and huge into my 'yak. They might be okay for a big Klepper or Folbot double, though.

One good way to reduce the worry is to take a semi-expendable camera. You can often find old, obsolete 35mm cameras for very little at pawnshops or camera shops (which may take them in trade) and then you don't have to risk your new expensive camera around all that water. Some of these old cameras are capable of astonishing results. I used to have a 1932 Argus C3 that cost me twenty bucks; before I lost it—dumping a kayak on a fast run, what else?—I took a lot of pictures with it.

Camera shops occasionally get more modern automatic cameras which for some reason refuse to automate, and sometimes they will sell them very cheap (having got them back on warranty) rather than go to the trouble and expense of repairing complex electronic systems. Some of these cameras will still work perfectly well with manual controls. I have a little Olympus which I got in this way for fifty dollars, and I carry it all sorts of places. With one of these or an old camera, you will need an inexpensive light meter or learn to guess. You may find that taking your own readings and setting your own exposures increases the fun of photography rather than detracting from it. I did.

Small, inexpensive pocket cameras are okay if you just want a few snapshots for the album. I have seen one of these in a rubber-covered waterproof design which ought to be very handy for a kayaker. If you're rich, try a Nikonos—a fully waterproof, professional-grade camera designed for divers. It can go around your neck, even in heavy rapids.

Get a relatively fast color film as light is often poor down in canyons and river valleys. Keep exposed film cool, which may not be all that easy; it gets astonishingly hot inside a wetpack on a sunny summer day. If the weather is hot, you may prefer to get Kodachrome, which doesn't go off from the heat nearly as easily as the faster films such as Ektachrome, though it is so slow that exposures may be difficult. Ektachrome, once exposed, will go black if it gets very hot. Print-type films are considerably more stable.

A wide-angle lens is worth having as it gives a much broader scope to the picture and really gives the viewer the feeling of wide open spaces. However, it won't be much good for stalking wildlife or doing close-ups of flowers. A clear UV filter will help keep stray droplets off the lens. Be sure to take lots of lens tissue and a soft cleaning brush.

ART

Instead of photography, or as a separate hobby, you might consider an older form of pictoral representation. Don't be too quick to say, "Oh, I can't draw," or assume you have no talent. You might surprise yourself if you'll study a few basic books—

Watson-Guptill have a line of inexpensive manuals that will explain the secrets in simple terms—and learn to look at things, actually <u>look</u> at them. Most of us don't really see things the way they look; we see them as we expect them to look or according to what we already know about them. What color is this page? Oh? Sit under a leafy green tree on a green lawn; what color is it now? See what I mean?

You ought to try it—at least a few times. Even if you never produce any acceptable pictures, you will discover that you have learned to see things more clearly, and this will greatly add to your enjoyment on trips. It will also improve your water reading ability; try drawing pictures of rapids and see if this doesn't force you to look at them more clearly.

And who knows, you may surprise yourself. I was in my late thirties before I ever even tried to paint or draw anything. One day my daughter Eileen picked up a simple oil painting set at a yard sale, got discouraged with her efforts, and gave it to me, and just for the fun of it I tried doing a few simple landscapes. Now, I wouldn't call myself an artist by any means, but I can at least occasionally turn out a painting that looks the way I want it to look and hang it on the wall without embarrassment. It might work for you too.

Whether you are just dabbling or already know how to draw and paint, you will find that water-based media are far easier to handle than oils in the field. Oils are too slow to dry, require delicate handling of the finished work, and you have to carry thinner too. Water colors are perfect if you're any good with them (I'm not), and there are tiny water color sets designed for sketching, which fit into a shirt pocket. And water is, of course, abundant.

Personally, I find acrylics work out best; you can use them thick, like oils, or thin them and use them as watercolors, and either way the picture is very tough and durable when finished. You can make up a small acrylic set to carry on your trips, protecting the soft brushes with lengths of plastic tubing.

NATURE STUDY

A kayak is a wonderful boat for watching birds and shore mammals as it lies so low in the water and makes so little noise.

However, the flash of a double paddle will spook wildlife at a considerable distance. If you are really into birds and the like, get yourself a small, short single-bladed paddle—the length of your arm or less—and carry it strapped to the deck. It will not work for real propulsion but it will get you much closer to a wary bird or animal than the standard paddle. If you use a breakdown paddle you may simply take it apart and use half.

The birds along a river or lake add a great deal to the pleasure of being there; even if you know little about them, they are entertaining to watch and nice company if you're alone. Once I spent a week in December sharing an island with, among other neighbors, a pair of loons, a family of wood ducks, and a bald eagle. On another trip, an osprey followed me for several miles, having noticed that fish often darted into the shallows when my paddle splash alarmed them.

I strongly recommend carrying at least one good bird book— Peterson's new one for choice—and maybe guides for flowers and trees as well. Another enjoyable adjunct to a paddle trip, particularly on open water, is sky watching. I got interested in the stars when a friend let me look through a telescope; I found that knowing the major constellations transformed the night sky from a cold, awesome, rather frightening spectacle into a panorama of old friends.

A good pair of binoculars is a valuable tool in many situations, and not just for watching birds and beavers and the occasional skinnydipper; it will be a great help in crossing large expanses of open water. I wouldn't get anything very fancy, though; kayakers' binoculars lead a very rough life.

FISHING

Fishing in order to catch fish to vary the evening menu, I know. Fishing as an elaborate ritual, I cannot discuss.

If you just want to be able to angle a little for the pan, though, or as something to pass the time on a rest day, the best all-around setup is a light open-face or closed-face spinning rig, with a small selection of lures appropriate to where you're going. River smallmouths, the fish I know best, go for little spinners and white-tailed jigs. Catfish and largemouths like rubber worms and, even better, real ones. Once I got a needle-nose gar on a rubber worm. I cut that line fast; a gar is nothing you want to share a kayak with.

Some kayakers have managed to rig up various straps and clips to hold their rods on deck, but I usually just take a collapsible rod, which will go into the cockpit handily. Those ultra-light pack rods that take apart and stow in a fitted case look very good for kayaking, too.

All of this assumes you will be bank fishing. As much as I hate to admit any fault in my beloved craft, a kayak makes a rather poor fishing platform. You just don't have much room in that cockpit to move around or cast properly. Kleppers and Folbots work out pretty well for fishing—I've seen ocean fishing done successfully from a Folbot, and it looked like great fun—but smaller kayaks really aren't the world's greatest fishing boats. And even if you do catch something, it's a bit awkward getting it in and extracting the hook and so on, in the confines of a kayak cockpit. Still, you can do it if you really want to.

Looks as if we've come to the end of the cruise, doesn't it? Except for the following appendices, I seem to have said all I had to say on the subject of kayak touring.

I hope you go. And I hope the winds are all from astern, the landowners all friendly, and the rocks all made of foam rubber.

Maybe I'll see you one of these days.

Appendix **A**

Sample Equipment Checklist

The following represents a typical outfit *for me,* on a solo cruise in moderate weather for up to a week. It is not necessarily what I advocate for everyone, and, since most people go in groups, some items such as stove and first aid kit may be shared to reduce the individual boat loads. Much will depend on the type of water and the type of boat. A large flatwater kayak will hold more gear and anyway, for serious whitewater, it is important to hold down weight to keep the boat maneuverable.

Sleeping bag, mummy type, synthetic fill
Lightweight, half-length air mattress
Lightweight, one-man tent or, in cool weather, light tarp
Stove with fuel supply as appropriate (usually Hank Roberts Mini
    in slalom kayak, Optimus 8R in larger boat)

Two aluminum pots, 2 quart and 1 quart
Cup
Large spoon
Plastic 1-quart water bottle
Small pocket flashlight (with batteries if on extended trip)
Folding candle lantern, with candles as appropriate
Butane lighters (minimum 2—1 kept for emergencies)
First-aid kit
Knife
50-foot hank nylon parachute cord
Personal toilet items such as toothbrush, comb, etc.
Small pair pliers
Iodine for water purification
Small sewing kit
Toilet paper
Sunburn lotion, insect repellent, as indicated by season
Personal recreation items such as camera, books, small fishing
    outfit, sketching materials, as may be desired and practicable
    for given trip
2 pairs wool socks
1 pair trousers, type and material depending on season (may sub-
    stitute shorts in extremely hot weather)
1 sweatshirt or thick cotton shirt
1 wool shirt or sweater
Cap or hat
Bandanna
(*Note:* Clothing may vary considerably according to season.)
Binoculars
Maps and compass if needed
Wetpacks
Boat gear: repair kit, duct tape
On extended trips, spare paddle and spare spray skirt
Food as required
To be worn while paddling: wet suit, paddle jacket, paddle pants,
    life jacket, helmet, tennis shoes over wet suit booties—in
    cool weather also wear wool shirt and pants under paddle
    suit, over wet suit

Appendix **B**

Useful Addresses

The companies listed in this section are merely a few whose products or services happen to be familiar to me. This is a large and still-burgeoning industry and space doesn't permit any sort of Whole Kayak Catalog here. It should not be taken as a criticism, necessarily, if a company isn't listed.

KAYAK MAKERS

Country Ways, 221 Water St., Excelsior, MN 55331 (Kits for wood-veneer flatwater kayaks, paddles; also finished wood-veneer boats.)

Easy Rider Boat Co., PO Box 88108, Tukwila Branch C, Seattle, WA 98188 (Several fine touring designs—their Dolphin is an excellent flatwater tourer.)

Eddyline, 8423 Mukilteo Speedway, Mukilteo, WA 98275 (State-of-the-art sea kayaks.)

Folbot Corporation, PO Box 70877, Stark Industrial Park, Charleston, SC 29405 (Folding and rigid wood-frame kayaks and bargain-price kits.)

Hans Klepper Corporation, 35 Union Square West, New York, NY 10003 (Finest folders around; also several very good conventional rigid kayaks.)

Leisure Products Marketing Systems, 1044 Northern Blvd, Roslyn, NY 11576 (U.S. distributors for the Metzeler Spezi inflatable kayak.)

Old Town Canoe Co., 58 Middle St., Old Town, ME 04468 (A venerable tradition among canoeists, OT also makes a few good kayaks.)

Pacific Water Sports, 16205 Pacific Hwy. South, Seattle, WA 98188 (Makers of truly beautiful sea kayaks; their Sea Otter also makes a fine flatwater cruising boat for inland waters.)

Perception, Inc., PO Box 686, Liberty, SC 29657 (Rotationally molded soft plastic whitewater kayaks; very popular make—if you want one, you'll have no trouble finding a dealer.)

Phoenix Products, 207 N. Broadway, Berea, KY 40403 (Excellent line of FRP kayaks, especially whitewater and touring designs; one of the oldest U.S. names in the modern kayaking movement.)

Sawyer Canoe Co., 234 South State St., Oscoda, MI 48750 (A canoe maker, but their Loon has characteristics of both the decked C-1 and the true kayak and definitely makes a superb touring boat.)

Seda Products, PO Box 997, Chula Vista, CA 92012 (Good line of FRP kayaks; also paddles and other accessories.)

Semperit Boats, 2 Herman St., PO Box 220, South River, NJ 08882 (U.S. distributors for the Dolphin inflatable kayak.)

MAIL-ORDER RIVER OUTFITTERS

Blackadar Boating, PO Box 1170, Salmon, ID 83467 (Extensive line of whitewater equipment, run by authentic river people.)

California Rivers, PO Box 468, 21712 Geyserville Ave., Geyserville, CA 95441 (U.S. distributors for the unique Minnow series of Kiwi kayaks; some other good whitewater equipment, despite the most *chaotic* catalog ever printed.)

Northwest River Supplies, PO Box 9186, Moscow, ID 83843-9186 (My own favorite supplier for many years—clear, honest catalog, first-class gear, and eminently fair prices. Stupid nine-digit zip code should not be held against them.

CAMPING GEAR

Eddie Bauer, 5th and Union, PO Box 3700, Seattle, WA 98124 (Mostly down clothes for incredibly rich people, but some first-rate serious outdoor gear, too.)

L. L. Bean, Freeport, ME 04033 (Has in recent years become mostly a source of high-status clothing, but still sells a lot of high-quality equipment too—good sleeping bags, for one thing.)

Eastern Mountain Sports, Vose Farm Rd., PO Box 811, Peterborough, NH 03458 (Extensive line of lightweight camping equipment, suitable for kayaking.)

Indiana Camp Supplies, PO Box 344, Pittsboro, IN 46167-0344 (General outdoor gear; also carries most complete line of medical supplies for wilderness trips up through expedition level. Publishes Forgey's first aid book, listed in reading section.)

Recreational Equipment, Inc., PO Box C-88125, Seattle, WA 98188 (General lightweight camping equipment, at very attractive prices—quality stuff throughout.)

ODDS AND ENDS

American Canoe Association Book Service, PO Box 248, Lorton, VA 22079 (Best single source for river guidebooks for all parts of the U.S.)

Mitchell Paddles, 4 King Hill, Canaan, NH 03741 (I recommend their wooden paddles.)

U.S. Geological Survey, Branch of Distribution, (*east of the Mississippi*) 1200 South Eads St., Arlington, VA 22202, (*west of the Mississippi*) Box 25286, Federal Center, Denver, CO 80225 (Topographic maps in often incredible detail—you must first order the free index map for the state in question, which will show you the quadrangles you want. Free guide to map symbols.)

Appendix **C**

Reading List

KAYAKING

Sure, there are other books, and I recommend you read them. I don't agree with some of the things they say, but the best way to gain a real understanding of any subject is to check out all the possible input, and, as you go, measure it against your own experience.

Canoeing For Beginners, by Stuart Ferguson. (Arco, 1976.) Australian book originally. Very, very basic, yet some good suggestions—only general kayaking book besides this one to explain deep-water remount. Some ideas on making your own paddle; might be worth trying.

Canoes and Canoeing, by Percy Blandford. (Norton, 1976.) Mostly obsolete, but does contain plans and directions for building several wood-frame kayaks with simple tools and easily available material. Built one of these myself, the one called Griffin, and it's quite a nice flatwater boat.

Kayaking, by Jay Evans and Robert Anderson. (Stephen Greene, 1975.) First good kayaking manual in the U.S., still around; outdated in many ways and instructions unclear in a few areas, but still has some good things to say. Mostly oriented toward competition, and should definitely be read if you want to get into racing.

Sea Canoeing, by Derek Hutchinson. (A & C Black [London], 1976.) Outstanding study of sea kayaking, but don't be confused by the British usage of canoe.

Sea Kayaking, by John Dowd. (University of Washington Press, or, in Canada, Douglas & MacIntyre, Ltd., 1981.) Another fine book on sea kayaking, my own favorite and easier to get in this country than the Hutchinson book.

Whitewater!, by Norman Strung, Sam Curtis, and Earl Perry. (Macmillan, 1976.) Whitewater technique for rafts, canoes, and kayaks, with a superb chapter on how rivers move. Earl Perry's section on kayaking is excellent. If you're going to get into really big stuff, Perry's discussion of heavy hydraulics is required reading.

Wildwater, by Lito Tejada-Flores. (Sierra Club Books, 1978.) Very popular guide to whitewater kayaking; oriented strictly toward the sporting kayaker whose interest is in whitewater for its own sake, not the tourist. Good instructions on many techniques, especially braces; directions are simple and illustrations are fairly clear. Irritatingly elitist in tone, like so many Sierra Club efforts, and not very useful on touring; still worth adding to any kayaker's bookshelf.

RELATED INFORMATION

All-Purpose Guide to Paddling, edited by Dean Norman. (Greatlakes Living Press, 1976.) Collection of mostly short introductory articles on various boats—mostly canoes, but some kayak material. Article by the late Walt Blackadar explains his unconventional techniques.

Wildwater Touring, by Margaret and Scott Arighi. (Macmillan, 1974.) Pioneer work on the subject, still one of the best; contains best discussion of river groups that I've seen. Information on equipment is mostly out of date, however. Descriptions of five eminently cruiseworthy Northwest rivers. No detailed advice on kayaking as such.

CAMPING

Harsh-Weather Camping, by Sam Curtis. (David McKay, 1980.) Outstanding study of how to cope with rough weather of all sorts—from simple rain to big storms, from heat to cold—which should be read by everyone who goes any farther outdoors than the city park. Material on weather forecasting is particularly important for flatwater paddlers.

High Peaks and Clear Roads, by Raymond Bridge. (Prentice-Hall, 1978.) General discussions of various aspects of lightweight camping for wilderness travelers, including kayakers.

Wilderness Medicine, by Dr. William Forgey. (Indiana Camp Supplies, 1979.) Exhaustive study by a doctor and an experienced wilderness traveler; contains valuable instructions on first aid for injuries and illnesses and making up your own first aid kit. Should not only be read but carried along on even slightly remote tours.

INSPIRATIONAL

Broken Waters Sing, by Gaylord Stavely. (Little, Brown, 1971.) Veteran river guide describes journeys on Western rivers—in drift boats, not kayaks—with great wit and perception.

Down the River, by Edward Abbey. (E. P. Dutton, 1982.) Utterly wonderful essays by today's leading environmental-gonzo writer.

Goodbye to a River, by John Graves. (Alfred Knopf, 1959.) One of the best pieces of river literature since Mark Twain. A solo journey down the Brazos, past and present. Authentic literature, not just a book. Read it.

The Heroes, by Ronald McKie. (Harcourt Brace, 1960.) Incredible true story of Australian commandoes in kayaks blowing

up ships in Singapore harbor in World War II. Epic journeys
across the Indian Ocean. If this sort of thing appeals to you,
try also *Cockleshell Heroes,* by Cecil Phillips (Heinemann,
London, 1957), about another bunch of iron-nerved kayakers
doing the same thing in occupied France.

Kayaks Down the Nile, by John Goddard. (Brigham Young University Press, 1979.) Journey down the Nile in foldboats;
oddly dull reading considering the subject matter. Great photo
of author in kayak being charged by elephants!

The Starship and the Canoe, by Kenneth Brower. (Holt, Rinehart,
1973.) True story of an eccentric visionary, who builds gigantic kayaks to cruise the Pacific Northwest seas, and his
astrophysicist father. This one is sure to move you.

Yukon Summer, by Eugene Cantin. (Chronicle Books, 1973.) Story
of a young man's solo cruise through Canadian-Alaskan wilderness in a Klepper. Of particular interest to novice readers,
as Cantin by his own admission had very little experience
before setting out. Mandatory for Klepper owners.

WHERE TO GO

I have not listed any guidebooks because nowadays they pro-
liferate like hamsters and would require something the size of the
Whole Earth Catalog. Any good outdoor shop will carry guidebooks, as do the better mail-order outfitters. The best guides are
locally produced, often by canoe clubs. Steer clear of thick guidebooks to the whole U.S. as most are terrible.

If you live in the West, however, I do recommend Ann Schaf-
er's two-volume *Canoeing Western Waterways: The Coastal States*
and *The Mountain States.* (Harper & Row, 1978.) The information
is too brief and sketchy to serve as detailed instructions for running any particular stream (with a few exceptions) but its cata-
loglike structure makes it possible to find plenty of places to go
and at least get some idea of how hard it may be. In the East,
John Kauffman's *Flow East* (McGraw-Hill, 1973), while primarily
a study of environmental problems—and very much worth reading on that account alone—might also provide some ideas on
streams worth checking out. And Bill McGinnis's *Whitewater
Rafting* (Quadrangle, 1975), while of course meant for rafters,

contains detailed descriptions of some of the best whitewater rivers in the United States, easily convertible to kayakers' terms.

MAGAZINES

Wilderness Camping used to be my favorite, but it's gone down the river, along with *River World* and *Mariah*. There remain:

Canoe, Highland Mill, Camden, ME 04843. Official publication of the American Canoe Association with much worthwhile information on kayaking and kayak touring. Has ads for products of real value, and ACA sells good books, including river guides, through the magazines. As part of the Nov./Dec. issue, but available separately for *Canoe* as well, *Canoe* publishes *The Buyer's Guide*, an extremely helpful guide to new boats. *The Buyer's Guide* lists over 100 touring and sea cruising kayaks, with complete specifications for each and retail prices. All known makers of touring kayaks are included.

Small Boat Journal, P. O. Box 400, Bennington VT 05201. Fascinating magazine, mostly oriented toward traditional wooden craft and sailboats, but often has canoe and kayak material too. Especially interesting to sea kayakers.

Glossary

BOW. The front end of the boat.

BRACE. A technique of stabilizing the kayak, in which the kayaker's weight is partly supported by the paddle blade acting against the water. This may be a *high brace,* in which the paddle shaft is held above eye level, or a *low brace,* in which the paddle is held at approximately its normal operating level.

BRACE ROLL. A variant of the Eskimo roll in which the paddle is swept downward, directly against the water, rather than around in a surface arc.

BRACE TURN. Turn executed by planting a paddle brace in such a way that the kayak swings around it; one popular variant is called the *Duffek turn.*

C-1. Single-seat decked whitewater canoe.

C-2. Two-seat decked whitewater canoe, especially racing versions.

CHUTE. Any point at which a stream is forced through a narrow passage, increasing force and speed; also, the deepest, most unobstructed passage through a rapid.

COAMING. The lip around the cockpit opening onto which spray skirt is snapped.

COCKPIT. The area where the paddler sits.

CONTROL HAND. In using a feathered paddle, the hand that retains its firm grip and executes the rotation necessary to orient the blades.

DECK. The solid covering of the top of the kayak. What many people believe kayakers aren't playing with a full one of.

DRAW. A lateral stroke which pulls the kayak directly to the side.

DROP. A distinct steepening of the river bed, much steeper than overall gradient; may be vertical or simply very steep, of any height.

EDDY. A phenomenon wherein the current is stopped or reversed by passing close to bank or large obstruction; also, the slack or upstream-flowing water next to the bank or just downstream from points or obstructions.

EDDY LINE. The boundary at which normal downstream current meets eddy area; it must be crossed with proper technique in strong rapids or an upset may result. Also sometimes called *eddy fence*.

EDDY TURN. The technique of turning into an eddy by bracing in the eddy itself.

ENDO. A trick by which a kayaker causes the kayak to be tossed upwards, stood on its end, and dropped upside down, to be righted with a roll. It may also occur accidentally. Planting the nose of the kayak in a suitable hole is one way to accomplish this. Short for end-over-end.

ESKIMO ROLL. Any of several techniques by which a capsized kayak is righted by the paddler (usually, but not always, with paddle action) without exiting.

FEATHERED PADDLE. A paddle in which the blades are set at 90-degree angles to each other on the axis of the shaft.

FERRY. Any technique of moving across the current of a stream. Includes *back ferry* when kayak is set at an angle to current while paddler backpaddles, facing downstream; *front ferry* is similar except that the kayak is aimed upstream and a forward stroke is used; and simple turn-and-stroke cross-stream maneuvers. Sometimes called ferry glide.

FLATWATER. Technically, a class of kayak racing events. In general usage, still, open, or slow-moving water, as distinguished from whitewater. Also used as an adjective to describe any boat intended for this kind of use.

GRADIENT. The amount of slope in a given stretch of river or stream, generally expressed in terms of feet of drop per mile; for example, a 30-foot gradient means the river bed loses 30 feet of elevation per mile. The figure is purely an average and takes no account of falls, etc.

GRAVEL BAR. A beach or bar composed of gravel deposited by floods. An excellent campsite unless flooding is possible.

HAYSTACK. Very large standing wave.

HOLE. A phenomenon in which moving water pours over a sudden drop in the streambed, such as a ledge or rock, and momentarily flows downwards, rolling back upon itself rather than downstream. Can stop and hold boat, and large holes can be extremely dangerous. Also called *reversal, suckhole, souse hole;* if it is large enough to hold boat and make escape difficult, may be called *keeper hole.*

HYPOTHERMIA. An extremely dangerous and potentially fatal medical condition in which the body's core temperature is lowered past the capability of metabolic mechanisms to restore normal temperature. This is especially possible in water.

INFLATABLE CANOE. A small *open* inflatable boat, with a canoelike hull form; it is sometimes incorrectly called an inflatable kayak.

K-1. Technically, a class of competition kayak holding one person. In general usage, any single-seat kayak.

K-2. Technically, a two-seat racing kayak. In general usage, any two-seat kayak.

K-4. A four-seat kayak used in flatwater racing.

LEAD BOAT. The first boat in line in an organized kayak group; also, the lead position itself. Sometimes it also refers to the general status and skills of the person in both physical and figurative leadership of a whitewater group, as, "He's good enough to run lead boat."

LINING. The technique of letting a small boat down a rapid at the end of a rope. Not recommended by this author with kayaks, which upset easily without human guidance in the cockpit.

PADDLE. An instrument with the river on one end and a neurotic on the other. Used principally to make already bad situations impossible.

PAWLATA ROLL. A type of Eskimo roll in which the paddle is held in an extremely extended manner, with one hand actually grasping the blade. It is named for Hans Pawlata, possibly the first modern white man to master the roll, though he later abandoned it for other techniques of rolling. Also called an *extended-paddle roll.*

POOL-AND-DROP. A type of stream configuration in which long, relatively slow stretches are broken by short rapids.

POP-UP. A trick, or accident, in which the kayak is bodily forced vertically out of the water, standing on end. Sometimes called an *endo,* but the true endo terminates in kayak falling backwards or forwards onto its own deck.

PUT-IN. The geographical point at which boats are launched at the beginning of a trip or run.

RAPID. Any point at which any stream becomes faster, more turbulent, and stronger of current than over its length, usually caused by narrowing of channel, and/or obstructions, and/or sudden drop in a gradient. Rapid refers to one such place, rapids to more than one; the use of rapids as a singular noun is obsolete.

RIFFLE. A small, regular patch of turbulence over a shallow bed or an easy drop; any very easy rapid.

ROCKER. Design feature in which bottom of boat is curved upwards toward ends to improve maneuverability.

ROCK GARDEN. An extremely rocky, obstructed rapid.

RUN. To negotiate a rapid; or, as a noun, the act of doing so or the route followed. Shoot as in to shoot the rapids is an obsolete term.

SCREW ROLL. A version of Eskimo roll in which hands remain in normal paddling position on shaft throughout.

SHUTTLE. The procedure by which vehicles are moved between put-in and take-out.

SKEG. Fixed, rudderlike fin under stern of boat; partial keel. Intended to increase directional stability. May be removable.

SLALOM. A type of formal racing event in which kayaks and canoes maneuver over a marked course—similar to a ski slalom. *Slalom kayak* refers to a kayak designed for this event, but the term is also used for any maneuverable, short-hulled kayak of this general type.

SPRAY SKIRT. A flexible covering for a cockpit, with an elasticized sleeve to fit paddler's waist. Snaps around cockpit coaming in use.

STANDING WAVE. A wave formed by pressure from water flowing down a chute and hitting slower water below, or flowing over a rock just below the surface. Unlike normal, open-water waves, standing waves do not move significantly in relation to fixed points on shore.

STERN. The back end of the boat.

STRAINER. An extremely dangerous type of hazard in which water flows through limbs, trees, fences, and the like. Potentially fatal.

SURFING. A technique in which the kayaker balances on the upstream face of a large standing wave, using a minimum of paddle force to remain there.

SURFING KAYAK. A short, specialized kayak designed for beach (not river) surfing.

SWEEP BOAT. The last boat in an organized river running group; it also refers to this position itself. The sweep boat operator has the responsibility for making sure everyone got through the rapid all right and helping to rescue those who did not.

SWEEPER. An obstacle which projects over moving water or downward into a current; it may cause an upset or sweep paddlers out of open boats.

SWEEP STROKE. A stroke used for turning the kayak by bringing the paddle out and around a large arc like a letter *C*.

TAKE-OUT. The point at which boats are removed from the water; the termination point of a kayak trip.

WET EXIT. Leaving a capsized kayak.

WETPACK. A watertight bag used to keep gear dry; also called a *drypack* by those who find the term wetpack illogical.

WET SUIT. A close-fitting suit of neoprene foam intended to keep an immersed person warm, or at least slow heat loss, in cool water.

WILDWATER. A racing event in which the object is to paddle straight downstream, through rapids, for the shortest possible time over a measured course. It's also called a *downriver* event. *Wildwater kayaks* (also called *downriver boats*) are those craft specially designed for this event. Some people, especially Europeans, use wildwater as a synonym for whitewater.

WILLOW JUNGLE. A very, very dangerous phenomenon in which willows take root in the streambed, usually during dry summers, and spread across a rapid, possibly blocking a chute completely. Common in Southern streams. Creates a huge strainer, often made worse by driftwood and fallen trees which may lodge in willows.

Index